JULIUS ROSENWALD

Julius Rosenwald

Repairing the World

HASIA R. DINER

Yale

UNIVERSITY

PRESS

New Haven and London

Frontispiece: Julius Rosenwald, 1917. Harris & Ewing Collection (Library of
Congress, Prints and Photographs Division)

Yale University Press books may be purchased in quantity for educational,
business, or promotional use. For information, please e-mail sales.press@yale.edu
(U.S. office) or sales@yaleup.co.uk (U.K. office).

Set in Janson Oldstyle type by Integrated Publishing Solutions.
Printed in the United States of America.

Library of Congress Control Number: 2017934017
ISBN 978-0-300-20321-9 (hardcover : alk. paper)

A catalogue record for this book is available from the British Library.

This paper meets the requirements of ANSI/NISO Z39.48–1992
(Permanence of Paper).

10 9 8 7 6 5 4 3 2 1

*Roads Taken: The Great Jewish Migrations to the
New World and the Peddlers Who Forged the Way*

*We Remember with Reverence and Love: American Jews
and the Myth of Silence After the Holocaust, 1945–1962*

The Jews of the United States, 1654 to 2000

*Hungering for America: Italian, Irish, and
Jewish Foodways in the Age of Migration*

Lower East Side Memories: A Jewish Place in America

*In the Almost Promised Land:
American Jews and Blacks, 1915–1935*

A Time for Gathering: The Second Migration, 1820–1880,
vol. 2 of *The Jewish People in America,* ed. Henry L. Feingold

*Erin's Daughters in America: Irish Immigrant Women
in the Nineteenth Century*

This book on the life of Julius Rosenwald,
an individual who cherished American democracy,
is dedicated to all of those who today are engaged in
resisting the forces bent on weakening it.

CONTENTS

ACKNOWLEDGMENTS

AMONG THE many pleasant aspects of writing a book, the conceptualization, the research, and the writing, the one I most look forward to is thanking the people who have helped me in my project. This brief section gives me a chance to express my gratitude.

First and basically foremost I want to say how grateful I am to Steven Zipperstein, the editor of the Jewish Lives series, for asking me to write this biography of Julius Rosenwald. JR showed up in several of my previous projects, including my first book, *In the Almost Promised Land: American Jews and Blacks, 1915–1935*, based on my dissertation written nearly a lifetime ago. In that book Rosenwald took center stage. He also had a cameo appearance in my most recent book, *Roads Taken*, a history of Jewish peddlers. So when Steve asked me to write this volume for the Jewish Lives series I wondered if I had anything new to say about Rosenwald, and I think I did. I appreciate profoundly his faith and support in me and I also am gratified that he considered Rosenwald a worthy inclusion in this library of notable Jewish women and men.

Secondly I want to thank Peter Ascoli, the author of the large, authoritative biography of his grandfather, which I cite often in this book. Peter's book differs from mine and we focus on different aspects of Rosenwald's life, but he always gave generously of his time, offering me pieces of advice and sharing sources with me. Aviva Kempner made her film about Rosenwald independent of my doing this book, but as the film and the book converged in time, she has been helpful to me, and I am pleased with how much she is doing to make sure that the name of Julius Rosenwald comes out of its obscurity.

I asked four special friends to read this book, and each one did so with her own individual and sharply trained critical eye. Marion Kaplan, Nell Irvin Painter, Shuly Rubin Schwartz, and Kathryn Kish Sklar came to this project with their vast expertise in German-Jewish history, African American history, the history of American Jewry, and the history of Progressivism, respectively. Each of these factors laid the contours of Rosenwald's life and I thank you all for your willingness to read. I so value your contributions and friendships.

Over the years I worked on this book I also had valuable conversations with Gennady Estraikh, David Sorkin, David Levering Lewis, Zohar Segev, Linda Borish, and Steven Diner. Steve was busy writing his own book, so for the first time in my career I did not bother him to read and edit my manuscript, but he gave me plenty of time to talk about JR and to share with me his own deep knowledge of Chicago in the age of Rosenwald.

Two of my doctoral students fed me a steady stream of citations involving Rosenwald that benefited me greatly. Judah Bernstein, now completing his dissertation, and David Weinfeld, already launched in his career, knew I was working on this, and they kept their eyes open for Rosenwald references in places where I would never have thought to look.

I want to give particular thanks to the staffs of the University of Chicago Special Collections and the Fisk University Library, which hold the Rosenwald papers and also the papers of the Julius Rosenwald Fund. Two goldmines of material, these libraries and their excellent librarians provided helpful advice and comfortable environments in which to work. Similarly, Erica Hanson of Yale University Press helped shepherd this project through.

I am completing this book at a trying moment in the history of the United States, a moment which gives me pause and allows me to rethink the meaning of Julius Rosenwald. He made many millions through business but never saw money as an end in itself, as a way to augment his own political power or that of his class of the wealthy and well-connected. Money, he believed, brought responsibility to those who had it, and that responsibility meant seriously thinking about how to make the world a better place. He had no interest in slapping his name on buildings, no desire to see it boldly projected on public spaces. His money let him expand opportunities for others, to foster the welfare of those whom prejudice had ground down. Not a meaningless antidote to the present moment.

January 20, 2017

JULIUS ROSENWALD

INTRODUCTION

◆◦◆◦◆

The Forgotten Millionaire

In 1929, the children of Julius Rosenwald, the Chicago prince of retail and among the city's preeminent philanthropists, contemplated commissioning a biography of their father, a man known worldwide, whose business and civic activism had improved the lives of millions. The book never came into being. The Rosenwald children should have realized that their father would never agree to the biography. He had for decades refused to allow his name to be affixed to the buildings, institutions, and projects he sponsored. He never even added his name to the immense company he took over, Sears, Roebuck. He gave lavishly and generously to a number of philanthropies but always insisted that his contributions be matched by others, never wanting to be the sole donor. Hardly surprising, then, that the biography project died. Yet his many achievements and the issues that engaged him, as laid out in the correspondence between the Rosenwald children and potential biographers, justify *this* book's inclusion in a series titled "Jewish Lives." As the children weighed the merits of potential biographers, they emphasized that a prime consideration was each writer's sensitivity to Jewish history in general and to the importance of his Jewishness to their father's work in particular. Although some Rosenwald family members favored the journalist David Lawrence, others endorsed the team of Jerome Frank, a legal scholar, and his wife, Florence Kipper Frank, a writer, poet, and playwright. David Levy, Rosenwald's son-in-law, wrote about Jerome Frank, "Qualifications Experienced Jewish knowledge," while Florence Frank promised Rosenwald's daughter Adele Rosenwald Levy that she would produce "not only a biography, but an attempt at the interpretation of that period of American industry which Mr. Rosenwald has influenced—also an interpretation of the Jewish background and of your father's significance as an American Jew."[1]

In *Julius Rosenwald: Repairing the World*, I tell the story of Rosenwald's life as an American Jew. Although I shall examine how he acquired his wealth and what he did with his fortune, I shall not cover the full range of his civic enterprises. Rosenwald, an apostle of good government and a progressive conservative, funded all sorts of undertakings such as public health projects. He actively advocated for his chosen city, Chicago, serving as one of its biggest boosters. All these aspects of his life merit attention, and I will focus on them, somewhat. But I am concerned here with his story as an American Jew, a man who devoted much of his life and fortune to Jewish causes, which for him also revolved around the project of improving the lives and circumstances of the nation's African American population. These two issues moved him deeply, more than any others, and to them he gave the greatest amount of his time and money. Rosenwald's belief in the chord binding the welfare of Jews and African Americans together defined his life as a Jew in early-twentieth-century America.

Julius Rosenwald—JR, as friends and family called him—grew up as a Jew in a community of Jews. He took his first steps in commerce as a manufacturer of men's suits. His commercial network consisted largely of other Jews, immigrants from Europe's German-speaking lands and their sons. The fathers of most of those with whom he worked and socialized had come to America as immigrant peddlers in the mid-nineteenth century. The majority gravitated to the garment industry, producing and selling ready-made clothing, replicating a pattern found throughout modern Jewish history worldwide.

After acquiring his wealth, Rosenwald declared that he no longer felt the need to make more money. His sons, sons-in-law, and an assortment of managers ensured that Sears continued to thrive, enabling the Rosenwalds to live in luxury. But JR instead concentrated on his real passion, improving the world by giving his money away.

In 1929, the year that the Rosenwald children proposed commissioning the biography, JR reflected on how he had achieved his success and the meaning of wealth, saying, "I am frequently asked for advice on how to get on in the world. I think that most of my interviewers have really been seeking a magic formula for making a million dollars. There is nothing occult about it. Any man can make a fortune from scratch if he has the opportunity, enterprise, and luck. No amount of ability will give a man success unless he gets the chance to use it constructively."[2] Having made his many millions from Sears, Roebuck and Company, he directed his very considerable resources toward undertakings he considered "constructive" that he believed would create a better world, a better America, and a better future for Jews everywhere.

Rosenwald's ideas about giving, principles that informed his decisions about how to give, how much to give, and to which causes, had their roots in his Jewish upbringing and worldview. Jewish law, commentaries, and other normative texts had much to say about these matters. As a boy Rosenwald attended synagogue with his parents in Springfield, Illinois, and as an adult he belonged to Chicago's Reform Sinai congregation, led by Rabbi Emil Hirsch, a Progressive activist. Rosenwald, in these places, would have heard much about the role of charity within Jewish culture, and likely learned that the Western, Christian concept had no place within Judaism. Hebrew lacked even a word for it. Rather, Jewish texts and tradition enjoined *tzedakah*, "righteousness," derived from the word for justice, positing it as an obligation for Jews. Giving did not emanate from the giver's good heart. Rather, Jews gave because doing so constituted a mitzvah, a commandment. The giver must give. Those in need were entitled to receive, and all, even the poor, carried the obligation of helping others who found themselves in even greater distress.

Giving as an obligation had historically run deep within Jewish culture, and mid-nineteenth-century American Judaism made relieving distress and serving the needy integral to its own development. Social service functioned as a key organizing principle for American Jews, bringing together emigrants from many European lands who sparred in their religious institutions over liturgical reform and ritual innovation. Rosenwald, a Jewish millionaire raised in this tradition, took his giving seriously, developing a vision of "public giving" that he set forth in an article published in 1929.[3]

We have no evidence that Rosenwald read deeply in Jewish history or knew much about Jewish thought beyond what he had acquired in his childhood home, in religious school, or from the sermons he had heard in his hometown synagogue in Springfield or Chicago's Sinai. Likely, however, he just absorbed certain lessons from that history, and these became fundamental to his very being and shaped his life as a philanthropist.

Starting in the late eighteenth century, Jews and their Christian allies in the German-speaking lands of Europe began to consider the Jews' anomalous state as a separate class. They debated prospects for Jewish Emancipation, a change in their status that while not exactly offering full equality involved making them more like the others around them. Molders of the Jewish enlightenment, the Haskalah, such as Moses Mendelssohn and his disciples argued that before Jews could be integrated into gentile society they had to change, in particular to acquire a secular education. Mendelssohn organized what may have been the first school for Jewish children that taught modern subjects, aimed at equipping them to function in German society. They had to master the dominant language, diversify themselves occupationally, and learn to adapt their public behavior. Mendelssohn hoped to steer Jews away from trade toward agriculture and skilled crafts. Only after they had transformed themselves could Jews expect to be emancipated.

While Jews bore the burden in this process, they and the Christian advocates of Jewish Emancipation argued that Christians had to be reminded of the Jews' innate abilities and their contributions to the society. Julius Rosenwald carried this tradition into his life as an American Jew. He named his first son Lessing, probably after Gotthold Lessing, a German playwright who in 1779 created the character of Nathan the Wise in his eponymous drama based on the life and career of Mendelssohn. Lessing's plea for tolerance accepted as truth that Jews had to change but argued that non-Jews of goodwill had a role to play in the transformation. Rosenwald's belief that as a white person he had a responsibility toward black people grew out of this history of his own people.

The projects of Jewish Emancipation and Enlightenment that shaped JR, despite his lack of interest in intellectual matters, had at their core two linked beliefs that informed everything he did and served as the basis of his philanthropic life. First he assumed as a given the existence of a basic rationality to the world. People needed only to be trained and educated to alter their behaviors and attitudes. This training not only involved the acquisition of skills by those marginalized by society, the Jews of central Europe for example. That faith in the rational would also lead the prejudiced away from their attitudes.

This rational view of the world existed in tandem with another belief Rosenwald inherited, an optimistic faith that the improvement of society lay just around the corner, and that good people could move it ever forward and upward, with conditions for all always getting better. Belief in the inevitability of progress, with its rational and optimistic framework, made a bridge between the American Rosenwald and the world of the European Mendelssohn and Lessing. As a Jew with considerable means, Rosenwald believed that he bore a responsibility to use his wealth to enrich Jewish culture, promote Jewish integration into the nation to which so many had migrated, root out anti-Semitism, and provide for Jews in distress abroad. The many projects he joined to ameliorate the situation of Jews, some of which his money launched, reflected his uncomplicated identification with his co-religionists. He evinced no anguish or ambivalence about his Jewishness. He embraced it and believed that as a Jew he had to help other Jews and enrich their culture.

At the same time he felt that he and other American Jews had a special relationship with and obligation toward African Americans, most of whom lived in the rural South in conditions of dire poverty. The glaring inequities of their circumstances stifled any chance for economic progress for the children and grandchildren of slaves. Their situation moved Rosenwald deeply, though he rarely explained why it mattered so much to him. From the moment he plunged into philanthropic work, he dedicated his wealth, reputation, and energy to what he identified as the African American cause.

Rosenwald's philanthropy extended beyond the needs of Jews and blacks. He gave lavishly to Progressive-era Chicago institutions, including such key institutions as the University of Chicago, glorying particularly in its School of Social Service Administration, led by the activist Sophonisba Breckinridge, Hull House, the renowned settlement house founded by activist Jane Addams, the Immigrants' Protective League, spearheaded by reformer Grace Abbott, and the Museum of Science and Industry, an institution he himself envisioned, pushed for, and funded. These projects also reflected his self-image as a Jew in early-twentieth-century America. They, however, could not compare in the size of his contributions and the scope of his energy with his Jewish and African American endeavors.

Rosenwald and other American Jews of his generation, native-born of immigrant parentage, most born around the time of the Civil War, aligned themselves with the Progressive movement of the late nineteenth and early twentieth centuries, which coincided with mass eastern European Jewish immigration. Their interest in Progressivism, dedicated to bringing a new order to American society that would rid it of its many social ills and narrow the chasm between the well-off and the "other half," fit their experience as Jews. As a successful but still fearful minority group, they considered that an orderly society in which all enjoyed a certain level of comfort would be to their benefit as well. Eager to avoid political extremes of right or left, middle-class American Jews worked through local and national organizations, both Jewish and general, to make America a place where anti-Semitism could not thrive.

Yet their philanthropic activity and public activism coincided with an era in which anti-Semitism rose to prominence in America. The decades during which Rosenwald launched his most highly publicized gifts to African American and Jewish institutions, as well as to a myriad of other causes, witnessed the arrest, trial, and lynching of Leo Frank, the imposition of quotas on Jewish admission at numerous private American universities, the rantings of Henry Ford in his *Dearborn Indepen-*

dent about the menace of the "International Jew," and the passage in the 1920s of immigration restrictions that, while not
aimed directly at Jews, included them in their nationally based
quotas.[4]

Much of the anti-Semitic rhetoric stemmed from the pur-
ported association of Jews with money-grubbing, an association that had long imbued European Christian culture, where
Jews traditionally fulfilled the role of moneylender forbidden
to Christians. In America, the image of the rich Jew who made
his money in unsavory ways surfaced in the despondent rumi-
nations of American patricians like Henry Adams, who scorned
wealthy Jewish parvenus who vulgarly flaunted their riches
while insinuating themselves into social institutions where they
did not belong. At the same time the poor and dispossessed,
such as farmers in the South and Midwest, blamed Jewish businessmen, reputed to control the railroads, the stock market, and
the other engines of finance, for grinding down native-born
Christian Americans.

Julius Rosenwald led a relatively uneventful life, devoid
of great earth-shaking events and dramas. But the same cataclysmic events that touched the lives of so many of the world's
Jews, including the epic Jewish migration from eastern Europe, World War I, the Russian Revolution, and the pogroms
which ravaged the Jews of Ukraine during the civil war that
followed, touched him as well. Despite viewing them from the
safety of his nicely appointed homes in Chicago's Hyde Park
neighborhood and Ravinia, on the city's wealthy North Shore,
these cataclysms played themselves out in his public life.

We have no record that Rosenwald faced any particular
crises or even difficulties, any anguish or trauma. In his personal life he enjoyed a happy nineteenth-century-small-town
childhood with no dislocations or losses. At age twenty-eight
he married Augusta Nusbaum, the sister of a business associate, and their marriage appears to have been placid until her

death in 1929. He then enjoyed a short second marriage, ended by his death three years later. He got along well with his five children, who remained loyal and loving to him and to one another. JR died peacefully in 1932 at age sixty-nine. He seems to have had no secret vices. No scandals ever attached to his name and never during his lifetime or subsequently did anyone accuse him of duplicity, deceit, or misdeeds. Even critics who disapproved of the causes he supported, or declined to support, never uncovered any sordid details of scandal or graft.

In his business life he moved steadily from modest circumstances to better ones, along the standard route taken by late-nineteenth-century American Jews. His acquisition of great wealth, which he always attributed to luck, differentiated him only in scale from his cohort of American Jews, who benefited from their communal networks and the opportunities they found in America, and who as white people faced few limitations, despite their immigrant antecedents and non-Christian religion. Most public commentary about Rosenwald both praised him for his generosity and emphasized his Jewishness, a fact that tells us much about the place of Jews in early-twentieth-century America. Writers and commentators, whether Jewish or not, viewed his Jewishness in a positive light, praising Jews for their contribution to American life. Despite the rise in anti-Semitism during these years, many Americans embraced Jews. Much of the discourse in America about Jews, Rosenwald's among it, lauded them for their solid families, their economic mobility, their sober lifestyles, and their generosity.

Throughout his life, Julius Rosenwald, with his distinctively Jewish name, took pride in his Jewishness, speaking openly about how his heritage had shaped him. When he declared that he hoped to alleviate in particular the situation of black Americans, he argued that his attention to the people most oppressed in America stemmed in part from his Jewish outlook. He demonstrated to white Christian Americans through his deeds that a Jew could show them how to be better Americans, even better Christians. In *Julius Rosenwald: Repairing the World,* I explore the ways Rosenwald's Jewish heritage and worldview shaped the philanthropy and social agenda of one of early-twentieth-century America's most unassuming of multimillionaires.

1

Taking Advantage of Opportunities and Luck

WHEN JULIUS ROSENWALD commented in print, in speeches, or in film, about his life and his spectacular success, he attributed his wealth to luck, describing himself as having been in the right place at the right time. Rather than claim great intellect or keen native abilities, he focused on having seen opportunities and grabbed them. He chose the word *opportunity* to tell the story of how he was—the passive intended—catapulted from a position as the son of the proprietor of S. Rosenwald, purveyor of men's clothing in a downstate Illinois city, to membership in America's wealthiest class. Yet, he did not define *opportunity*, offering only a vague statement that "the opportunities of life are too varied to be confined to rigid programs." He speculated that, like himself, "the man who starts from scratch has an inestimable advantage over the rich young man in that he knows the value of money."[1]

In January 1929 he appeared on screen in a Movietone news

story in which he shared some thoughts about wealth. With a twinkle in his eye, comfortable in front of the camera, he declared, "Most people are of the opinion that because a man has made a fortune that his opinions on any subject are valuable. For my part, I always believe most large fortunes are made by men of mediocre ability who tumbled into a lucky opportunity and couldn't help but get rich and that others, given the same chance, would have done far better with it."[2]

The chance he grabbed came his way when he was thirty-three. In 1895, Rosenwald, a mildly successful Chicago-based manufacturer of men's summer suits, went along with his brother-in-law Aaron Nusbaum's suggestion that they pool their resources and buy, for seventy-five thousand dollars, half-ownership in a cash-strapped mail-order house with good name recognition, Sears, Roebuck and Company, founded in 1886. JR agreed to invest in the company, which had started out selling watches and jewelry but had recently expanded into the selling of more varied and sundry items and needed funds. JR had a hunch that the gamble might pay off.

Lacking the money, he turned to a friend and business associate, Moses (Mo) Newborg, for half his amount. Newborg made the loan, and Rosenwald chipped in the rest with money from his own firm, Rosenwald and Weil, a stable but middling partnership he maintained with his cousin Julius Weil.

Rosenwald already knew the Sears operation through earlier business dealings. He and Weil had sold their suits through the Sears, Roebuck's catalogue, and JR had confidence in the company. He calculated that a partnership might prove profitable. Albert Loeb, a lawyer and friend of Rosenwald and Nusbaum, drew up the papers, launching Rosenwald's lifetime association with Sears.

From 1895 until Rosenwald's death in 1932, the names of Rosenwald and Sears, Roebuck and Company went together as the company spread throughout the United States. Within five years of the buy-in, Rosenwald and Richard Sears, one of the founders, had nudged out Aaron Nusbaum, and then Rosenwald eclipsed Sears, who stepped down in 1908 for a combination of reasons, including ill health. Rosenwald then assumed sole control of the retail behemoth, among the nation's largest businesses. He retained the familiar brand name, Sears, Roebuck, recognizing that customers coast to coast associated it with high quality, low cost, good service, reliable communications, and efficient delivery.

The opportunity Rosenwald "tumbled into" ought to be seen as more than the random chance affair he proclaimed it, nor did he start "from scratch." Rather, he benefited from advantages that had come his way decades earlier. A convergence of forces, American and European, offered him options that he seized upon to further his spectacular career. Those forces had propelled the mass migration of young Jews in the mid-nineteenth century from central Europe, especially the German-speaking lands and Bohemia, Moravia, Hungary, Galicia, and elsewhere in the Austro-Hungarian empire, even as far east as Lithuania and parts of western Russia, to the United States, where they found doors opening to them, the obverse of those they found closed in the old countries.[3] Relying upon Jewish communal networks, the new immigrants discovered that as white Europeans they could partake of the benefits America had to offer, including dynamic economic growth, room to expand, and increased personal rights. Julius Rosenwald, like others of his generation, reaped and built on the benefits of the success their fathers made, augmenting private fortunes and engaging in projects of public life.

AMERICA FEVER

Julius Rosenwald's parents, Samuel and Augusta, had joined the exodus of young Jews out of central Europe, from places like

Bünde, Bedereska, and countless towns throughout Westphalia, Hesse, Posen, Bavaria, Württemberg, Baden, and Silesia, regions that in 1871 united to become Germany. Samuel hailed from the Ruhr Valley village of Bünde in Westphalia, controlled by Prussia after the 1815 Congress of Vienna. He arrived in Baltimore in 1854. Augusta Hammerslough and her brothers made a similar journey somewhat earlier from Bedereska, near Bremerhaven, a Hanseatic port on the Baltic. Drawn by the dynamism of the United States economy and the desire of Americans for consumer goods, the Hammerslough brothers had departed for America one by one when they turned thirteen, sent by their parents to join an uncle in Baltimore. They began in America as peddlers, outfitted by the uncle. Augusta, the youngest, like many other unmarried women in her circumstances, made the transatlantic journey after her brothers had settled down to a stable and sedentary life.

The conditions that drew them to America represented the opposite of those that pushed them out of their home communities. The Jewish economy of central Europe had dried up with modernization and industrialization, the spread of the railroad, and the demise of peasant agriculture. Jews, long Europe's middlemen, peddled goods, traded in cattle, and dealt in other farm products produced by peasants, carting foodstuffs, for example, to markets in exchange for manufactured items. But as the system that had supported them, if not particularly well, crumbled in the early decades of the nineteenth century, young Jews realized that they could not make a living if they stayed home, as too many of them competed for dwindling opportunities. Those with some capital and education, who spoke, read, and wrote German at a higher level instead of the vernacular western Yiddish (Judeo-German), moved to the cities of central Europe, where business possibilities existed and they could take advantage of expanding political and civil rights for Jews. Those who could not or would not stay in Europe turned to America.

The Jews who caught "America fever" came from a world of commerce. Whether as cattle dealers or peddlers, as shop-keepers or handicraft workers, they found their livelihoods in the marketplace. Particularly in central Europe, Jews had for centuries forged communities through commerce, exchanging credit and goods, making marriages based on commercial considerations, and interacting with non-Jews through buying and selling. Samuel Rosenwald and the Hammerslough brothers brought that same experience on their transoceanic voyages.

The exodus from the 1820s through the 1870s that brought some 250,000 Jews to America also grew out of state restrictions on Jewish life promulgated in numerous regions. They particularly suffered from the implications of the hated *matrikel*. Literally a list or registry, these statutes limited how many Jews in a single town or province could marry. In order to suppress the number of Jews, a people with high birth rates, governments instituted rules designating the number of Jews allowed to marry, permitting marriages only when an officially registered Jew emigrated or died, thus opening up a vacancy. Not attractive to young people eager to get started, the twin burdens of shrinking opportunities to earn their bread and severe limitations on their ability to wed and start a family enhanced the appeal of the new world.

Samuel Rosenwald seems to have emigrated alone, but like many of his peers, he turned to other Jews to get started in business. Landing in Baltimore, he made contact with the Hammersloughs, who provided him with credit and his first bundle of goods to peddle, selling house to house from a pack on his back. The Hammerslough business that helped the newly arrived Samuel Rosenwald resembled that of numerous other Jewish male immigrants who had been attracted by the burgeoning American economy and the development of waterways and roads that allowed merchants to get goods to people who lived in the hinterlands. These companies supplied the newly arrived immigrant peddlers with consumer goods such as needles, thread, buttons, lace, cloth, mirrors, eyeglasses, and other popular luxuries. These peddlers went into the homes of women who lived beyond the reach of the urban marketplace but craved such items. Like other recent immigrant Jewish merchants in ocean and river port cities, they also opened stores in the small towns that cropped up around the country. They furnished their stores with goods and staffed them with even newer arrivals, mostly young Jewish men who had served apprenticeships in peddling.

America had for these young Jews everything their home communities lacked. Immigration enabled them to get started in business, marry, have children, build homes for themselves, and enjoy the rights of citizenship. The fact that they had white skin enabled Jews like Samuel Rosenwald to traverse the road as peddlers without hindrance. Samuel Rosenwald could knock on the doors of potential customers' homes, cross their thresholds, and display his goods without fear of enslavement or other violence. When they married they could decide where to set up their homes and shops.

Although Jewish-owned stores across the country carried an array of merchandise, many specialized in dry goods. The stores served their customers' material needs, offering many commodities that Americans wanted. But if one kind of good trumped all others in demand, clothing did. The buying and selling of clothes, whether for men or women, at retail or wholesale, new or used, occupied Jews all over America. It constituted their economic métier. For some peddlers, the clothing trade eventually led to the launch of a grand department store. Gimbels, for example, arose out of the peddling years of Adam Gimbel, from Rheinland-Pfaltz, who hawked his wares to the farm families around Vincennes, Indiana. But even Jewish families that never made it into the upper commercial echelon tended to specialize in clothing, a trade that offered immigrant Jews a way to make something of themselves in their new land.[4]

The Hammersloughs eventually developed peddler routes, customers, and stores throughout the mid-Atlantic, the upper South, and the Midwest. Like others of their class, immigrant status, and Jewish affiliation, once settled, they brought over sisters as potential brides for the largely male, unmarried migrants. Throughout the United States, once a Jewish immigrant peddler decided to get off the road, his thoughts turned to marriage, and the Jewish business networks helped supply the brides.[5]

ON TO SPRINGFIELD

Samuel Rosenwald and Augusta Hammerslough married in August 1857. For a wedding gift, her brothers gave them a store to manage in Peoria, Illinois. The Baltimore Clothing House, a Midwestern outlet for goods shipped from Augusta's family in Maryland, bound the family even more tightly to commerce and to one another. As with many American Jews of the mid-nineteenth century, this expansion brought them into towns and cities in the newly opened regions in the American heartland, beyond the Atlantic seaboard. In the volatile nineteenth century, many businesses opened with great expectations and closed soon afterward. The Rosenwalds' shop in Peoria suffered that fate, but the Baltimore Hammersloughs, not abandoning their kin, sent them to another store, in Talladega, Alabama. This venture lasted even less time than the Peoria shop, and within a year Augusta and Samuel and their son Benjamin (a first child had died in infancy in Peoria) relocated to Evansville, Indiana, where, once more under the auspices of the Baltimore family, they took over the Oak Hall Clothing Company, renaming it S. Rosenwald and Company. Here the Rosenwalds lived for six years, successfully selling men's suits.

At the outbreak of the Civil War the Rosenwalds' benefactors sent them on a final journey, to Springfield, Illinois, the state's capital as of 1839. Three Hammerslough brothers had moved to Springfield in 1856, and the brothers had just opened a store that conducted a brisk business, particularly in the sale of military uniforms. Needing an experienced and trusted manager, they tapped Samuel Rosenwald. He and Augusta remained in Springfield for the next quarter-century, and there she gave birth to their second child to survive infancy, Julius, on August 12, 1862.[6]

In Springfield, the families joined a small but thriving Jewish community. Enough Jews had settled there that by 1858 they could form the Springfield Hebrew Congregation, although they did not charter a synagogue until 1863, when they founded B'rith Sholom. Samuel later served as president of that congregation, and Julius grew up in it, receiving there lifelong lessons that shaped his ideas about the core of Judaism.

The growth of the Jewish population paralleled Springfield's boom times. The city benefited from the capital's move from Vidalia, and agriculture in the surrounding countryside supported town businesses. Lutherans, mostly Germans, constituted a good portion of the white residents. Local investors opened banks, created law firms such as Lincoln and Herndon, and persuaded a number of railroad companies to open lines to link the city to the rest of the state and the nation. The local economy flourished with the rise of manufacturing. Mills and tanneries cropped up, and new mining enterprises in the area led to population growth. Not just immigrants from Europe but both white and black Americans arrived to take advantage of employment possibilities.

All these new residents, regardless of their origins or occupations, needed clothes, which Samuel Rosenwald and his fellow Jews happily provided. The Jews, among their other skills, had enough German at their command that they could handily converse with Springfield's German speakers. The Jewish merchants had also acquired English as peddlers, and now this, their second language, enabled them to deal with others who came into their stores.

In later years writers profiling Julius Rosenwald liked to emphasize his humble origins, reinforcing the idea that in America an impoverished childhood did not hinder future success. B. C. Forbes, a financial writer, included Rosenwald in his pantheon of "men who are making America," listing him among other poor boys who became rich men.[7] But in fact Rosenwald grew up in modest but comfortable circumstances.

The family business thrived during the Civil War, selling uniforms to officers. Samuel Rosenwald prospered enough to buy out his brothers-in-law and become sole proprietor of the emporium in the heart of Springfield's business district. He bought his family an ample wooden house on Eighth Street, across the street from the home Lincoln lived in before leaving for Washington, D.C. Although not wealthy, particularly when measured against Julius's phenomenal treasure of later years, the Rosenwald family never knew deprivation or want.

Julius and his siblings, one older brother and five younger ones, attended the local public school, the Fourth Ward School. He then finished two years of high school. The boys received their Jewish education in the afternoons, for some years offered in rooms above a grocery store owned by a Mr. Salter. Long after he had achieved his great wealth and renown, a number of institutions of higher learning offered him honorary degrees in recognition of his largesse and his notable career in business and philanthropy. He almost always refused such honors, with genuine humility. As he wrote with regard to one such award, "It would embarrass me to accept" the honorary doctorate proffered to him by Illinois College in 1929, not because of "over-modesty" but because "I have a strong feeling, not being a college or university man, I am not entitled to a doctor's degree."[8] (He did accept an honorary degree from the University of Chicago, where he served on the board of trustees, although he expressed discomfort with the honor.)

That he had not finished high school, let alone college, made Rosenwald a typical young Jewish man of his generation, most of whom entered business and succeeded. These young men trained in their parents' shops, learning the business in stockrooms, on the selling floors, and behind cash registers. The Rosenwald family, like many Jews of their era, ignored the religious prohibition on doing business on the Sabbath, and opened their store on Saturdays, when most people shopped. For a merchant specializing in men's clothing, no other day could be as important in moving goods. On Sundays, most American men and women attended to church and family, and some states mandated that businesses cease operations to honor the Lord's Day. From Monday through Friday, male customers worked and married women tended to home chores, but Saturday brought them into the stores. Julius spent Saturdays helping out in his family's shop, deriving basic lessons in merchandising from the experience.

He also found ways as a youngster to make extra money. He played the organ in the local Congregational church, and on one occasion in 1874, at the age of twelve, earned some change by hawking a pamphlet through the streets titled "History of the Monument," a brochure written to mark the dedication of the Lincoln monument in Springfield's Oakwood Cemetery. Julius worked the crowd assembled to witness the unveiling of the massive marble tribute to the Great Emancipator, touting a set of lithographs depicting the memorial structure and declaring them "suitable for framing." He even glimpsed former general U. S. Grant in the gathering, and later remembered as particularly impressive that the future president wore "yellow kid gloves," a fitting recollection by a man who spent his life from childhood on surrounded by men's clothing and whose keen eye for consumer goods helped him make millions.[9]

The Rosenwald family enjoyed a good life in Springfield, as did most Jews there. Certainly if measured by the vitality of their businesses, the Illinois city had smiled on them. In 1872 Samuel Rosenwald reported to his family in Bünde that "last year my business was very satisfactory" and noted, "If one does not do a fairly good business one soon loses out."[10] Less than ten years after putting down his peddler's pack, he owned property, including a store and a house in Illinois as well as a shop in Kansas City, testimony to his success and the beneficence of America. Success in business put Samuel and the other Jewish residents of Springfield in an above-average economic bracket. The wealthy Springfield Jews used their resources in 1876 to move their congregation out of its rented space into a dedicated synagogue building, costing $7,500, and employed a full-time rabbi, Samuel Wolfenstein, a graduate of the rabbinical seminary in Breslau.

Samuel Rosenwald and his Jewish neighbors achieved their success in part because of the city's openness toward Jews, Springfield's only non-Christian residents. Outside business, however, social slights occasionally disturbed their relative comfort. In an 1881 letter to his German relatives Samuel wrote, "I quite forgot that you wanted to be exactly informed about the Jewish question. Although there is not much in the way of *Rischus* [literally, "evil," but here meaning anti-Semitism] here, we are not on the same level with the Christians. . . . In business one hardly ever hears anything like that, but the children often hear about it, and that is unpleasant enough."[11]

The father's words shed some light on how his son would understand the place of Jews. Samuel Rosenwald conveyed a sense of ambiguity as he provided information about the "exact" extent of the problem. He pointed to the *almost* complete absence of anti-Jewish sentiment, and noted that in business it held no sway. Yet he backtracked a bit by stating that "there is not much" anti-Semitism, indicating that there must have been some. American Rischus did not seem to upset Samuel greatly, but he did not like that the children heard the occasional anti-Jewish taunt. This bothered him, and he oscillated between positive and ambivalent feelings, a typical response to the condition of Jews in America.

Why did the Rosenwalds in Germany ask about anti-Semitism? We can only conjecture that they might have read in the widely circulating *Allgemeine Zeitung des Judenthums* that a few years earlier, in 1877, the Jewish financier Joseph Seligman, an immigrant from Bavaria and a former peddler, had been refused admission to the Grand Union Hotel in Saratoga Springs, New York, on the grounds that having "colonies of Jewish people" vacationing in the posh facility would be "obnoxious to the majority of the guests."[12] They could have gleaned from this publication other examples of acts of anti-Jewish exclusion or read the rantings of anti-Semites in various locations around the United States. Yet that same newspaper, like the rest of the European Jewish press, more often heralded Jews' triumphs in the United States, extolling it as a place where Jewish immigrants and their children "have an opportunity to learn a lot," and this luxury, "along with full civil liberty," leads them to prosperity. In the United States, according to the newspaper, "an Israelite has an opportunity to comply—unhindered—with all religious prescriptions." Novels and other published works, as well as letters from emigrant relatives, declared America to be a land of few liabilities for Jews, proliferating in opportunities for economic mobility, religious freedom, and personal liberty.[13]

The German Rosenwalds may have wanted to know whether America in truth conformed to the nearly utopian image spread in Jewish publications. They may also have queried Samuel about conditions in Springfield because despite the march of Jews in Germany toward integration and new rights, anti-Semitism not only flourished all around them but had created a toxic political environment. In 1879, for example, Wilhelm Marr founded his League of Anti-Semites, dedicated to using politics to defeat the growing power of the Jews over Germans. Two years later the eminent German historian Heinrich Treitschke declared in *A Word About Our Jews*, "The Jews are our misfortune." Against the backdrop of a severe economic depression, several anti-Jewish political parties entered German civic life, launching a discussion as to the worthiness of the Jews for citizenship. Publications and gatherings questioned whether Jews could ever become true Germans, a question which mainly elicited negative responses.

The question raised by Samuel Rosenwald's relatives might have reflected contrasts between America and Germany, but Rosenwald's response can be understood as indicating his awareness of the conditions of life for Springfield's other group of others, its African American population, and the dramatic difference between the way Jews, as religious outsiders, fared in the city and the way black people, as racial outsiders, did. Almost all Springfield's black residents made their living as laborers and servants. An 1865 act of the Illinois legislature, passed several years after the Rosenwald family came to Springfield, repealed the Black Laws, which had specifically banned African Americans from settling in the state, but although a substantial number of the capital city's African Americans owned property by the 1870s, they lived in segregated neighborhoods. Until 1873, Springfield strictly segregated schools, and continued to do so even after Gertrude Wright, an African American teenager, secured permission to attend the city's only high school, the one from which Julius Rosenwald later decided to drop out. When the city created its public school system in 1854, town lawmakers declared that they would "furnish gratuitously, to all white children and youth, resident of the city, between the ages of five and twenty-one, a free course of instruction; the cost of which to be defrayed by public taxation." They deliberately left out black children. Springfield's black churches compensated for the educational needs the city denied, although in 1858 the school board did vote to "organize a school for the Colored children within the City." The school facilities soon became overcrowded, and the professional staff could never meet the needs of the community.

Springfield's Jews, by contrast, ran their stores, bought their houses, and organized their communal life wherever and however they wished, unimpeded by law or custom; Springfield's African Americans bought their property, maintained their homes, sent their children to school, worshipped in churches, supported themselves, paid taxes, and participated in the public life of a city whose politicians, newspaper editors, and other leaders defined Springfield as the domain of white people. Springfield newspapers consistently linked black men to crime and deviance. Like many Germans who doubted that the Jews could ever be true Germans, white residents of Springfield, consonant with most white Americans, defined African Americans as different, inferior, innately criminal, and outsiders, unworthy of the full rights of true Americans.[14]

Samuel Rosenwald had noted in his letter that his children "hear about" anti-Jewish rhetoric at school but gave no specifics. Probably the ugly words repeated in Springfield differed little from those Bernard Drachman, later a rabbi, heard in the 1870s as a schoolchild in Jersey City, New Jersey. As he recalled it, children would taunt him with cries of "Jew," "sheeny," and the well-worn "Christ killer." So too Henry Morgenthau, who later shared a rooming house with Julius Rosenwald in New York City, recalled of his Brooklyn childhood: "I had my little difficulties in school. I well remember how one of the boys told me that he deeply sympathized with me, because I would have to overcome the double handicap of being both a Jew and a German."[15]

Did these words bruise the boys who heard them? What

damage did they inflict? Morgenthau considered them "little difficulties," and Samuel Rosenwald as "unpleasant enough." None of these boys changed his religious affiliation or altered his name as a result of schoolyard jibes. Neither did they distance themselves from the Jewish people. Drachman, Morgenthau, and Rosenwald all went on as adults to participate publicly and vigorously in Jewish affairs, at home and abroad, while they held prominent places as Jews in the larger American world.

No doubt the young Bernard, Henry, and Julius and his siblings, the objects of this hostile language, found it painful, but such slights paled beside the constant brutality faced by Springfield's and indeed all of America's black citizens, whether children or adults. Additionally, if their families discussed global Jewish politics, the boys could not but measure the ugly playground slurs as different in degree and kind from the attacks taking place in Germany, contrasting perhaps the Americans' verbal slings with those of Wilhelm Marr, who spoke of the need to lead the German people "the way to victory of Germanism over Judaism," prophesying an inevitable struggle between Jews and Germans.

To Marr, "Judaism" meant the Jews' racial essence. In the America of Julius Rosenwald's youth, "Judaism" conveyed something entirely different. It represented the practice of a religion, the rites of a faith tradition brought by the immigrants to their new home. As a religious system it provided Julius Rosenwald and his peers with a way to exercise their Jewishness and affirm their modernity. The Springfield Hebrew Congregation followed the traditional German rite of *minhag Ashkenaz*. The designation "orthodox" had not yet entered the American Jewish lexicon, but it fit the congregation, the town's only organized Jewish entity. During its first two years, B'rith Sholom, the successor congregation, used a prayer book redacted by the moderate reformer Marcus Jastrow, *Avodat Yis-*

rael, published in German in 1863 and in English in 1865. They later switched to the stridently Reform text *Olat Tamid*, edited by David Einhorn, which prompted a break away from the small congregation by a handful of traditionalists, though not the Rosenwald family. Those who left B'rith Sholom then formed a separate institution, the Young Men's Hebrew Congregation, in protest against the other's slide toward Reform.[16]

Samuel and Augusta Rosenwald participated actively in B'rith Sholom. Samuel served as president for seven years starting in 1867. Julius marked his bar mitzvah a year before the building opened its doors. At fourteen, like most young men and women in Reform congregations, he celebrated his confirmation, a Reform innovation, in the newly dedicated space. Looking back, he reminisced about B'rith Sholom and its meaning to him and his family. He recalled that they "attended Friday evening services regularly and kept the greater holidays." He thus participated in a distinctively American development, the Friday night service. Because Jews in America predominantly made their living in retail and had to operate their stores on Saturdays, American Reform congregations adapted the Friday night service greeting the Sabbath as the main weekly religious rite, rather than the more conventional Saturday morning service. In addition, they transformed synagogue life into a family affair, not just the business of men. After describing his family's Friday night synagogue attendance and congregational membership, Julius speculated, "I always believed that the respect in which the Jews of Springfield were held by their Christian fellows was largely the result of the congregational life," noting that "the Rabbi represented the Jews when an occasion arose."[17]

Julius Rosenwald offered an important insight into nineteenth-century American attitudes toward Jews. He realized that Christians increasingly saw Jewish life as built around religion and housed in synagogues, with rabbis the embodiment of the group. Americans understood the Jews' difference in religious terms. Despite the occasional "Christ killer" invective, Jewishness as a religion in a nation of many denominations proved comprehensible to Americans and enabled immigrant Jews to integrate into American society more easily.

The positive relationships forged across shop counters between Jewish merchants and their non-Jewish customers helped secure a comfortable place for Jews in America, and Julius Rosenwald had no desire to leave his father's occupational niche, the slot of nearly all Springfield Jews. But he wanted to do so on a bigger scale and in a more exciting place than Springfield. In 1879, the seventeen-year-old made his way to America's largest city, where he opened a new chapter in his life.

OFF TO NEW YORK

However pleasant Springfield might have been for Julius and however strong his love for his parents and siblings, he yearned for greater prospects than could be found at his father's clothing store. So, like many a young Jewish man who had grown up in a hinterland town as the son of immigrant peddlers turned shopkeepers, in 1879 he headed to New York to live with and learn from his Hammerslough uncles, who had left Springfield earlier, after having sold their Capitol Clothing store to Samuel, who put up a new sign, "S. Rosenwald, the C.O.D. One Price Clothier."

The uncles, now manufacturers and sellers of men's clothing, had managed to capitalize on the recent invention of the sewing machine, which revolutionized industry in America and left an indelible mark on modern Jewish history. It enabled the mass production of clothes, and the commercial possibilities this heralded spurred several million Jews in eastern Europe to immigrate, an influx that started in the 1860s with migrants from Posen and Lithuania. The garment industry took off, primarily in New York, with Chicago a second center. East European Jews created a vast, constantly growing labor force in America, frequently working in the factories that now belonged to the earlier immigrant Jews from central Europe.

Ensconced in his uncle's opulent home, a four-story townhouse on East 58th Street, JR benefited from the concentration of Jews in the garment industry, a business not solely run by Jews but in which they predominated. His uncles put their nephew to work in the stockroom, a low-level position but excellent training for a man who would eventually build mammoth warehouses crammed with goods for shipping to customers across the country. But Julius yearned for more opportunity, responsibility, and earnings, and worked part time at several other Jewish-owned retail clothing firms. He also started traveling for the Hammersloughs to stores outside New York with which they did business, bearing suitcases stuffed with wares.

In 1881, Julius moved out of the Hammerslough home and took a room in a boardinghouse, where he met other young rising Jewish men, sons of immigrants whose family histories resembled his and who also moved on toward positions of prominence. He shared accommodations with and befriended Henry Morgenthau, a banker whom President Woodrow Wilson would later name the U.S. ambassador to the Ottoman Empire, Henry Goldman, later a partner in the investment house of Goldman Sachs, and Mo Newborg, JR's friend from Springfield and the future founder of the banking house Newborg Company. Morgenthau had immigrated to New York from Germany at age ten, had acquired a substantial American education, and had already entered the banking industry. Goldman was the son of an immigrant peddler who, after selling his wares in the Philadelphia area from a horse-drawn wagon, had become a broker of IOUs in New York and then, in 1882, had founded M. Goldman and Sachs, a bank and investment house, with his son-in-law Samuel Sachs. Henry joined the family concern in 1885, renaming it Goldman Sachs. Moses Newborg's father, also a Jewish immigrant from central Europe, supplied goods to Samuel Rosenwald's store—not bad contacts for a small-town young man eager to move up in the world.

Within a few years, JR took his first steps toward striking out on his own, opening in 1884 his own store in partnership with his brother Morris. Aided by a loan from his father, they launched J. Rosenwald and Brother. When that store failed, JR hatched another scheme. With a line of credit provided by his uncles, he returned to the Midwest, but not to Springfield. Instead, he settled in Chicago, the city the meatpackers had chosen for their massive slaughterhouses, and the railroad barons deemed the ideal hub for the nation's freight. Here JR launched a business manufacturing men's summer suits, the "Special Order Firm" of Rosenwald and Weil. His father helped out again, as did the father of his cousin and partner Julius Weil.

Rosenwald and Weil's suits, like the clothing produced and marketed by most manufacturers, depended on the countless sweatshops springing up in New York, Chicago, and other large cities. Sweatshop labor, condemned by unions and social reformers, allowed Rosenwald and other factory owners to sell goods cheaply and affordably to customers of modest means. The manufacturers and retailers could set low prices because they paid their workers, nearly all immigrants from Italy and eastern and central Europe, pittances. Laboring under dark, unsanitary, and unsafe conditions, adults, women and men alike, as well as children sewed for long hours in their own apartments or in those of contractors and subcontractors. In Chicago, JR and Weil employed workers who had emigrated from Italy and from Lithuania, Bohemia, and Galicia. Rosenwald and Weil apparently felt no sense of concern about the working conditions of their employees or any communal responsibility toward their fellow Jews. Like other manufacturers, they considered immigrant workers necessary to the system from which they hoped to profit.

In his social life, however, Julius Rosenwald put a premium on Jewishness. After he relocated to Chicago, Rosenwald befriended the large family of Emanuel Nusbaum, neighbors on the city's South Side, in Hyde Park. Nusbaum, like Samuel Rosenwald, hailed from the German-speaking lands and had arrived in America as a young man and begun his American life as a peddler. Nusbaum had settled in the small town of Plattsburgh, New York, and made a living as a shopkeeper. Eventually he left upstate New York for Chicago, where he set himself up in the garment business. Through his friendship with Emanuel, JR met two individuals who would change his life, Augusta (Gussie), one of the seven Nusbaum daughters, whom he married in 1890, and her brother Aaron, who became his partner in the Sears venture, the basis for his later fortune.

Aaron Nusbaum had done well in the clothing business, but, a go-getter, he enjoyed hunting for new opportunities. In 1893, during the Chicago World's Columbian Exposition marking the four hundredth anniversary of Columbus's voyage to the Americas, he found one. He obtained a concession to sell carbonated water to the crowds thronging the Midway extravaganza, earning a quick $150,000 profit from the 27 million thirsty fairgoers. He then invested the money in the Bastedo Tube Company, manufacturer of pneumatic tubes, a technological innovation pioneered in the 1830s to shoot messages and money from one floor of a department store to another.

Nusbaum, searching for customers to buy his tubes, approached Richard Sears. Sears, however, in need of a substantial loan, cared less about Nusbaum's tubes than Nusbaum's money. A Minnesotan, Sears had been working as a railroad station agent when he stumbled upon a cache of unclaimed watches. He bought the whole box from the manufacturer and sold them at a nice profit. Deciding that he could distribute other consumer goods via the railroads, he expanded his merchandise, selling watches, clothing, including suits made by JR's company, jewelry, and sewing machines through a catalogue. By the time he met Aaron Nusbaum, Sears had taken on a partner, Alvah Roebuck, who made and repaired watches. The thriving business kept the two so busy they could not handle the volume of orders.

Although not the first of this kind, having been preceded by that of Montgomery Ward in 1872 and the Spiegel catalogue of 1865, the Sears catalogue boasted some distinctive and innovative features. Sears and Roebuck designed their catalogue to be smaller than the others, not in page length but in height, on the hunch that people who had in their homes several catalogues would stack them in a single pile, putting the smallest on top. Thus they would find the Sears catalogue first, whether looking for a specific item or just browsing. The Sears catalogue carried instructions not only on ordering but on sending back unwanted goods, and promised low prices, in part because the company started manufacturing much of what it sold.

Recognizing a good business opportunity, Nusbaum talked his brother-in-law into joining him. A friend, the lawyer Albert Loeb, drew up the partnership documents. In return, he received four shares of Sears stock, which enabled him to break a tie if the partners disagreed. He also served as general counsel to the company through his firm Loeb and Adler. (In the 1920s Loeb briefly became the subject of painful publicity when his son Richard, in partnership with a friend, Nathan Leopold, on a lark kidnapped and then killed a neighbor's child, Bobby Franks. The trial, in which the youths were defended by Clarence Darrow, made news around the world. Three weeks later, Albert Loeb died of a heart attack.)

Nusbaum stepped in as general manager, secretary, and treasurer, while Sears continued as president. JR, despite the money he had brought in, started out in a decidedly inferior position, overseeing the men's clothing department. But almost from the moment Rosenwald and Nusbaum took up their offices at Sears, irreconcilable frictions developed between them, pitting Sears and Nusbaum against each other. Nusbaum, according to one history of Sears, tended to be haughty, not particularly adept at working with others, and uninterested in promoting a pacific working environment. Rosenwald and Richard Sears soon forged an alliance against Nusbaum, whose style they considered harmful to the business.[18] Sears in particular, unhampered by family connections to Nusbaum, found the situation intolerable, and in 1900 decided that he could no longer work with Nusbaum. Sears reportedly came into Rosenwald's office and declared, "Someone's got to go. Either you and Nusbaum buy me out or you and I buy him out."[19]

So JR, despite the close family relationship, cast his lot with Richard Sears. Albert Loeb, who in short order became corporate secretary of Sears and then vice president and treasurer, drew up the papers, and the two partners offered Nusbaum a million-dollar buyout. Nusbaum persuasively demanded more, a million and a half. Nusbaum's departure gave JR and Sears full control of the company. A rare cloud on his otherwise sunny personal life, JR, though he regretted the way financial considerations had disrupted the family solidarity, never spoke to Nusbaum again, causing much sorrow for Gussie, who also severed connections with her brother.

That Rosenwald and Richard Sears could pay this amount to get rid of a problematic partner testified to the company's robust business and the widespread popularity of its name. That success had been stimulated in part by Julius Rosenwald's insistence that the company focus on instilling trust in its customers. Farm families in remote regions, Rosenwald reasoned, had to know that products bought from Sears would be of good quality at a fair price. The woman in her home anywhere in America had to be certain that the company stood behind every item she bought and that if anything fell short of her expectations, she could easily return it for a full refund.

Rosenwald himself spent his first years at Sears managing the operation of the company, including customer relations. He relished his role, and Sears boomed, becoming so successful that in 1904 the partners realized that the company needed a significantly larger physical plant to handle operations. Without more space, Sears could neither fulfill current orders nor grow.

The company undertook a mammoth construction project, which Rosenwald oversaw, of a new headquarters spread over forty acres on Chicago's west side near the railroad yards. The work took only a year to complete but exceeded the company's financial resources. Needing cash, JR tapped into his contacts, turning to his one-time flatmate Henry Goldman, now head of Goldman Sachs, for a loan. Goldman convinced Rosenwald that Sears, Roebuck would be better served by transforming itself into a publicly owned company and issuing preferred and common stock. Sears, Roebuck became the second retail company in American business history to issue an IPO, an initial public offering. Goldman's advice transformed Rosenwald and Richard Sears into millionaires.

Rosenwald in that first decade of the century turned his attention to the inner workings of the company. He came up with the idea of offering veteran employees the chance to buy the company's first publicly traded shares, a strategy which a decade later germinated into its trademark extensive employee profit-sharing program, something businesses nationwide would replicate.

Rosenwald launched this project, as well as an array of other employee programs, after he had been running the company singlehandedly for several years. As partners, Rosenwald and Richard Sears differed over several matters, including expansions and marketing strategies. Sears had a bold, daring vision of where and how the company could grow, while Rosenwald tended to be more restrained and cautious. He particularly worried about Sears's idea of opening plants outside Chicago, a plan that Sears proposed during the Panic of 1907, known as the Bankers' Panic or Knickerbocker Crisis, when shares on the New York Stock Exchange tumbled by nearly 50 percent, hitting the company hard.

Rosenwald worried that the company would overextend itself, and most of the employees, many now shareholders, agreed. Richard Sears tended to think big. He proposed opening a branch in Dallas and offering incentive programs to steady customers. Rosenwald opposed both plans, considering the expansion too risky and the incentive program too expensive and not worth the potential negative consequences of loss of business rather than growth. (American business historians have sided with Sears.) A 1988 history of the company described the tension between the two men and their temperamental differences through a series of dichotomies: Sears was "an opportunist and immediate benefit tactician," Rosenwald "a strategist, always with a long-term plan. Sears was a star and Rosenwald a team player. Sears overshadowed others. Rosenwald developed them. . . . Sears lived for the mail-order moment and Rosenwald for the long-term pull."[20]

Such differences poisoned the air at Sears headquarters, causing Rosenwald concern about the future. Beset by personal, family, and health problems, Richard Sears resigned in 1908, though he served as chairman of the board until his death six years later, in 1914. For the next ten years, the son of a former peddler and impecunious immigrant Jew from Bünde reigned supreme at one of the nation's largest companies, stepping back from active leadership in 1924 when his civic work and philanthropic projects consumed him more than the drive for wealth.

During his active years at the company, particularly once Sears moved aside, Rosenwald oversaw the nation's largest mail-order house, earning double Montgomery Ward's profits. Sears not only sold goods of nearly every kind, small and large, including houses that customers could assemble on their own, it owned or maintained an interest in twenty-five factories, which churned out every product a customer could conceivably want. From 1908 until 1924, Julius Rosenwald *was* Sears, the embodiment of the company. He attended to details of the entire process from manufacturing to shipping. Rosenwald decided what Sears would carry and what it would drop. He abhorred patent medicines, for example, and discontinued their sale, and removed guns and ammunition from the catalogue.

In 1910 Sears, Roebuck employed over six thousand employees. Three years later that number grew threefold. In 1920 the company's mammoth operation earned $245 million in sales. To enable Sears to produce most of the goods it sold, Rosenwald went on a factory-buying spree, acquiring facilities around the country to produce goods at a volume much larger and a price much lower than he could have negotiated with other manufacturers. He devised a scheme to upgrade pre-existing factories, providing new machinery and modernizing facilities. His scheme worked. Large items like pianos and organs made in Louisville, Kentucky, or buggies, churned out in a factory in Evansville, Indiana, went directly to customers. Smaller items traveled from the Chicago plant via railroad.

Part of the company's success lay in employee relations. Even before Rosenwald's accession to sole leadership, he pioneered an employee benefits program, the Sears Mutual Benefit Association. Initially open only to workers who had been with the firm for at least five years, it later became available to anyone with three years' service. Intended to build a loyal workforce, the plan addressed an acute problem in early-twentieth-century America: the loss of disgruntled workers to better jobs. Constant worker turnover hampered smooth operations and cut into profits. Rosenwald wanted to maintain the flow of business and therefore needed to create and retain a contented workforce.

In the Sears arrangement, workers had the chance to buy company shares. The company offered them paid sick days, and all enjoyed a week's paid vacation. In 1912, Rosenwald instituted a system in which workers with five years of service received bonus checks of 5 percent of their salary as tokens of thanks. These checks helped induce both the women of Sears, who earned on average $9.12 a week, and the men, who, typical of the time, earned more, on average $15.41, to stay on, rather than look for other jobs. The following year the bonus climbed to 6 percent, capped at 10 percent after ten years of service. Rosenwald also established an employee savings bank with a guaranteed 5 percent interest. As befit a patriot who took a leave of absence during World War I to work for the government in Washington, D.C., Rosenwald paid in full any worker (presumably male) who left temporarily to serve in the National Guard.[21]

But Rosenwald's corporate benevolence, indeed paternalism, sprang from more than a fear of losing workers. He operated his business at a time of increased labor militancy, when around the country unions embarked on energetic campaigns to convince workers that they should join together. Unions sought to recruit members to unite and demand that their employers agree to collective bargaining. The workers sought higher wages and better work conditions. They hoped to win over governments, state and federal, to support unionization. Labor activists knew Chicago, the headquarters of Sears, to be a union town, where organized labor enjoyed wide support among workers and their neighbors, and they targeted non-union businesses for their organizing campaigns.

In the first decades of the twentieth century, labor demands roiled American society, while union activists argued that laissez-faire economics, in which business pursued profits unchecked and unregulated, could not hold. In the 1910s union membership rose, and with it wages. Sears employees, women and men drawn from working-class families and neighborhoods, would have seen friends, peers, and kin reaping the benefits of unionization in their places of employment. Many Sears employees worked in factories, making the goods sold under the Sears name. Sears warehouse workers labored under industrial-like conditions. Sears workers would have appeared to union campaigners as excellent candidates for unionization. But JR abhorred unions.

Even after he became deeply entrenched in Chicago's reform community, funding many of its most outstanding projects, and developed close political and personal relationships with reformers such as Jane Addams, Grace and Edith Abbott, Sophonisba Breckinridge, and Graham Taylor, all supporters of the Women's Trade Union League, Rosenwald balked at unionization. Business for Rosenwald constituted business while social reform, in which he believed deeply, meant something different. Strikes he considered bullying tactics that deprived people of their livelihoods. Even when immigrant Jews, with whom he empathized, stood on the picket lines, as they did in the 1910 action by the Amalgamated Clothing Workers Union against Hart, Shaffner, and Marx, he condemned the protesters. Two leaders of that strike, Bessie Abramowitz and Sidney Hillman, had come from the east European Jewish immigrant community in Chicago, which rallied behind the strikers. (Hillman worked at the Sears warehouse infant-wear department, from 1907 until 1909.)

Edith Abbott, a towering figure of Chicago reform and JR's close ally in many Progressive endeavors, noted in her unpublished diary, during the strike, "Mr. Rosenwald did not agree with Grace [her sister] about trade-unions, and we all felt sorry during the garment workers' strike to think that he wasn't with us." She continued, "Some of the girls who came to the meetings at [Jane Addams's] Hull House were from the shops of Mr. Rosenwald's company." The *Chicago Tribune* reported that over a hundred young women from Sears joined the strikers. Rosenwald insisted on keeping his business life and civic activism separate. During that famous strike, Rosenwald and Grace Abbott sat together at a board meeting of the Immigrants' Protective League, which she headed and which he almost singlehandedly funded. As Abbott got up to leave the meeting early in order to deliver a speech at a union demonstration, Rosenwald said, without embarrassment or irony, "I know where you're going and I wouldn't agree with what you are going to say. But I want you to get there safely." He then directed his chauffeur to drive her to the gathering so she could advocate for a position he opposed.[22] (He had softened his position a bit by the 1920s. Although he still refused to give money to the Women's Trade Union League, he admitted that "there is no question of its worthiness," something he would not have said a decade earlier.)[23]

His eagerness to forestall unionization helped push him to create in 1916 his widely touted and nationally copied profit-sharing plan. Some of his Chicago-based shareholders who favored unionization and who believed that business ought to manifest a social conscience also influenced him. These few individuals worked with JR in various Progressive reform activities and they leaned on him gently to rethink his position that business and good works ought not mix. Louise de Koven Bowen, a pro-union reform-activist shareholder, wrote JR in 1915 acknowledging that while she appreciated the robust size of her Sears dividend check, she "must also confess to a feeling of responsibility as a stockholder—and perhaps some sense of guilt—that in these hard times so large a sum is to be distributed among the stockholders and that the employees are to have no share whatever in it."[24]

Most shareholders probably did not experience her "feeling of responsibility" or "sense of guilt," rejoicing mostly, or even exclusively, in the heft of their dividends. But in the heady days of Progressivism, labor agitation, and reform activities, Rosenwald, an opponent of unions, a Progressive, and by all accounts an employer who cared about his workers, hit upon a scheme to combine profit with benevolence. When in 1916 Sears, Roebuck initiated the Employees Savings and Profit Sharing Plan it had no equal. Although not the first of its kind, it proved the boldest. The *New York Times* at the end of the year declared it "the most liberal and comprehensive" such plan in the nation. Instituted by Rosenwald, with the assistance of Albert Loeb, the Sears profit-sharing venture allowed all employees who had worked for Sears for three years to contribute 5 percent of their annual salary to the overall pool. Sears matched that amount of money. To ensure that higher-paid workers did not benefit more than those who earned less, the arrangement forbade anyone from putting in more than the 5 percent.

Rosenwald envisioned the scheme as a way to aid employees when they retired, assuming that they had worked for the company long enough. Heirs could access this money if the employee died before drawing it after retirement. Before the passage of the Social Security Act in 1935, the cessation of the family breadwinner's active work imperiled the entire family.[25] Rosenwald's plan proved an immediate success. According to the *New York Times* article nearly all who qualified joined at once. It also had the effect Rosenwald had hoped of inspiring job longevity. Sears workers apparently felt that they functioned as something other and more than employees. One secretary told the *Times* reporter (possibly to curry favor with management), "My dear sir, we are now part of the firm."[26]

In the ensuing years, Sears faced both good and bad years,

and how Rosenwald navigated these testified to the degree to which he considered the company an extension of himself, demonstrating concern for employees and customers. When 1919 promised to be a high profit year, following record sales during the war, a soaring volume of business, and the stock's rosy health, JR moved ahead with a plan to open a branch in Philadelphia to operate as a massive catalogue supply center. He placed his twenty-eight-year-old son Lessing, who had started working for him in 1911 as a shipping clerk, in charge.

Then in 1920 the nation suffered a dramatic, if brief, deflationary recession. Lasting eighteen months, it produced a sharp rise in unemployment and a precipitous drop in production. This downturn hit Sears particularly hard, as a company that encouraged people of modest means to spend money on items they could generally live without. In particular, the depression hit farmers, who made up a large part of the Sears customer base. Falling sales in 1921 forced layoffs, as company officials contemplated lowering prices to offset tumbling stocks.

Faced with a number of unpalatable choices, JR decided that orders made before the downturn could not in good faith be canceled. Doing so would amount to a moral and ethical breach. Instead, he instituted a new strategy to stimulate new markets, to compensate for declining agricultural sales, and to develop a new customer base. Previously both Sears and its biggest rival, Montgomery Ward, had advertised solely through their catalogues, assuming that most of their customers lived in rural areas. Now the two firms decided to reach out to urban and suburban dwellers by opening city outlet stores for the stock of goods farm families could not afford, a wise move, since according to the U.S. Census Bureau, the 1920 census indicated for the first time that a majority of Americans lived in cities. To encourage city shoppers, Sears began an advertising campaign in newspapers.

Rosenwald also examined the company's internal workings to ferret out inefficiency and mismanagement. Executives, himself included, now had to arrive by eight in the morning and stay until late at night. He streamlined the Sears bureaucracy and put a stop to his highly paid executives' practice of taking time off whenever they felt like it. But despite these efforts, by year's end Sears still faced the danger of failing, as stocks dipped further and the factories producing its goods closed down. For JR this called for a drastic measure to stem the decline and possible death of his company.

Encouraged by Albert Loeb, JR boldly announced that he would donate $5 million of his own wealth to save the company. He would also personally purchase the Homan Avenue property which Sears occupied. In dipping into his own resources to offset company losses, Rosenwald placed the welfare of his employees and shareholders, as well as the city of Chicago and the nation, ahead of his personal acquisition of wealth, although he worried about his own future and that of his children. Harry Sachs, son-in-law of Henry Goldman, dubbed this "one of the most generous acts" in the commercial world "that has ever come under my notice." Rosenwald, he wrote, had evinced a most "remarkable attitude towards the company's stockholders."[27] Likewise, C. W. Barron, a Boston newspaperman who in 1912 had purchased the Dow Jones Company, informed readers of his publication, the *Boston News Bureau:* "There is a broader lesson of the sort of trusteeship shown by the man whose commercial genius did so much for the almost romantic upbuilding of the concern known to thousands of farmer families. In that same sweep of country it has been the fashion for many to conceive of men of wealth and captains of industry as utterly selfish and as given to preying on the misfortunes of others. Here is the chivalric answer!"[28]

Rosenwald's move, though risky, demonstrated his commitment to the company that had enriched him. It saved the jobs of his workers and the investment of the company's many stockholders, while enabling Sears to serve the huge buying public that had come to rely on its products.

His actions grew out of a complex of motives. The salvation of Sears, of course, meant economic benefit for Rosenwald and his family, so in this his move could be seen as one of self-interest. But it also reflected a deep concern for the common good. Whether judged as privileging one over the other, he followed no precedent in taking this action.

His generous gamble paid off. Shortly after his seemingly impetuous leap into uncharted waters, the economy rallied and the nation entered into eight years of prosperity, fueled by a frenzy of consumer spending on nondurable goods. Rosenwald's decision to nurture a nonrural customer base proved a canny reading of demographic trends. As Sears began opening retail stores in cities and suburbs, throughout the 1920s young people from rural communities began moving in, forced out by the crisis in agriculture, which did not share in the country's prosperity. These new urban dwellers now found in Sears stores the goods and brands they had grown up with.

Meanwhile, Sears did not abandon the farmers despite their declining numbers and the loss of sales. Rosenwald had been working for the relief of his best customers since 1912, when he had contributed money to the Crop Improvement Committee, which placed agents in rural counties around the country. These agents assisted farmers with advice on seed improvement, crop choices, and related matters. Rosenwald offered to donate a thousand dollars to every agricultural county that wished to hire a local agent as long as residents of the county raised some of money themselves to pay the experts' salaries. In time 110 counties, the first in Rosenwald's home state of Illinois, received such funding, as he spent more than one million dollars, mostly in the Midwest.[29]

The Sears, Roebuck Agricultural Foundation, founded in 1923, followed upon this earlier work. The foundation provided expertise to farmers who sent in queries on technical and economic problems. It offered cash grants to groups of farmers who worked together to tackle common concerns and paid youth leaders to work with girls and boys in what became a forerunner to the 4-H clubs. In 1924, Sears launched its own radio station, WLS (referencing the company's well-deserved brag, the "world's largest store"), aimed at the nation's farmers. Broadcast initially from the Sears headquarters on Homan Avenue, it offered farmers a chance to use this newest, hottest technology to enhance their lives and livelihoods, broadcasting the kind of advice and information that farmers needed in their work.

In the 1920s mass consumption in the United States soared. Household appliances in particular proliferated, sparked by the spread of home electrification, making refrigerators, washing machines, toasters, and vacuum cleaners both desirable and available to many families of modest means. This period, when so many Americans seemed to taste prosperity, might be seen as the golden age of the American consumer, and Sears, with Julius Rosenwald at the helm, made their material dreams a reality.

Rosenwald put a great deal of emphasis on marketing, feeding the public a steady stream of articles with stories about the company and the positive impact of consumption and by extension the positive value of capitalism. The mass purchasing of goods, these articles declared directly and by implication, unified Americans, erasing differences that had separated them, including rural versus urban, and even well-off versus the less well-off. If most Americans could live in private homes, furnished with tables and chairs, couches and comfortable beds, wallpaper and rugs, and could put cars in their garages and vacuum cleaners in their closets, then differences in class became less onerous. Mass production, distribution, and consumption, these articles proclaimed, heralded the end of social conflict.

An *American Magazine* article detailed the volume of Sears's annual sales, glorying in the catalogue's heft and reach. The catalogue now weighed five pounds, ran over a thousand pages, and contained one hundred thousand items. Over 32 million people had purchased something from it during the previous year, ordering, for example, 20 million rolls of wallpaper, enough to circumnavigate the globe four times. These millions of customers clearly trusted the name Sears, and the articles linked the company name with that of its most visible representative, Julius Rosenwald.

The articles emanating from Sears, frequently written by Rosenwald himself, emphasized his humble origins, simple tastes, loyalty to Sears employees, and hard work and long hours put into the company. Clearly serving as company public relations, the pieces, regardless of where published, asserted that Rosenwald's employees did not work *for* him but *with* him, that he depended upon them as much as they relied upon him, and that together they had made Sears "the world's largest store." These articles emphasized that the millionaire eschewed luxury and ostentation. In 1905, early in Rosenwald's years at Sears, *Architectural Digest* had reviewed his newly constructed home in Chicago's Hyde Park neighborhood and depicted it as "plain and even severe," imbued with "dignity without the slightest pretension."[30] In 1920, the *Independent*, a nationally circulating New York magazine, in an article on Sears fittingly titled, "Satisfaction or Your Money Back," described him as a man who "wears no jewelry or other marks of wealth. . . . He works ten or twelve hours a day, setting a pace that few of his young employees can follow; the only thing that appeals to him more than work is a personal affection or a philanthropic duty. . . . He holds that employees require few written laws; their own sense of right should govern them; it is better to have a principle of right in man's heart than a rule of conduct in his head. Principles not rules are the guiding force of the company."[31]

The magazines portrayed a genial, humble man who had climbed to the loftiest rungs of American industry not despite but because of his small-town modesty. They connected his character to the nature of his business. He had become rich because he knew how to appeal to the public, giving it, in all of its diversity, what it wanted. He, as the embodiment of Sears, recognized that Americans not only yearned for material things; they wanted nearly boundless choices of goods. And if Americans did not yet want these things, he could teach them to do so. Simultaneously the articles praised him for instituting employee practices that had undermined the appeal of the labor movement. The press coverage joined the names of Sears and Rosenwald, conveying a positive impression of a highly successful but consistently humane capitalist.

Occasionally negative articles appeared that countered the celebratory portrayal that predominated. References to Rosenwald as a man who had made millions while his nonunionized workers groveled for corporate handouts jarred with the company's portrait. Particularly after the image of Rosenwald the philanthropist began eclipsing that of Rosenwald the businessman, articles began chiding him for giving away millions while his employees earned meager wages. Joseph Fels, a millionaire soap manufacturer and philanthropist, and like Rosenwald the child of Jewish immigrants from German-speaking lands, alerted JR to a vitriolic attack published in a Manitoba newspaper, *The Grain Growers' Guide*, titled "One Form of Philanthropy." It sneered, "No wonder some Great Moguls in the realm of commerce have money for charity. Julius Rosenwald, president of the Sears Roebuck Company . . . has made quite an enviable name for himself as a philanthropist. Yet his fortune is based on a system in which the Golden Rule does not play a conspicuous part. Girl employees of his wealthy firm testified before the Illinois Senate Committee that they work ten hours a day for $4.50 a week. Forewomen, called 'Scotters,' were employed to speed up the tired girls with threats of dismissal whenever their overworked frames sought a moment's rest." Referring to JR's "perverted ideas of charity," the author called him a "would-be-philanthropist . . . trying to buy back respectability with blood money." Rosenwald, he counseled, ought to turn his "attention to working out justice in business."[32]

Rosenwald never responded to such criticisms, continuing to oppose unions, and articulating an unswerving commitment to his moral vision of good employee policies and to capitalism. In this, as in his civic undertakings, once he made up his mind about a course of action, attacks did not faze him, regardless of their source, logic, or moral underpinnings.

AN AMERICAN SUCCESS STORY

How might we explain Rosenwald's business success? What made him so adept a marketer? He himself consistently placed an emphasis on circumstance, stating in 1929, "If I had followed a definite program instead of taking the lucky breaks I would still be in a modest clothing business in the Loop," Chicago's central city hub. Ironically, on the eve of the Great Depression, he went on to predict, "America is just as ready for any new ideas today as it was nearly thirty years ago for the mail order idea," and to assert that anyone who so desired could become a millionaire. Rosenwald's optimism seemed boundless, and it shaped his approach to life as well as to business.[33]

Some of his success no doubt depended on that optimism, as well as on his intellect, intuition, sound judgment, and ability to size up people and markets. In ways that could not be learned in the classroom, he figured out how to evaluate situations with acuity, and brought to his decisions warmth, humility, and a sense of humor. He surrounded himself with talented people, and his sure touch in interpersonal relationships served him well as a manager. He seems to have genuinely, if paternalistically, cared about others and to have looked out for his employees' welfare in both large and small measures. He ate his lunch almost every day in the employees' cafeteria, and he made a policy of promoting from within. One business writer of the time attributed Rosenwald's success to his "unflagging and unfailing thoughtfulness. . . . He has infused into business a soul and impulse that serve the highest and best ethical purpose."[34]

Edwin Embree, who would play a crucial role in Rosenwald's philanthropic work, heading the Rosenwald Fund founded in 1924, observed of Rosenwald's place in the growth of Sears: "It is difficult to assess Julius Rosenwald's contribution. . . . He was quick and astute, but never pretended to be a business genius. He had a gift for judging the worth of other men and putting them in responsible posts. . . . He held firmly to the policy of rigorously honest dealing. And he had an intuitive sense that continually astounded his associates. Frequently, at business conferences, after listening quietly to a proposal, he would shake his head and say with conviction, 'I can't tell you what's wrong with it, but I don't like it.' Almost invariably he was found to be right."[35]

But his business practices alone cannot explain his enormous success. Rather, a complex web of historical circumstances created an environment in which Julius Rosenwald could use these qualities to their best advantage. Rosenwald came to Sears at a particularly propitious moment in American business history, just as railroads, automobiles, and trucks enabled retailers to ship almost everything they stocked almost anywhere in the country.

Trucking provides a good example. Until 1900, the distribution of goods to consumers outside cities depended on railroads, which conveyed the merchandise from its point of manufacture to an urban depot. From there, loaded on horse-drawn wagons, it laboriously traversed poor roads to remote outposts where a few customers awaited it, relying on animal-driven vehicles that limited the size of the items that could be carried. But technological breakthroughs in the early twentieth century, just as Rosenwald moved into sole leadership of Sears, changed all this. The first decade of the twentieth century saw the birth of modern trucking, with the development of gasoline-powered engines, new forms of transmission, and gear drives that allowed large trucks to go where railroads could not with goods that horses could not carry. By 1914, one hundred thousand trucks plied America's roads. Trucks had become so prevalent and crucial to the life of the nation that the previous year, states began limiting the permissible weights of the loads they could carry.

Innovations in the United States Postal Service also played a part in transforming Sears's business. In 1906 Congress instituted the rural free delivery system, liberating farmers from having to go to town to pick up the mail. Now a postman came to their front door bearing packages containing items chosen from the catalogue. They could do this because so many roads had been paved outside cities, and these two factors enabled Sears—and Rosenwald—to move more goods farther and more quickly.

When Rosenwald bought into the firm it already enjoyed the blessings of good name recognition, made possible by wide customer satisfaction with its wares, goods that defined American consumerism. He enlarged and expanded the range of products, at the same time expanding the consumer base. Despite the nation's periodic panics and downturns, class inequities, lack of meaningful government regulation, and absence of protection for consumers and workers, early-twentieth-century Americans, including industrial laborers, immigrants, farmers, and modest shopkeepers, consumed goods at levels unimaginable to their European counterparts. They ate more food, and enjoyed a more varied diet; they lived in larger dwelling spaces, filling them with more objects, practical and whimsical, useful and aesthetic, than any other people in the world. They stocked their homes with dishes and cutlery, clothing and shoes, toys and appliances, pianos and furniture, sheets and towels, rugs and curtains. And having more, they wanted more. Their level of consumption did not seem remarkable to them, though it astounded immigrants and other visitors from abroad. David Potter, a 1950s historian, characterized Americans as a "people of plenty," a collectivity which defined access to material goods as essential to national identity. He traced this aspect of the American character back to the country's earliest years, even before independence.[36]

That well-known love of goods had inspired Samuel Rosenwald, the Hammersloughs, and tens of thousands of other young Jewish immigrant peddlers to head for America. They had heard that if they strapped packs on their backs and went into the American backcountry, they would find customers for whatever goods they carried. Only the magnitude of the selling distinguished Julius Rosenwald from his peddler and later modest shopkeeper father. Efficiency of production, scale of distribution, and ease of transportation made JR a multimillionaire.

The Jewish communal infrastructure of social contacts, family ties, common ancestry, and shared values offered another factor in the success of both father and son. With the exception of Richard Sears, up to the moment JR became the undisputed head of the company, everyone he worked with, turned to for money or advice, or relied upon came from his familiar and familial world. Networks of kinship and trust helped and supported these immigrants and their sons, enabling many to prosper in their new home.

Most of JR's peers in the American Jewish community operated in the same economic niche that he did. Retail, especially of clothing, lay at the heart of the American Jewish economy. Reared in a tradition of salesmanship, they took their expertise to their new land. It did not matter that their customers back home had spoken German, Czech, or Polish, while the new ones spoke English. These immigrants arrived knowing how to assess people's material wants, how to cultivate suppliers and keep accounts, and how to make the sales.

Rosenwald's fame and fortune flowed from his circumstances. They cannot be separated from his parents' migration to America from a particular place at a specific time. His personal, family, and communal heritage of commerce shaped his American success story, and his achievement owed as much to historical contingency as to his own endeavors or the luck he often credited. That he far outstripped all of his peers ought to be seen as a matter of degree. They shared the common history of a generation.

How can we measure Julius Rosenwald's success? One 1990 compilation assessed his wealth, measuring him against other Americans of stupendous wealth, individuals who came both before and after him. In *The Wealthy 100, from Benjamin Franklin to Bill Gates*, Rosenwald sits nearly in the middle of an exclusive club. Coming in at number 57, JR tops his former partner Richard Sears (89), and stands alone among his highly successful fellow Jews, with names like Lehman, Schiff, Fels, Warburg, Seligman, Goldman, Sachs, Straus (Levi, Nathan, Oscar, and Isidor), and Guggenheim, names recognizable for decades to come.[37]

Rosenwald would not have cared about his ranking. He valued success and loved the life that wealth brought him, but he reveled in using his riches to do good.

A NEW DIRECTION

While the name of Julius Rosenwald would continue to be linked to that of Sears, a major change in their relationship took place in 1924, when Rosenwald, who held a $150 million personal interest in the company, stepped down from the presidency, although he stayed on as chairman of the board. From this time on, he dedicated the largest share of his time and energy to his philanthropic and civic work. While he continued to play a substantial role in the company's affairs, especially after the 1929 crash of the stock market and the Great Depression of the 1930s, making money and the minutiae of the company took a backseat to his bigger work of repairing the world.

JR had been involved in many civic concerns well before 1924. During World War I, for example, he had taken leave from Sears to work in Washington, D.C., on a commission that advised the Council of National Defense. He chaired the council's Committee on Supplies, overseeing the purchase and distribution of goods to the army. This work not only appealed to his patriotism, it made use of his extensive knowledge of ordering, stocking, and allocating materials. It also brought him into contact with a group of nationally prominent Jews, including the future U.S. Supreme Court justice Felix Frankfurter and the financier Bernard Baruch.

The seven-member Advisory Commission of the Council of National Defense marked an important moment in American Jewish history. For the first time in American history, Jews played visible roles in national affairs, and for the first time the federal government looked to Jewish experts for national guidance. President Wilson appointed three Jews to the commission: JR, Baruch, and Samuel Gompers, the president of the American Federation of Labor. Rosenwald served enthusiastically, but became frustrated by the reports of waste and lack of coordination between suppliers of goods and the army, which caused chaos in the materiel flowing to the troops in France. In 1918 he decided that he could better serve by going to France to work directly with the troops. So he donned a uniform and went "over there," quipping that with this assignment, people should address him as "General Merchandise."

Rosenwald's war work, following more than a decade of activity in civic affairs, influenced his decision to step back from running the company. He now turned his attention to work of a different order, and from then on the public would know him as a philanthropist, a molder of public life through his program of giving, and an individual eager to change the world around him.

2

Not by Bread Alone

WELL BEFORE his ascendancy into the city's and nation's merchant elites, long before he became, according to *The Wealthy 100*'s list, the fifty-seventh richest man in American history, Julius Rosenwald thought about how best to use his wealth, should he be fortunate enough to acquire it. In the late 1890s he had mused with friends about the future, when he might earn, say, fifteen thousand dollars a year (approximately $14 million in 2010 dollars). He figured that he would expend a third on living expenses, ensuring a comfortable life for his family and himself. Another third would "be laid aside," for the future. The final third would, naturally, "go to charity."[1]

The individual who envisioned a future in which he could dispose of a substantial chunk of his yearly earnings to benefit others, for what he then called "charity," would probably have been pleased to know that he would one day find a spot on a 2013 list, "American History's Great Philanthropists," published in the magazine *American Philanthropy*. No doubt the caption accompanying his picture would also have brought him joy. The profiles, organized in alphabetical order in the "Philanthropy Hall of Fame," presented Rosenwald as a person who had directed his vast wealth toward "reinforcing the unity of America," nudging "the nation closer to fulfilling the promise of its founding." Bringing Americans together and reminding them of that promise gave him a guiding principle which informed his philanthropic work, from his first ventures in Chicago to his later national and global causes, chief among them assisting America's black population and Jews worldwide. His understanding of the obligations imposed on him as a Jew in particular guided his philanthropic mission and the projects he embraced. His philanthropic work reflected his deep belief in America and his desire to make it a fairer, more inclusive and humane place that would offer safe haven for Jews. Being publicly identified as Jewish meant that whenever he gave away his money or embraced a cause, others viewed him as a representative of all Jews, and his act as a manifestation of Jewishness.

HOW TO GIVE AND WHY TO DO SO

Rosenwald did not believe in simply handing out money to worthy causes. He directed his wealth toward countering prejudice, easing poverty, and promoting civic unity, and his gifts reflected an ideology of philanthropy, in which each contribution would ideally spur equivalent donations from others. Rosenwald's philosophy of philanthropy, therefore, never took the form of the anonymous gift. He did not hesitate to let the world know about his donations—both the causes to which he gave and the amount of the gifts. In one article, written for the *Saturday Evening Post* in 1929, he reported: "The program of public welfare for which I stand sponsor and which provides for the spending of a sum in round figures, both capital and interest of at least seventy-five million dollars" ought to attract others with means and a civic consciousness. This declaration did not reflect a desire to boast about his great wealth. He did not need to give his money away to do that. Rather, by publicly announcing the amount of his gifts to various causes, he hoped to stimulate further contributions, large and small.[2]

He nearly always made his bequests in the form of matching funds. Beneficiary institutions had to raise equal or at least sizable contributions from others. He wanted those organizations to reach out to a wide base of supporters and as such demonstrate the degree to which they spoke to a broad public. Whether Hull House, the University of Chicago, or the many Jewish institutions he supported, such as the Jewish Joint Distribution Committee, he expected that all the recipients of his gifts would be able to appeal to large numbers of other donors, developing a wide base of contributors. Even if that public chipped in small amounts, their participation betokened a cause worth supporting and an institution which knew how to pitch its message. He used his name to encourage others to give. Rosenwald never wanted to be the sole support of an institution, however worthy, and he expressed his frustration when an organization he admired relied too heavily on his help. He collaborated closely with the Abbott sisters and Sophonisba Breckinridge, founders of Chicago's Immigrants' Protective League, but chided them for failing to interest others in their project. If a program had merit, he reasoned, more than one person ought to fund it. A project that did good work should market itself to a wide public, soliciting many supporters.

But though he lent his name to advertise causes, he did not, unlike so many of America's great philanthropists, including J. P. Morgan, John Paul Getty, Meyer Guggenheim, Andrew Carnegie, and Leland Stanford, among others, put it on buildings or emblazon it on walls. The University of Chicago once chiseled his name on a new building while the Rosenwalds happened to be on an extended out-of-town vacation. Upon returning to Chicago, JR expressed dismay at seeing the words "Rosenwald Hall" on the building's exterior, but he felt unable to ask the institution to sandblast it off.

He did not just give his money and walk away. Once he decided to contribute to an organization, he maintained a lively interest in it. But although he might make suggestions on how the money be used, he mostly deferred to those who ran the settlement house, school, hospital, or other organization, recognizing that they knew better than he what the project needed.[3] Usually Rosenwald contributed to a cause or an organization because a person he respected, a Jane Addams, Booker T. Washington, Edith Abbott, Emil Hirsch, or another reformer, suggested it. If he liked what they said, he gave.

In rare cases he suggested projects of his own, although even then he confined the use of his name to fundraising. A notable case involved the creation of one of Chicago's premier institutions, the Museum of Science and Industry. What museumgoers informally called "the Rosenwald museum" grew out of a vacation Rosenwald had taken in Munich with his youngest children, William and Marion, in 1911. Noting how bored the youngsters had become with sightseeing, JR offered to take each child on a special private outing. His son William chose the Deutsches Museum and fell in love with it. Showcasing Industrial Age achievements, the museum encouraged visitors to touch exhibits, pull levers, and press buttons so that they could experience firsthand how these technological wonders worked. Visitors did not have to speak in hushed and reverential tones. No aura of elitism permeated the rooms. Rather than celebrating rare artistic genius, the Deutsches Museum boasted of and showcased the innovators, inventors, workers, and captains of industry who together had fostered technological progress.

A decade after this memorable visit, the Commercial Club, which among its activities promoted the city, asked members for suggestions about new projects it and the city might undertake. Rosenwald, recalling the German museum, replied, "Chicago should have, as one of its most important institutions for public usefulness, a great Industrial Museum or Exhibition in which might be housed for permanent display, machinery and working models illustrative of as many as possible of the mechanical processes of production and manufacture."[4]

Planning began in 1926. Rosenwald envisioned locating the museum in the vacant Palace of Fine Arts, a relic from the 1893 Columbian Exposition on the Midway, at the southern edge of Jackson Park overlooking Lake Michigan and adjacent to the University of Chicago, where Aaron Nusbaum had once peddled his carbonated beverages. The dramatic Beaux Arts building had narrowly escaped demolition, and the city's art lovers eyed it for a future art museum. But Rosenwald's offer of $3 million, which eventually climbed to $5 million, for an institution to replicate the Munich museum and display machines, gadgets, even a coal mine, won out.

If ever an institution deserved to carry the name Rosenwald, the Museum of Science and Industry qualified. Members of the board and other notable Chicagoans encouraged him to allow the naming, but he refused. The museum thus became an anomaly in Chicago. Aside from the Art Institute of Chicago, founded in 1879, all the Chicago museums founded in Rosenwald's day bore the names of their donors: the Field Museum of Natural History (1893), named for the retailer Marshall Field; the Adler Planetarium (1930), for Max Adler, once an associate of Rosenwald's at Sears; and the Shedd Aquarium (1930), for John G. Shedd, a protégé of Marshall Field's.

Rosenwald not only refused to have his name immortalized, he did not like being called a philanthropist. In his *Saturday Evening Post* article, he laid out his philosophy of giving. Employing the passive voice, he acknowledged that "I am often called a philanthropist." But the pronoun *I* did not often appear in his lexicon.⁵ In describing his work for the public good, he generally preferred *we*, as in a 1915 piece in *Harper's* in which he described all the shareholders in the civic undertakings he supported. By using *we* rather than *I*, he portrayed himself as part of a team of "organized charity leaders." His money did not put him at the head of that group. He declared to the contrary that he "served in the ranks" with "the citizens and social experts" who hoped to change on a permanent basis the conditions of "the poor, unfortunate and afflicted."⁶

Rosenwald's philosophy set him apart from most other big givers of his era, such as Rockefeller and Carnegie. Not only did those plutocrats create institutions which carried their names, such as Rockefeller University, Carnegie Mellon University, and the Carnegie libraries which proliferated across America, they established foundations which funded projects well beyond the lifetimes of their creators.

Not so Julius Rosenwald, who detested perpetual endowments. One of the few entities which went by his name, the Julius Rosenwald Fund, had been designed to go out of operation within a set period of time. The Fund first met formally in 1917. Up to that time Rosenwald's donations had come directly from him as an individual, but after this most of his contributions, though not all, flowed through the Fund. Administered by Edwin Embree, whom Rosenwald poached from the Rockefeller Foundation and who articulated the Rosenwald ideology of giving, the Julius Rosenwald Fund was chartered with $20 million in assets, making it one of the ten largest of the nation's philanthropic foundations. Dedicated to projects to enhance "the well-being of mankind," it differed from the other foundations in one straightforward and simple way: its charter stipulated that it must cease twenty-five years after Rosenwald's death. It charged the trustees to dispose of both principal and interest in that time. Nothing, the charter mandated, could remain. Fearful of the influence long-serving trustees might exert on more recent board members, JR, who actively involved himself in the Fund's work throughout his lifetime, stipulated in setting it up that other than himself and Embree, no trustee could sit on the board for more than six years.

The Fund's work reflected Rosenwald's concerns for particular social issues, and operated in accordance with his ideas about philanthropy and its impact on both givers and receivers. "I am not in sympathy with [the] policy of perpetuating endowments and believe that more good can be accomplished by expending funds as Trustees find opportunity for constructive work than by storing up large sums of money for long periods of time," he declared in 1928 to a recently augmented board of trustees. Disliking bureaucracies, he believed that this time-limited program of philanthropic involvement would allow his generation to fund what it considered essential while freeing future generations to support whatever undertakings they deemed important. "Coming generations can be relied upon," he predicted in his typically optimistic style, "to provide for their own needs as they arise."[7]

Rosenwald's commitment to giving during his lifetime stemmed from his profound worry about the conditions he saw around him, the inequities of the contemporary world, and his belief that he and other privileged men and women had a mandate to act. The ills of society, local, national, and global, needed solutions that money could help supply. Yet he balanced his pessimism about present ills, including poverty, racism, anti-Semitism, disease, and corruption, with confidence that knowledgeable people could guide society toward improvement. Experts with insight derived from education and firsthand experience had the ideas needed about how to address these problems. They lacked only the money to put them into practice.

Rosenwald's ideas on philanthropy, before and after the Fund's creation, exhibited other distinguishing features. JR embraced the thousands of requests that poured into his mailbox with a sense of hopefulness, with an assumption that a person who gave well and strategically would receive as much as the recipient. Direct, flexible, pragmatic, and people-oriented, he strove to develop a way of giving that "ennobles life, not because of what it does for others but more what it does for ourselves," the "ourselves" being those with means. He shared in his era's widespread belief in progress and in the power of informed individuals of goodwill to use their resources to create and sustain institutions that would improve their world. He preferred to support organizations that sought "permanent rather than palliative measures," and he embraced undertakings that might add "to the sum total of human progress."[8] As donors, he averred, "we should give not grudgingly, not niggardly. But gladly, generously, eagerly, lovingly."[9]

He valued institutions that he believed would erase divisions in society, and embraced projects that narrowed the chasm between givers and recipients. Throughout his philanthropic life he stipulated that he would "contribute to an institution or project only in proportion to the recipients' willingness to contribute an equal and, where possible, even greater share." While many of the institutions he supported handsomely worked with very poor and distressed people, he insisted in general that beneficiaries also contribute something to their own well-being. When they did so, those who gave the money and those who used it forged a partnership.[10]

One person's giving, according to the Rosenwald philosophy, should stimulate another's, creating a ripple effect among the wider public, among the well-off, and indeed among those not so well-off who could still find ways to participate in civic improvement. "I am a great believer," he declared, "in the influence of one man upon other men for good or bad and I give not only with the idea of stimulating others to giving, but to proper giving."[11] As he moved from small gifts to local organizations in the first decade of the twentieth century to large donations for national and global concerns in the 1910s, he pioneered in asserting the principle of the matching gift. He would announce his willingness to donate money as long as others joined him. Individuals might not be able to give as much as he did, but as an aggregate they should match his contribution. In the Rosenwald worldview of giving, enshrined in the Rosenwald Fund's charter, donors should think beyond the boundaries of their immediate community, city, or ethnic or religious group and work instead for "mankind."

Rosenwald also recognized that the problems plaguing modern society had far outstripped those of earlier eras, and individuals, no matter how charitably inclined, could no longer make a significant difference on their own. Along with other Progressives of his era, JR put little faith in the solutions of the past. Spontaneous, unstructured giving would have little impact on modern social problems. Indeed, such charity, the progressive-minded asserted, Rosenwald among them, reinforced social divisions. Whether focusing on immigrants, health care, housing, the efficient functioning of local governments, or the needs of Jews or African Americans, Rosenwald looked to experts for guidance through the thicket of competing issues and warring interest groups about how much to give and to whom, which boards to serve on, and which institutions to fundraise for among his wealthy peers.

Despite the breadth of his giving, with the list of institutions he supported running pages long, he did not give to endowment funds. Endowments, he believed, saddled people in the future to the values and visions of the present. No matter how deeply he believed in a particular cause or respected its leaders, he drew the line at supporting its endowment. Jane Addams urged him to help endow Hull House, but though he appreciated both Addams and her work, even joining in an effort to persuade the Nobel committee to award her the Peace

Prize, he turned her down for assistance to the settlement house's endowment fund. Similarly, he admired the University of Chicago for its commitment to urban reform, its service to Chicago, and its absence of discriminatory practices against Jews, but he consistently refused requests made by its various presidents and trustees to contribute to its endowment fund. In a 1929 *Atlantic* article, "Principles of Public Giving," he stated forcefully that as a loyal University of Chicago trustee, he had said no when asked to "contribute to the fund" for the endowment, "but instead turned over a sum of which the principal may be exhausted." He glowed with pride, sharing with readers that he had been "assured" that his money "has been of considerable service. It has been used for such diverse purposes as the purchase of the library of a Cambridge professor; for paying part of the cost of Professor Michelson's ether-drift experiments; for reconstructing the twelve-inch telescope at Yerkes Observatory; for a continuation of research in glacial erosion in the State of Washington, and for research in phonetics." Had he given that money to the endowment, as requested, "some of the objects could not have been achieved."[12]

THE PROGRESSIVE MOVEMENT

Julius Rosenwald's philanthropy dovetailed with contemporary political and cultural trends embodied in Progressivism, which by the 1890s had begun to exert strong influence on American society. The Progressives, a loosely organized constellation of reform-oriented women and men, asserted that the modern age had generated problems whose solutions demanded new civic institutions and social practices. They launched projects to refashion society, advocating for causes in which the well-off and the dispossessed work together toward their mutual well-being. The Progressives believed strongly that the poor, immigrants, and others in distress would be transformed by encounters with the educated and well-off. Like Rosenwald, they had no doubt that the poor would benefit from adopting middle-class values and mores. Helping them in this pursuit depended on creating and investing, sometimes with state aid, in new institutions, including schools, playgrounds, community centers, settlement houses, clinics, libraries, and urban gardens, to provide the necessary social and legal services that through the expertise of the few would improve the lives of the many.

Advocacy of this type of Progressivism allowed Rosenwald and his allies to distinguish themselves from still prevalent ideas promulgated by Social Darwinists in the late nineteenth century, who felt equal certainty that poverty reflected the defects of the poor and that those with means had no obligation to interfere with the natural order that had created the haves and the have-nots. Buttressed by a deep-felt American belief in individualism and self-reliance, Social Darwinism thrived in a nation that celebrated the man who raised himself up from poverty by means of his innate sterling character, hard work, and clean living.

This widely accepted American worldview, associated with the Yale sociologist William Graham Sumner and articulated most fully in his 1884 book, *What the Social Classes Owe Each Other*, propelled the Progressives into action. Sumner's succinct assertion—that "a drunkard in the gutter is just where he ought to be, according to the fitness and tendency of things. Nature has set upon him the process of decline and dissolution by which she removes things which have survived their usefulness"—encapsulated the view that Rosenwald and other Progressives fought against.[13]

When it came to the plight of "the drunkard," Rosenwald supported Prohibition, implying that the state had a powerful role to play in directing civic life, but he and other Progressives dissented from Sumner in arguing that society owed it to itself as well as to the drunkard to help him. Society, too, suffered from the drunkard's affliction and had to understand what role it had itself played in creating the problem. Why, Progressives asked, had the drunkard turned to drink? Why could he (or she) not stop? How many drunkards languished in the gutters of every city or neighborhood? What programs or treatments existed to rehabilitate the drunkard? Who else suffered as a result of the drunkard's actions? What price did the family pay? How did the drunkard harm society at large, including those who traversed city sidewalks and thereby, no matter their abstemiousness and sobriety, risked their own safety and comfort? How did basic economic inequalities drive some to such levels of desperation that they would find solace in drink? By thinking in terms of such questions, training experts to answer them, and creating institutions to address them, the Progressives hoped to improve the social order rather than, like Sumner, to justify it.

Progressivists chafed at the conventional American belief that help for the distressed, including the drunkard in the gutter, might best come from women and men with kind hearts and Christian souls dispensing charity, on a case-by-case basis. As the Progressives saw it, offering the drunkard a warm bed, clean clothes, a bowl of hot soup, and a prayer or Bible message might provide immediate relief, but did nothing to solve his or her problem for the future. Without systemic change, the drinker would go back to the bottle.

Conventional charity built around small-town Christian benevolence had been under attack since the 1830s, America's first age of reform, and spearheaded by such individuals as Dorothea Dix. By the 1870s the rise of the Scientific Charity movement had further eroded belief that the complex thicket of social problems could be resolved by simply pricking the consciences of individual Americans, particularly through sermons delivered from church pulpits.

But the methods and philosophy of Scientific Charity differed fundamentally from those of the Progressives, as the former considered idleness to be the cause of poverty, advocated moral regeneration, and relied on volunteerism. The drunkard, according to Scientific Charity advocates, should first prove himself worthy and willing to change in order to get relief.

Progressivism called for fundamental changes in the American system of laissez-faire. It saw economic inequality as the core problem and advocated a vastly increased role for the state in ironing out the divisions and distresses which plagued modern America. Relying on trained experts, the Progressives launched a hydra-headed assault on America's deep commitment to individual solutions generated by the goodwill of kind-hearted people. Advocating child labor laws, minimum wage and protective legislation, and Prohibition, among other remedies, Progressivism envisioned state bureaucracies as agents of change. Not that all Progressives agreed on all these matters, but they united in seeing that American responses of the past to social problems did not fit the complex, diverse, and disorderly industrial age.

As the Progressives saw it, Americans' attitudes in the 1890s toward poverty and other social ills still reflected the nineteenth-century emphasis on individual responsibility and the belief that individual solutions would be enough. Yet Progressive reformers recognized another reality. They recognized the widespread exploitation of workers by factory and business owners concerned only with profit. In Chicago, the major industries, such as meatpacking, railroads, steel, and garment manufacturing, depended on the availability of large pools of low-paid, unskilled workers, mostly immigrants. These workers lived in substandard housing and labored under unsafe conditions. Julius Rosenwald set up his business and began his civic work in the same Chicago which Upton Sinclair depicted in his 1906 exposé *The Jungle*, a harsh and hopeless novel of life among the Slavic immigrants in the city's stockyard neighborhood, often described as "the *Uncle Tom's Cabin* of wage slavery."

Where Chicago's social and economic divisions could be seen most clearly were in attitudes toward worker-employer relationships. Employers like Rosenwald denied that workers had the right to engage in collective bargaining for better pay and working conditions. One of the more extreme expressions of this view came from Philip Armour, of the meatpacking plant, who proclaimed in 1879, "As long as we are heads of our own houses, we shall employ what men we choose, and when we can't, why, we'll nail up the doors—that's all." Marshall Field's, the city's signature department store, fired employees seen with unionists, while other employers recruited private security forces as their private, personal armies to break up union meetings. Even the anti-unionist JR recoiled from such tactics and attitudes.

Rosenwald and many other Progressives, including those whom he worked with but who did support unions, positioned themselves not just against the forces of laissez-faire capitalism but also against the politics of the left, a force palpable in places like Chicago. The Progressives argued that American capitalism could be made humane, and they warned that without serious and well-thought-out alterations to the system, anarchism and socialism would upend the social order. Proof of the danger could be found in the streets of Chicago, a flashpoint for clashes between the forces of the entrenched social and economic classes and political militants, many articulating a Marxist message, from the left, with their calls for revolution.

Beginning with the founding of the Workingmen's Party of Illinois in the 1870s and the creation of the International Working People's Association (IWPA) in the 1880s, strikes, marches, and demonstrations advocating the destruction of capitalism punctuated city life. In the 1890s Chicago still carried the scars, both physical and psychic, of the May 1, 1886, Haymarket Street affair, a police riot which resulted in the arrest, trial, conviction, and execution of eight IWPA leaders. Although Chicago socialists consistently polled poorly at the ballot box, they formed robust membership clubs in ethnic neighborhoods, infiltrated the city's strong labor movement, and launched a lively press, which chronicled daily abuses against the working-class masses. In 1886 anarchists founded the Central Labor Union, incorporating under its umbrella many of Chicago's largest labor organizations. At the turn of the twentieth century, radicalism exerted such a strong hold in the city that Rosenwald's close friend Jane Addams, herself a union supporter, felt compelled to declare, "I am not in any sense a Socialist, have never belonged to the party and have never especially affiliated with them."

Rosenwald and his peers in the city's Progressive movement positioned themselves in the middle, between the radicals to the left and the recalcitrant factory owners to the right, sharing neither the wish to topple capitalism nor the urge to leave its abuses unameliorated. Rather they sought to create a system, in Chicago and across the nation, based on fairness and a commitment by those with means to aid those without. The former would provide crucial services to the latter, helping to raise up the workers and the poor and thereby maintain civic peace. Julius Rosenwald shared this Progressive vision, and once he decided that he had earned enough money, he used it to further that ideal.

Historians since the 1960s have debated about the origins and the implications of the Progressive movement, seeing its complexities and contradictions as its advocates sought to chart a position midway between extremes. Historians have for the most part seen the movement as falling between efforts to mitigate the abuses of industrial capitalism and efforts to preserve the status quo by imposing middle-class white Protestant standards of behavior on the working classes and the poor, who often came from different backgrounds and adhered to other values.

The historians agree on one point: Progressivism, like other reform movements of the era, emphasized that Americans shared a common fate. Whether considering poverty, crime, disease, or other social ills, the Progressives believed that all people, across lines of race, religion, nativity, and class, needed to find a solution. Progressives' solutions varied along a spectrum, but converged on the proposition that these problems affected everyone, and unless people in a position to help, either with funds or expertise, took steps, the ills plaguing the poorest classes would overwhelm all society. Progressivism reflected a belief on the part of the white well-off classes that to preserve their own comfort and welfare they had to restructure the society around them. Rosenwald shared this belief.

THE ROLE OF THE STATE

Rosenwald, despite his belief in the importance of the voluntary sector in solving social problems, did not oppose pushing the government to play a part as well. The agencies he funded and the leaders of the institutions his money made possible recognized that private organizations, no matter how amply supported by philanthropy, could not adequately address escalating social needs. He and other Progressives advocated for government to take a more active role in social reform than it had in the nineteenth century. They encouraged policy changes in which the government would assume more responsibility for people in need. In 1915, for example, in a response article in *Harper's Weekly*, Rosenwald defended his brand of Progressivism against accusations that it opposed such demands as a state-mandated minimum-wage policy. The institutions he served, noted Rosenwald, stood "unequivocally in favor of minimum wage legislation." Additionally, he de-

clared that several of the organizations in which he participated
most actively, including the United Charities of Chicago, of
which he served as vice president, had actively lobbied the Illinois legislature to pass the Parents Funds Act, which created
what has been more commonly known as Mothers' Pensions,
by which the state gave monetary benefits to mothers who had
no means by which to support their children. He and other
Chicago activists had also been working for "unemployment
and public insurance against old age, disease and lack of work,"
and he commented that the city's philanthropic community
was currently "in mourning for one of our most capable and
self-sacrificing leaders . . . Dr. Charles R. Henderson, a Social
Gospel minister and professor at the University of Chicago,"
who "gave his life in an endeavor, backed by many others, to
relieve unemployment through public agencies." He hoped
that "more and more the greater governmental units, like the
county, city, state, and nation, will take over and operate tried
and true social agencies for the betterment of mankind."[14]

Rosenwald used this article to make another point about
the motivations underlying his civic work and his participation
in Chicago's Progressive community. He told the readers of
Harper's Weekly how, as a Jew, in conjunction with the city's
Jewish agencies, he had nurtured the growth of Chicago's welfare infrastructure both within and beyond the Jewish community. Rosenwald proudly identified himself as the president
of the Associated Jewish Charities and "Honorary President
of the Federated Orthodox Jewish Charities." The former, he
wrote, had years ago pioneered in creating the Jewish Home
Finding Society, which devised programs for "compensating
widows with dependent children and caring for motherless
children." Since the recent passage of the Parents Funds Act,
the Bureau of Personal Service, another Jewish association,
founded and run by his friend Minnie Low, "has cooperated to
the fullest possible extent with the Funds for Parents Depart-

ment in the interest of widows entitled to compensation under our law." So too the Associated Jewish Charities, he explained, maintained the "connecting link in the matter of service between our charities and the public bodies throughout the city, county, and state."[15]

Rosenwald's defense of Chicago's private charitable sector and its embrace of state engagement did not need these references to Jewish charitable work. He could have described the role played by the nonprofit sector in pushing for government action without details of his involvement in Jewish social welfare work. But these connections showcased the link between his self-understanding as a Jew and his civic activism. He did the work he did because he thought it benefited society and because it constituted work a Jew should do.

JUDAISM, PROGRESSIVISM, AND PHILANTHROPY

In his attitudes toward wealth and social responsibility, Rosenwald followed in the traditions of his Jewish upbringing. Rosenwald and his peers in the Jewish community recognized that they, the successful and well-off children of the first wave of Jewish immigrants, bore a responsibility to assist those who arrived later. They participated with other like-minded Americans in general social reform, as they accepted the self-imposed task of lifting immigrant Jews out of poverty and ensuring the vigor of Jewish life in America. They had the means to do so, and they articulated a coherent vision of how to go about it. Additionally, beginning in the early twentieth century, Rosenwald's generation of American Jews assumed much of the responsibility for aiding Jews in other lands who faced difficulties and dislocation. They did so not simply to flaunt their achievements as Americans or gain influence in world Jewish politics, but because they realized that they represented the largest and wealthiest sector of world Jewry.

The currents of his religious life ran through Rosenwald's philanthropy, as it did for the others of his generation. Most belonged to the Reform movement, a stream of modern Jewish life which asserted that ethical monotheism constituted the heart of Judaism, functioning as its fundamental core. As the Reform movement in central Europe and the United States renegotiated many cultic and legal elements of Rabbinic Judaism, including the dietary laws, the laws of family purity, and strict observance of the Sabbath and holidays with their detailed behavioral proscriptions, it focused on the elements of Judaism that Reform Jews believed distinguished Judaism from other religions in positive ways. Reform thinkers saw in their Judaism a way to hasten the remaking of the world into a more just and ethical reality.

The Reform movement grew stronger in the second half of the nineteenth century in part as a conservative reaction to the integration stimulated by the Jewish Emancipation, and the integration of Jews into general society. Movement leaders feared massive defections from Judaism as Jews increasingly found comfortable spots for themselves outside the boundaries of Jewish life. They fretted over intermarriages between Jews and non-Jews as a result of greater acceptance, worried about Jews converting to Christianity. They trembled at the birth of the Ethical Culture movement in the late 1870s, a break from Reform orchestrated by Felix Adler, a rabbi in their denomination. Adler proclaimed that Judaism, even the liberal Reform strand, remained too narrow, parochial, and centered on God as an actor in history. Unlike Adler, the rabbis of Reform and many lay members, committed Jews and believers in modernity, progress, and integration, decreed that Judaism should reform itself to survive and stay vital.

The congregation in Springfield, Illinois, that Samuel and Augusta Rosenwald belonged to, like many around the country, moved away from its traditional roots and joined the Union of

American Hebrew Congregations, the association of Reform synagogues. Here JR got his first lessons in Jewish thought and the Reform message. JR no doubt had learned as a young man that the Reform rabbis had gathered in Pittsburgh in 1885 to proclaim their vision of the movement. Judaism's conception of God, they insisted, constituted "the central religious truth for the human race," not for Jews alone. Reform Jews hoped, as stated in their conference platform, to facilitate the "establishment of the kingdom of truth, justice and peace among all men." The platform went on to declare that "in full accordance with the spirit of the Mosaic legislation, which strives to regulate the relations between rich and poor, we deem it our duty to participate in the great task of modern times, to solve, on the basis of justice and righteousness, the problems presented by the contrasts and evils of the present organization of society." Jews, according to Reform rabbis and thinkers, including Rabbi Emil Hirsch, who led the Chicago Sinai congregation that Julius and Augusta Rosenwald and their children belonged to, had inherited a religious system based on moral values.

Declaring Jews a "religious community" and "no longer a nation," the Pittsburgh Platform staked out a distinct ground for Reform Jews. The message further delivered in sermons, in editorials in Reform publications, and in pedagogic material emphasized Progressive values and the triumph of reason over superstition. The world of American Judaism, specifically that created and inhabited by immigrants from central Europe and their descendants, resounded with calls for universal justice, despite their own economic success. The imperative to seek justice constituted much of what they proclaimed it meant to "be" Jewish.

Reform Jews found that by focusing on the ethical principles associated with the Hebrew Bible, in particular the prophetic sections, they could further two projects. They could integrate Jewish beliefs and culture into the larger culture in which they lived, combining their bourgeois American social culture and their identities as Jews. They could, by conceptualizing Judaism as an ethical system which melded universalism and Jewish particularism, connect present to past. No matter that other traditionalist Jews viewed Judaism very differently, Reform Jews like Julius Rosenwald experienced no dissonance between their Progressive American commitments and their Jewishness, an inheritance bestowed on them by the tradition.

Emphasizing the call for justice also allowed Reform Jews to take pride in their faith community. As asserted by their rabbis and texts, Jews and Judaism had given much to the world, specifically in the matter of ethics. Locally, their accomplishments in the civic arena, undertaken in unity with others, helped justify the preservation of Judaism against increasing anti-Semitic attacks. The Rosenwalds probably heard strains of this message at the Sinai congregation, listening to Hirsch, a movement leader and a signer of the "Call," which in 1909 launched the National Association for the Advancement of Colored People. They would have absorbed the message in the *Reform Advocate*, a Chicago Jewish newspaper he edited, and no doubt they would have followed the rabbi's writings in other general publications. In 1901 Hirsch editorialized: "In certain ways the Jews of Chicago may claim the credit of having been among the first to inaugurate the better methods according to the truer standards of the new philanthropy in the dispensation of relief or the provision of education of the young. . . . The Jews of this city can proudly point to the fact that they were the first to bring about the systematic co-operation among the various agencies for the administration of charities."[16] Hirsch wanted Jews to know that *they* had a role to play in progressive reform and had risen to the task. He complimented them on setting the best, most modern standards in civic improvement, standards that became a model for others. They had given something important to the larger society, and Hirsch wanted them to take a particular pride in their accomplishments.

Many American Jews hoped that participation in Progressivism would increase the respect non-Jews accorded to Jews and Judaism. Historically, Christians considered Judaism parochial, legalistic, and inward-looking, for centuries contrasting Christianity's emphasis on love with Judaism's emphasis on law. Reform Judaism, which had rethought the idea of Jewish law and elevated ethics, provided a vehicle for American Jews to prove themselves generous to others, willing to act in support of people outside their own community, and giving to their non-Jewish neighbors. Hirsch made this case in the pages of the *Chicago Tribune* in 1899 when he encouraged well-off Chicago Jews to give to city institutions. "Nothing," he predicted, "would redound more to the honor of Chicago and the Jews than if the names of some of our wealthy Jews were written on the campuses of our universities as patron of the gentle arts and the classics." At this moment in time the man who would become his most famous, and wealthiest, congregant had not yet achieved riches or acclaim. When Hirsch threw out this challenge, Rosenwald still aspired to earn enough money so that he could donate five thousand dollars a year to charitable causes, once having attended to the needs of his family and the health of his business.[17]

Most nineteenth-century Jewish writers and community leaders on both sides of the Atlantic, though particularly in America, taught that the Judaic tradition, whether derived from the Bible or from later writings, commanded its adherents to do good in the world. Reform Jewish leaders, rabbis in particular, more than any other Jews at the time, stress, in articles and books, sermons and school lessons, the message that the sacred texts demanded that Jews provide for the poor and care for the needy, the widowed, and orphaned, whether their own or "the strangers" who lived among them. Rabbis, teachers, writers, and journalists, inspired by late-nineteenth-century Reform doctrine, repeatedly drew attention to the words of Hillel, a rabbi of the first century BCE, who taught, "If I am not for myself, who is for me? If I am only for myself, what am I?" and "That which is hateful to you, do not do to your fellow. That is the whole Torah: the rest is commentary: go and learn."

The first of Hillel's aphorisms, invoked by American Jews in Rosenwald's time and beyond, concluded, "If not now, when?" This charge too inflected JR's philanthropic vision, as it resonated with the Reform teachings of his synagogue. Rosenwald's refusal to give to, or create, perpetual endowments could be read as an echo of Hillel's "if not now." Chicago and America needed money today to protect immigrants, train social workers, and provide the finest medical care for the poor. A sense of urgency coursed through Rosenwald's work as a civic activist.

One moment encapsulates this attitude. Sitting around in the 1910s with Cyrus McCormick, Jr., Charles Crane, Samuel Insull, and John G. Shedd, all city titans, Rosenwald mused, "We five are probably the richest men in Chicago at the present time. It may be that in the future some of us or all may lose a part or all of our wealth and thereby the opportunity to do great things for Chicago." His suggestion? "I propose that each of us put $5 million in a jack-pot and agree to spend it in the course of 5 or 10 years for various philanthropies." Only Crane agreed and the scheme remained unrealized, but the proposal revealed much about Rosenwald's view of philanthropy. (Ironically Insull lost much of his wealth with the 1929 stock market crash and he had to stand trial, accused of purposely selling worthless stock to unsuspecting customers.) The imperative of "if not now, when?" reverberated. Monetary wealth, however much he enjoyed it, could be ephemeral. The mercurial nature of the economy, plagued by booms and busts, could strip a rich man of his treasure. Giving should be the priority of the now, when the money lay on the table.[18]

JR's philanthropy, regardless of its object, suffused his life just as it flowed through the world of Reform Judaism. His activism bound him more tightly to other activist Jews, and Jewish institutions and causes embraced the Progressive ethos. Progressive organizations and institutions provided a meeting place for Jews to get together with each other, but Progressivism also connected JR and other Jews to many of the city's and nation's elite non-Jews. JR in fact met these non-Jewish reformers often through other Jews who had already been involved.

Rabbi Hirsch played a pivotal role in JR's inauguration into the world of Progressivism. The European Hirsch had married the daughter of an earlier Reform rabbi, David Einhorn, who had been notable for being among the few Jews who actively defended abolitionism, agitating in slave-owning Maryland against "the peculiar institution." An enraged mob drove Einhorn out of Baltimore. As Rosenwald embarked on his philanthropic career he remained close to Hirsch, never deviating from the rabbi's message that his Jewish heritage imposed upon him the privilege of seeking to do or bring about justice. Hirsch served as Rosenwald's first philanthropic mentor, his guide to Chicago reform. He introduced JR to Jane Addams, whom he invited to speak at Sinai. He assisted in founding the nation's most significant civil rights organization, the NAACP, offering the synagogue as the venue for one of its first national meetings. He worked with Booker T. Washington, who educated JR about the issues concerning black Americans.

Other important associates from the Sinai Congregation included Judge Julian Mack, another child of central European Jewish immigrants and the creator of Chicago's first juvenile court, situated across the street from Hull House, and Minnie Low, sometimes called the "Jewish Jane Addams." She and Mack introduced JR to many of the city's child welfare advocates.

Rosenwald's philanthropy focused on many issues, but always he concerned himself with the situation of Jews, in Chicago, America generally, and worldwide. Acutely conscious of anti-Semitism, although he himself seems to have not experienced it aside from the playground Rischus, he paid close attention to manifestations and outbreaks elsewhere, fretting over episodes of anti-Jewish rhetoric and actions. He recognized that Jews like himself had benefited from the migration to America, which had made possible their remarkable successes, their untrammeled freedom of movement, and their integration into larger society. But he also realized that these benefits could be taken away.

Like most American Jews of his generation and background, Rosenwald viewed philanthropy as a mechanism to demonstrate that Jews defied the centuries-old stereotype of them as greedy, clannish, dishonest, particularly in business dealings, money obsessed, and unconcerned with the needs of others. In the common idiom of the day, after all, the word *Jew*, as a verb, meant "to cheat," "to engage in sharp bargaining or disreputable business practices."

When he declared in a speech that "the Jew must be a pillar of civic well-being and moral capacity," he might have been hearkening back to Hillel. But he also manifested an anxiety about the present. If the Jew "falls short of this standard," Rosenwald predicted, "he will himself have brought into being the monster which will one day destroy him and unseat him from his position of safety in America." By invoking "the monster" in his call for Jews to accept their civic duty and demonstrate their commitment to a better society, Rosenwald laid bare the Jewish bedrock of his philanthropy.[19]

This attitude also helps explain his refusal to make anonymous contributions. Not only would "the influence which the name of the donor would exert" be lost if the contribution lacked the name of the donor, but perhaps more important, as he told a 1912 gathering of the American Academy of Political Science, "if a man contributes to a worthy cause, his name should go with the contribution." When Jews made common cause with non-Jews to serve the public good, they served the Jewish people as well. When a Jew made an anonymous gift, he or she robbed the community of an opportunity to demonstrate its commitment to the greater good, its virtues as a collectivity of generous people whose moral vision extended beyond their own needs.[20] Clearly he valued Progressive activism for its own sake, as evidenced by the treasure he gave away and the time and energy he expended on the boards of civic associations and Progressive organizations. But Rosenwald believed that doing good should enhance the welfare of the givers no less than of the recipients.

Rather than appealing to reason, Rosenwald's strategy for defending Jews relied on action, on philanthropy, not words, generous actions, not arguments. Those who held anti-Jewish sentiments, could, he hoped, be enlightened when they saw Jews like himself giving to others, working to reshape society to benefit all. Thus could they keep the monster from coming into being.

3

Some Little Touch of the Divine

Julius Rosenwald invested his time, money, and reputation in the problems facing the Jewish people. He felt a deep, personal concern for the welfare of Jews worldwide, and he involved himself in many undertakings to protect Jews and keep Jewish culture vibrant.

His self-identification as a Jew did not require punctilious religious observance, however. He did not abstain from work on the Sabbath, nor did he forgo foods he liked. He seems to have devoted no time to studying normative Jewish texts. No meticulous observer of Jewish law, halacha, he enjoyed his life as an American at ease among non-Jews in social and business settings. Still, he placed his Jewishness at the center of his philanthropic vision, considering his work an embodiment of the moral obligations of Jews. He had a responsibility, he believed, to protect and assist Jews worldwide and to strengthen Jewish life. He extended a willing hand, offering assistance that conformed to his overall philosophy of giving and the traditions in which he had been raised, and he also engaged broadly with other Jews across lines of class, place of origin, and ideology.

Despite his somewhat secular way of life, Rosenwald described his commitment to giving in terms that invoked the sacred. Philanthropy ennobled, he claimed, launching the giver on a spiritual journey. In a speech to the Associated Jewish Charities of Chicago, a body he funded, actively served as president, and solicited for among his wealthy friends, he described the life he might have chosen. He and his peers might, he noted, have devoted "the few precious days of our existence only to buying and selling, only to comparing sales with the sales of the same day the year before, only to shuffling our feet in the dance, only to matching little picture cards so as to group together three jacks or aces or kings, only to seek pleasure and fight taxes, and when the end comes to leave as little taxable an estate as possible."[1]

But he had chosen a different path, having opted for "something better and finer in life, something that dignifies it and stamps it with at least some little touch of the divine." JR did not spell out here how he conceived of the divine. He had probably never fretted over theological questions, including the Jewish conception of God. Rather, he measured his religious obligations by the totality of his civic and philanthropic activities. By working to address the ills of the world, to improve them, he fulfilled his obligations as a Jew. From the first moment he could afford to give "not grudgingly, not niggardly, but gladly," he turned his attention to Jewish needs, at home and abroad, and for him such work constituted the essence of the "divine."

The connection between Rosenwald's sense of his Jewish identity and his philosophy of philanthropy remained with him lifelong. Rosenwald's personal story might be considered the ultimate success story for American Reform Judaism. In his life can be seen the breadth of opportunities available to American Jews and the power of Reform Judaism to inspire its members. He took deeply to heart its message, which exhorted women and men to use their increasingly ample resources in pursuit of justice. He never deviated from his goal of helping Jews as a people, of strengthening their culture, of sustaining Judaism. His Jewish interests began with organizations in Chicago but quickly moved out to encompass the country and later the world. He gave to causes he believed in and participated in Jewish activities he appreciated. But he did not withhold his generosity from Jews and Jewish organizations that reflected the sensibilities of Jews from other social classes or places of origin and who did not fully share his views.

Not all Jews appreciated the causes he supported, considering his choices flawed, wrong, or even harmful to the Jewish people. Such views did not cause him to cut off their organizations. He still gave money for their projects even when they did not follow his leadership or advice. When, for example, he campaigned in the Jewish wards of Chicago in 1911 for Charles Merriam, the Progressive reform candidate for mayor, he failed to carry Jewish voters with him, even though he generously funded many of their institutions. He appealed to them to vote for Progressivism, beseeching them that only reform politics would make a better city. But local interest-group political alliances swung their support to the political machine that granted them favors. Rosenwald's push to reform the system failed, yet he continued to support their many social service and cultural projects.

As in most American cities, immigrants from eastern Europe and their children made up the vast majority of the Jewish population. Enthusiastic supporters of labor unions, they had no sympathy for Rosenwald's pro-business, anti-labor stance. They believed that unionization would serve their interest as Jewish members of the working class. Although Rosenwald's money sustained many of the activities in Chicago's immigrant Jewish enclave, the Jewish masses led and participated in the garment workers' union he opposed. They vigorously criticized him and his policies, labeling him a traitor to Jewish workers. Similarly, Rosenwald's decision not to support Zionism provoked criticism from the many Jews in Chicago, nationally, and globally, who either paid dues to Zionist societies or sympathized with the idea of establishing a Jewish homeland in Palestine. Advocates for Zionism, some of Chicago's and the country's most prominent Jews, resented JR's refusal to endorse their cause, one that, particularly during World War I and into the 1920s and early 1930s, they believed offered the only solution to the increasingly precarious situation of Europe's Jews. They questioned the sincerity of Rosenwald's commitment to Jews and Judaism. Yet they still depended upon him to fund their other undertakings, and he gladly and generously supported them.

Even after his death, with tributes pouring in, saturating the Jewish press with a wave of adulation, some commentators noted that his stance on Zionism, in particular, had generated criticism. The Chicago *Jewish Sentinel* depicted him as a "great and good man," a "prince . . . whose life and works are unequalled in the history of Chicago Jewry" and whose gifts of time and money to Jewish causes had "electrified" the world. Yet the article noted that Rosenwald had been "much misunderstood and often criticized." Despite that, the article continued, "he emerges alive and untarnished while his critics and detractors long have been forgotten."[2]

Rosenwald's Jewish involvements, from the smallest to the most massive, from Chicago's West Side to the Crimea, sought to facilitate the integration of Jews into their surrounding communities without loss of their Jewish identity. However much antagonism toward Jews prevailed, however inhospitable the environment for them, he believed that circumstances could change and Jews could expect an improvement in their condition. Even America, he believed, could become a better place for Jews if society as a whole improved and if it treated its Jewish citizens as equal to its white gentiles. Such transformations did not oblige Jews to give up their Jewish culture or identity. Rather they could find ways, supported by individuals like him, to adapt as Jews.

His projects encouraged Jews to participate with their non-Jewish fellow citizens in projects for the common good to lessen animosities between them. He envisioned a day when the Jews' non-Jewish neighbors would change their minds, when those harboring anti-Semitic views or engaging in anti-Jewish practices would recognize their errors. American society had to root out anti-Jewish practices and attitudes wherever they existed, and he aimed to employ his money and public standing to facilitate this process.

He deployed his resources both for positive reinforcement and punitive action, supporting, for example, non-Jewish institutions that did not discriminate against Jews, rewarding their good practices to encourage others to follow and adopt them. His generous support of the University of Chicago, for example, constituted a Jewish cause in his eyes. While he praised the school because of its service to the city, he also applauded it for refraining from the discriminatory practices of many of its contemporary American universities, which imposed quotas on Jewish students, hired no Jewish faculty, and denied Jews seats on their boards of trustees. At the same time, he openly chastised institutions and individuals that discriminated against Jews, monitoring legislation, expending his political capital, and supporting campaigns to prevent or end such practices.

Rosenwald also expected Jews themselves to work toward integration into their communities. Jews had to show themselves as productive members of the larger community, contributors to the common good. They would prove their worth through their conduct. Through their generosity, civic involvements, and contributions to the general culture, they would expose the lies and ignorance of their enemies. He often described his own philanthropy as a rebuttal of those who considered Jews parochial and self-serving, interested only in themselves. Jews, like members of any despised group, had to conduct themselves impeccably, be above criticism, disarming their detractors. Whether holding them to a higher standard seems fair or not, Jews, according to JR, had no choice but to prove that they constituted not a burden or threat to their larger communities, but a benefit to all.

Americans in Rosenwald's era worried about mass immigration, class discord, and the consequences of assimilating huge numbers of poor people, who seemed to be pervading the nation, threatening its basic character. They included Jews among those who could disrupt the nation's true identity and values. Rosenwald's plan, though he gave it no such formal designation, called upon Jews to participate in their own rehabilitation, creating communal institutions that worked for the public good, funding them at the highest levels, and equipping them with trained professional staffs. Non-Jews would hail these Jewish institutions as exemplars of social service, models worthy of emulation. He worked toward a future in which others would recognize and acknowledge the good work Jews did not only for themselves but for all people.

The first three decades of the twentieth century, the most intense years of Rosenwald's philanthropic juggernaut, opened up strains in the relationship between America and its Jews. In a fraught era, anti-immigrant sentiment proved problematic for a community made up of immigrants. Discrimination against Jews in colleges and universities, in housing, and in certain forms of employment became routine, and while such setbacks did not stop Jewish economic mobility, they still rankled, and according to Rosenwald and his peers such practices needed to be stemmed. He approached his American undertakings in the main with a sense that Jews had benefited from living in America, that Americans should be seen as people of goodwill in their relationships with Jews, and that these harmonious relationships would continue so long as Jews took an active role in making their dealings with others positive and productive.

Rosenwald's commitment to Jewish advancement involved much more than mere defensiveness or group public relations, although in the early years of the twentieth century, American and world Jewry did need to be defended. Jews rightly felt compelled to emphasize their accommodation to America and their service to the larger society. All of America's Jewish defense organizations, such as the National Council of Jewish Women (founded 1893), the American Jewish Committee (1906), the Anti-Defamation League (1913), and the American Jewish Congress (1917), came into being in the years of Rosenwald's communal activism, and much of the political advocacy of and for American Jewry during those years can be traced to their fears over increased discrimination and anti-Jewish rhetoric, which lent to their efforts a sense of urgency. Rosenwald's activities hardly deviated from those of other Jewish activists.

But his involvement in Jewish causes transcended a simple response to anti-Semitism. By all indications, he truly believed that as a Jew he had an obligation to assist other Jews, wherever they lived. He felt that advocacy for Jews consisted of more than ensuring their physical safety, and he also worked to invigorate Jewish culture and sustain Judaism as a religion. He responded positively, for example, to an appeal for funds from YIVO, the Vilna-based Jewish Scientific Institution, even though he had no connection to the Lithuanian city or involvement in the world of Yiddish-language activities. He rejected few appeals from Jewish causes, whether cultural or eleemosynary. When he did say no, he did so according to a consistent vision.

In the main, Jewish institutions which did not foster Jewish integration did not appeal to him, and he politely declined to support them. Zionism offered the most dramatic example of a project to which he would not give money or lend his prominent and respected name, something many American Zionists considered as valuable as his dollars. Zionism he considered antithetical to integration. The movement proclaimed the principles of the "negation of the diaspora," a repudiation of, and expectation of the end to, Jewish life outside of a Jewish homeland. This central tenet of the movement predicted that Jewish life in the diaspora had no future, as a result belittling the advances made by Jews around the world over the previous centuries. Rosenwald did not approve of the Zionist mission and he would not support it or the agencies working for its advancement.

His philanthropic vision for Jewish causes followed his philosophy of giving for other Chicago and American causes. He would not make donations in perpetuity and he would not let his name be attached to institutions or programs. In addition, when he donated to a cause, he usually took an active role in the project, holding office on boards and regularly attending meetings. While he deferred to experts whom he trusted to know more than he did about a specific cause, he reacted quickly to suggestions about which causes to support, impervious to criticisms by those who disagreed with his choices. He challenged others to give as well and offered his contributions based on the ability of the recipient institution to raise matching funds, whether one large donation from a single donor or many small gifts from a broad public. He embraced projects which shrank the distance between givers and recipients, preferring to fund endeavors in which the recipients had a voice in the use of the funding and functioned as shareholders in the project or organization.

Rosenwald gave money to Jewish communal undertakings

like so many of the Jews of his class, combining conservative Progressivism, Reform Jewish ideals, and American concerns. But much of his activism brought him into contact with Jews who held different views from his, had immigrated more recently to America than his parents had, from places far removed from their home villages, and who could not begin to match his economic achievements. Some of his largest and most celebrated Jewish associations involved institutions that bridged gaps between diverse segments of the Jewish world. The important role he played in the creation during World War I of the American Jewish Joint Distribution Committee offers a notable example. The word *joint* in the organization's name referred to the combined participation of well-off American Jews, mostly Reform like Rosenwald, representatives of the Orthodox community, and the *landsmanshaftn*, the local mutual-aid societies formed by recent migrants from eastern Europe built around premigration hometown affiliations. The Joint, despite differences of opinion and internal squabbling, has functioned for over a century and from its earliest decades reflected the ability of Jewish groups to overcome differences so as to serve the needs of fellow Jews.

Through his Jewish philanthropic work he encountered, developed positive relationships with, and expressed respect and admiration for individuals who subscribed to ideologies different from his. While his family and social life, whether in Hyde Park or at his summer home in Ravinia, a lovely area north of Chicago, operated almost exclusively within a world of rich Reform Jews whose parents had come from German-speaking lands, Rosenwald's Jewish network came to include men and women born in Lithuania, Ukraine, Galicia, and elsewhere in eastern Europe who had spent their early years in America in immigrant enclaves. Many worked as Jewish communal professionals, and they taught Rosenwald much. He invited Alexander Dushkin, for example, a Jewish educator born in the Lithuanian province of Suwalk and a committed Zionist, to accompany him on a trip to the Tuskegee Institute, the African American school he funded and on whose board of trustees he sat. JR in turn happily accepted Dushkin's invitation to attend the Dushkin family's Passover Seder. Their disparate backgrounds and ideologies did not prevent the two from finding common ground, nor did they deter Rosenwald from embracing a fellow Jew, despite his strong aversion to Zionism.[3]

Rosenwald made Jews and the Jewish world central to his personal, philanthropic, and communal goals. His sentiments as a Jew and his concern for Jews seemed boundless. In 1904, he went alone on an ocean voyage to Europe, his first trip abroad, and recalled in a letter to his wife a moment of involvement with some east European Jewish immigrants, revealing his intense reaction as a Jew to the treatment of other Jews. As he related to Gussie, a man he met onboard, a "Mr. S.," told him that "they—the other steerage passengers—were mistreating the Russian Jews in steerage. We went at once, and gave a few of them—the offenders—the mischief, and since then there seems to be no trouble. Mr. S. and I went into the steerage this morning and had a pleasant half hour with some of the Russians. They are mostly men who having made some money . . . are going back for their wives and children." Rosenwald used this brief encounter to meet and engage with Jews with whom he presumably had little in common, aside from their Jewishness.[4]

By the time Rosenwald started directing his wealth toward Jewish causes, the majority of the world's Jews were centered in two places, the United States and Europe. About one-third of world Jewry had immigrated to the United States during the long nineteenth century, producing a robust, growing, and pluralistic Jewish culture which generally harmonized with American life. In large cities like Chicago, the second-largest in the nation, and in small towns like Springfield, Jews supported a variety of organizations and institutions expressing their many iterations of Jewishness, deeply inflected by their mostly positive interactions with their non-Jewish neighbors. In America at that time, voluntary institutions, religious, ethnic, or other, provided nearly all the social services, a reflection of the absence of strong state involvement, and Jews moved to fill that need. Rosenwald, whether explicitly or implicitly, considered this an ideal to be nurtured and strengthened.

Rosenwald's Jewish concerns did not stop at the shores of the United States, and he had much to say about, and many millions of dollars to give to, the Jews of Europe. Large concentrations of Jews continued to live there, primarily in the Austro-Hungarian Empire and its successor states, Poland in particular, and the Soviet Union. Rosenwald undertook projects for European Jews which shared features with initiatives he funded for Jews in the United States. But he recognized an important difference between their respective situations. He did not consider that the gentiles among whom European Jews lived, whether Poles, Ukrainians, or Russians, resembled American gentiles. Rather, they seemed to be more like the white southerners who had erected a system that kept African Americans in a state of near servility, decades after the end of slavery, through intimidation and violence.

In the years Rosenwald operated in the global Jewish philanthropic network, countless Jews suffered grievously, experiencing vast outrages perpetrated against them in central and eastern Europe. Over a quarter of a million Jewish civilians died in violent attacks during World War I and in the subsequent decade. The Jews in Poland and in Ukraine had been subjected to pogroms and other forms of physical brutality, unimaginable in America. Jews functioned there as the despised "other," and Rosenwald believed that he had to participate in, and indeed sponsor, projects to deter further assaults against them and to prevent any deterioration in their condition.

As a young man, the owner of a modestly successful men's suit company and the support of a growing family, JR exhibited little of the philanthropic zeal that would dominate the rest of his life. But even with limited means, he supported Jewish causes, volunteering at the Russian Aid Society, which provided temporary lodging for new Jewish immigrants in the 1890s, and contributing to his temple.

But after his move to Sears, and particularly after the departures of Aaron Nusbaum and Richard Sears, things changed, and Rosenwald's public life began centering on civic engagements, with Jewish causes prominent. Rosenwald provided massive financial contributions, used his influence, and made a vast expenditure of time for a number of Jewish organizations and agencies. As with his other projects, Rosenwald did not believe in acts of individual largesse benevolently disbursed on a case-by-case basis by kindhearted individuals, but favored institutions that offered systemic solutions and reflected a wide basis of support by donors and beneficiaries. He leaned toward organizations that operated on efficient and rational principles. In his Jewish philanthropic work, as in his other concerns, he believed in the scientific principles of Progressivism and good business.

This bias notwithstanding, Rosenwald also responded to personal requests to help individual Jews in distress. Minnie Low, the head of the Bureau of Personal Services, frequently told him about specific cases of concern, and Rosenwald usually gave her the help she needed, sometimes for years on end. She and her assistant Minnie Jacobs Berlin distributed Rosenwald money in a number of personal cases, reporting back to him on how they had spent the funds. At times he took an interest in a specific individual's situation, requesting minute details. He offered three hundred dollars, through Low, to the Klaff family in 1910, to enable them to buy a small drugstore. He paid the salaries of some of the workers in her office. In 1914 he responded positively to her note that she found herself in "need of a great deal of additional help, which we cannot get." His money made it possible for her to hire "a young lady . . . a Vassar graduate," who sought a social work position.[5] Chicago Jews learning about immigration problems besetting family members still in Europe or already en route to America would also turn to JR, who willingly used his influence with members of Congress and the Department of State to facilitate the family reunification. And Chicago Jews who believed that they had been discriminated against in employment appealed to him, considering him their representative to the larger world.

Chicago's non-Jewish Progressives, meanwhile, relied upon Rosenwald when they needed help addressing problems facing individual Jews in distress, such as immigrants who had gotten caught up in some bureaucratic morass of the system of immigration enforcement. Grace Abbott, for example, of the Immigrants' Protective League asked him to intervene with Jewish immigrants, relatives of Chicago residents, facing deportation. In the summer of 1914 she asked for money to support the two children of the Kipnis family who had just landed in Baltimore. Diagnosed during the standard medical examination with ringworm, they could stay in the country, officials ruled, only if someone would pay the cost of their hospitalization until cured. Rosenwald agreed to help, offering to pay for their care however long it took. When the children's situation became more complicated legally, and immigration officials wanted to return them to Europe, JR intervened. The two children had been placed on a boat to go "back to the old country," but when hostilities broke out in Europe, the boat sailed instead to New York. Abbott asked Rosenwald if he would now assume the cost for a hospital stay there, and he again, with not a moment's hesitation, agreed.[6]

But in the main he directed his attention to associations founded by and for Chicago Jews. The first of his Chicago Jewish charities, the Associated Jewish Charities, one he embraced before he had much to give, had been brought to his attention by Rabbi Hirsch. The Associated had been founded as an amalgam of a number of earlier, smaller Jewish charitable associations, and it became a centerpiece of his local Jewish giving and involvement. By 1905 JR had emerged as its single largest contributor, and in 1906 he became a director. By 1908 he had became its president, a position he held until 1912. Following a one-year break he returned to that position, serving until 1917. After he stepped down, he lent his name as honorary president. Along with other Jewish Progressives involved with the Associated, Rosenwald used it as a model not just for the provision of services to Jews but as an exemplar of the highest standard for the provision of social services. He derived tremendous satisfaction from the fact that non-Jewish social workers and scholars of social service, such as faculty at the School of Civics and Philanthropy (later the University of Chicago's School of Social Service Administration) held it up as an exemplar of service provision to be studied and copied.

Before the formation of the Associated Jewish Charities, Chicago Jews had been inundated with multiple appeals from many small organizations, most of which had something of value to offer to a small number of needy recipients. The Associated, one of the first such bodies in the country, Jewish or gentile, brought together representatives of the many constituent groups and launched a single fundraising campaign directed at the Jewish public. It then disbursed the funds based on detailed reports submitted by subsidiary agencies documenting the needs and the size of the populations they served. The Associated included both organizations of long standing that went back to the mid-nineteenth century and some newer ones founded by immigrant Jews. The organizations had previously had to appeal to their own constituencies for funding, which limited the amount they could raise, and according to Rosenwald, reflecting the Progressive imperative, this kept divisions in the community alive. Those divisions, he and others of his class believed, harmed rather than helped the Jewish cause.

Rosenwald criticized this practice as wasteful, annoying to those being solicited, and out of keeping with the Progressive age. Pressed by JR, the Associated increasingly adopted a solid and sober business model which emphasized efficiency, appealing to a broader donor base than any organization could solicit on its own. The Associated used paid professionals, trained social workers in particular, to provide what it considered the best services to those in need. Funding depended on organizations keeping accurate records of how much they took in and what they spent, with the idea of maximizing resources. According to Rosenwald, who referred to it in 1911 as the cause "nearest my heart," the Associated accomplished several things. It provided Jews in Chicago, children, the elderly, the ill, new immigrants in need of work, widows, orphans, the unemployed, with assistance. It also, as he noted, "place[d] the raising of money for Jewish charity in a class by itself, and thereby reflect[ed] credit on the Jewish community."[7] According to Rosenwald, the Associated stimulated good public relations for Jews among other Chicagoans and made "Chicago . . . the best and most progressive Jewish community in the world."[8]

JR celebrated his fiftieth birthday by the presentation of several gifts of $250,000, and he earmarked one of these for the Associated, a tribute to his belief in the organization and to the work it did in improving conditions for its beneficiaries, highlighting the Jews' contribution to the evolving world of American social service, and boosting Chicago's importance in the field of Jewish philanthropy.

As a generous supporter and energized member of the board,

Rosenwald campaigned for the Associated among his affluent friends, urging them to support it as well. He focused particular interest on several institutions under its umbrella, such as the Jewish Home Finding Society. Rosenwald, much influenced by Progressive thinking, wanted Chicago Jews to stop supporting orphanages and other institutions for children whose parents could not care for them. He, in the Progressive vein, thought it better to place orphans in private homes with families and to fund other families, mothers in particular, so they could care for their children in their own homes. His campaign against orphanages put him into conflict with the board of the Nathan Marks Orphanage, a struggling institution founded and supported by the city's Orthodox Jews, mostly recent immigrants from eastern Europe, who in other large cities as well had created a number of small orphanages.

The Nathan Marks home needed funds and had turned to JR to bail it out. As he typically did, he agreed to help but put conditions on his donation. He in this case made his gift contingent upon modern methods of care, of bookkeeping, and of fundraising in the future. This appeal involved him for the first time directly in the affairs of the immigrant Orthodox Jewish community. Rosenwald developed a tremendous appreciation for the group's leaders and for the communal activism of the immigrant enclave of Chicago's West Side.

He offered financial assistance to a number of their projects, assisting them in creating an equivalent of the Associated, the Federated Orthodox Jewish Charities of Chicago, a central body that collected and disbursed funds, directed and supervised by the city's Orthodox Jews themselves. JR attended a contentious 1911 meeting of the representatives of the city's many small Orthodox Jewish charities and spoke up in behalf of federation, aligning himself with the *Kurier*, Chicago's Yiddish paper, a voice of the Orthodox population. In return, the leaders of the Federated, perhaps hoping that JR would continue to fund them or perhaps because they genuinely valued him, moved by the fact of a millionaire Reform Jew working with them, elected him president, a position he held for years. He addressed the various constituent organizations, touting the importance of unity within the Orthodox world and the betterment of relationships between them and the American, mostly Reform, Jewish community in Chicago. He attended board meetings and presided over the organization. Chicago newspapers, both Jewish and secular, reported on his appearances before the groups that belonged to the Federated. While an address by Julius Rosenwald to the Young Men's Federated Jewish Charities paled in comparison to the meetings, also reported in the press, that he had met with U.S. presidents, other millionaire businessmen, and the nation's great leaders in philanthropy, business, and education, such publicity generated much greater attention for these Orthodox immigrant organizations than they would have received without him. His participation mattered greatly to them.

While the men and women of the Federated never became part of JR's social circle, he felt that all Jews, like all Americans, ought to work together rather than separately. As he saw it, each faction brought something of value to the life of Chicago Jewry. The well-established native-born American Jews like himself had money and influence with the city's power elite, while the newcomers had numbers, which translated into voting power. The newcomers also represented the future of Chicago Jewry. Each needed the other.

So in 1912, as part of his fiftieth-birthday give-away spree, he designated $250,000 to build the Central Administration Building to house the offices of both the Associated and the Federated, defining the common space as a venue for fostering communal unity. The two organizations might maintain separate offices, but sharing the building offered opportunities for activists from the numerically unequal sectors to interact with each other. Over the course of the next decade, amid all his other civic and philanthropic involvements, JR maintained an interest in both bodies and spent much time orchestrating a marriage between them, considering the bifurcation of Chicago's Jews, and of Jews elsewhere, dysfunctional and increasingly unnecessary as the American-born-and-raised children of the east European immigrants came of age. In 1923, Rosenwald's efforts to engineer a match between the two finally succeeded, and the Associated and the Federated merged into the Jewish Charities of Chicago, erasing at least bureaucratically and institutionally the idea of "German" and "east European" Jews as separate. With the merger, he expected Jewish identity to be tied to Chicago, or, more broadly, to America.

The merger took place at a crucial demographic moment. Two years earlier, the U.S. Congress had passed the Emergency Quota Act, which specified as a temporary measure the system that would be instituted in 1924 reducing European immigration to a trickle. No longer would new Jewish immigrants from Poland, Russia, and elsewhere in eastern Europe make their way to the United States in large numbers. By 1930, a majority of the Jews of the United States had been born on the American side of the Atlantic, a reversal of a century of immigration. Likewise, the rapid movement of the children of the earlier immigrants into the middle class via education meant that poverty diminished as an issue for the agencies of the Jewish communities. Those communities could focus instead on the professionalization of social services, medical care in particular, as well as the enhancement of Jewish cultural life.

Representatives of both bodies considered Rosenwald the ideal candidate to lead the now unified Jewish Charities. An editorial in the Chicago *Jewish Chronicle*, "It's Up to You, J.R.," spelled out the reasons why he, the one person associated with both bodies, would, despite his American, wealthy, and non–eastern European origins, make the best president of the new institution. The newspaper editorialized that "his leadership . . . moral vision . . . and brilliant personal example" had been "a tremendous personal influence in both groups," and went on to state the perhaps obvious point: "There is perhaps no other man in Chicago whom both sides will accept each as its own, and certainly no one whom both will trust as implicitly and follow as enthusiastically." That the *Chronicle* referred to him as one of their own required no stretch of the imagination for members of the Associated, but that members of the Federated could also accept it reflected JR's ability to move beyond conventional categories.[9]

The year after the merger, which resulted in a successful $2.5 million campaign for Chicago Jewry through the campaign of the newly created Chicago Jewish Charities, a combination of the Associated and the Federated, Hyman L. Meites published *History of the Jews of Chicago.* The Odessa-born Meites, an Orthodox Jew who claimed to be America's first official Zionist, the president of the Illinois Jewish Historical Society and publisher of the *Jewish Chronicle*, could not contain himself as he lauded Rosenwald for his ability to bring together the two segments of the city's Jewish population. "In this historic achievement," he proclaimed, "Rosenwald's efforts are universally recognized as the decisive factor." Rosenwald had one goal in mind: "to eliminate divisions and distinctions in the Jewish community and unite the two organizations into a single, all-embracing whole."[10]

Immediately after the merger the new Jewish charitable body raised millions for two massive projects. It created a school for nursing at Michael Reese Hospital, one of the jewels in the crown of the Associated, and amassed enough to expand the activities and facilities of the West Side's Chicago Hebrew Institute (CHI), an institution that JR had long supported, which represented his ideal kind of institution for Chicago's Jews.

Founded in 1903 by a group of young men from the immigrant community, and decidedly Zionist in orientation, the CHI listed as its purpose to "provide a social centre for the native Americans as well as to the immigrant; to encourage education; to promote physical welfare and arouse civic interest; to give freely moral and spiritual rather than material aid; to strive for the elimination of class distinction; to prevent rather than cure societal ills" for the city's Jews.[11] As one of the premier institutions on the West Side, the CHI functioned as a kind of Jewish Hull House. The Orthodox rabbis enthusiastically supported it, perhaps because it kept Jewish youngsters away from Addams's institution, which they mistrusted for its supposed Christian orientation. While they erred in seeing Hull House as a center for evangelical activity, they endorsed CHI as a place where adults, young people, and children could take classes, join clubs, listen to lectures, and watch plays with almost exclusively Jewish themes. Here they could exercise, take out books, view works of art, and develop the skills needed for American citizenship in an all-Jewish environment. An early director, Philip Seaman, summarized the institute as "frankly Jewish and staunchly American." It contained within its walls a modern synagogue that, although traditional in format, injected some English into the Hebrew liturgy, provided a Hebrew school for girls and boys together, sponsored the Hebrew Oratorio Society, and offered classes which stressed teaching how to be "a good American Citizen."[12]

The Hebrew Oratorio Society offers a small but instructive example of the deeply Jewish projects undertaken by the CHI and JR's hopes of fostering Jewish culture in America. The group, to which Rosenwald, against his usual practice of not funding individual organizations within the CHI, donated directly, allowing it to benefit from the focused gift as well as from his large contributions to CHI, could not have been more overtly Jewish in its goals. Established by the institute in 1917, it laid out its purpose in a letter to JR: "to cultivate, develop and produce Jewish music in all its branches, extending from ancient to modern times." The Oratorio Society drew a direct line from Jews in the present to their ancient past. Without saying so in precise terms, the CHI, the Hebrew Oratorio Society, and Rosenwald sought to demonstrate to Chicago Jews their tradition's relevance in twentieth-century America.[13]

Why did JR embrace the CHI and make it a focus of his philanthropic largesse and his time commitment? Founded by Zionists, CHI might seem to incorporate much that Rosenwald considered antithetical to his vision of Jewish integration. It contained an Orthodox synagogue, albeit a modernized one. It staged Yiddish-language plays. It provided a place for socialist and union groups to hold meetings. It stressed the Jewish aspect of the immigrants' lives, highlighting it over integration into the wider American life. It provided Chicago's poorer Jews with an alternative to Hull House, an institution he prized highly and a place where they would have socialized and interacted with non-Jews, something he sought to promote.

Rosenwald stated what he liked about the CHI in his acceptance of the invitation to serve on the board: "It is unnecessary for me to say that I am in sympathy with any movement that will tend toward breaking down the social barrier which seems to exist between the Russian and German Jews, and with the thought in mind that my connection with the Hebrew Institute will be a step in that direction, I have concluded to allow my name to be used as a Director."[14] He also appreciated that much of CHI's revenues came from the users of the institution, rather than as charity from rich donors.

The institute balanced its efforts to foster Jewish culture with the message that immigrants and their children should at the same time embrace America and modernity. JR provided funds for the CHI gymnasium, a place where girls and boys from immigrant families could engage in activities which presumably would not have been open to them had they not come to America. A May 1909 article in the *Chicago Tribune*, aptly titled "Urge Race to Build Muscle," reported that CHI's first director, David Blaustein, commented that "the Jew has never been an athletically inclined person, but with the erection of a gymnasium" funded by Rosenwald, "an athletic interest in physical activities would be aroused."[15] So too at the CHI, immigrant Jews, adults and children, would learn how to observe American holidays, to speak and read English, and to prepare for the citizenship test, and would be ushered into the world of their new American home.

The programming of the CHI and Rosenwald's larger project of fostering Jewish culture indicate a mutuality of purpose between ushering the immigrants into American life and sustaining their Jewishness. As Rosenwald commented, "The process of Americanization takes care of itself. But it is their Judaism that the people lose so rapidly."[16] He admired the CHI for being able to foster both identities and for contributing to the enrichment of both American and Jewish life. What the CHI and other, similar institutions aimed for might be seen as a Progressive-era effort intended to channel the inevitable road toward acculturation along, as they defined it, suitable and appropriate paths for the purpose of maintaining Jewish life in America.

They hoped that their efforts would create common ground between immigrant parents and their American-born children, something Jewish social workers and other communal commentators recognized as a problem, a cause of familial discord. They sought to guide Jewish youth away from the negative influences of the city streets and expose them, through recreational activities, Progressive education, and the expressive arts, to the best of America while keeping them connected to the Jewish world. Echoing the concerns of Jane Addams, who wrote of Chicago's immigrants in her 1909 *The Spirit of Youth and the City Streets*, the leaders and backers of the Chicago Hebrew Institute considered reconciling American-bred Jewish youth with their immigrant parents as essential to their work. The city streets as Addams depicted them lured young people with tawdry amusements, commercial entertainments, and crime, posing a direct challenge to the authority of parents who expected deference from their children. Immigrant parents, according to Addams and the CHI, did not understand the psychological and cultural outlook of their American children. Institutions like Hull House and the CHI embraced modern American ideas, particularly about adolescence, a relatively new concept of the Progressive era, but they also celebrated the world of the immigrant parents, a world inherited from the past.

Additionally, CHI, like many of the other Chicago-based Jewish organizations that Rosenwald funded, brought together under one roof, literally and figuratively, Jews who differed in their political ideologies, religious views, places of origin, and class. These institutions, as he saw it, fostered Jewish unity, solidifying communal cohesion, projects that JR considered crucial to Jewish integration into American life.

FOSTERING JEWISH CULTURE

Whether considering Jewish culture as a matter of the expressive arts or Judaism as a religion or Jewish history, Julius Rosenwald considered it his responsibility to use his money to encourage projects intended to promote it. To these cultural projects he brought his familiar vision, stressing the importance of Jewish unity and erasing boundaries between people who might be thought to have little in common.

That Rosenwald handsomely supported his own religious institution, Sinai, hardly made him unusual among Jewish philanthropists. But that he did so to stimulate other Jews to become more active in Jewish religious life generally made his generosity noteworthy. Early in his career, Rosenwald provided special funds to Sinai to devise programs to encourage all Jewish young people, not just the children of members, to join the congregation and through it to become more active Jews. By giving to the temple he hoped to strengthen Jewish life. So too his contributions to CHI, one of the rare projects to which Rosenwald gave to an endowment fund, bespoke his sense of the importance of enriching Jewish culture in Chicago and beyond. That it sponsored and staged performances of Yiddish drama, that it housed not only the high-culture Hebrew Oratorio Society but also the Jewish Singing Society, the Jewish Socialist Singing Society, and the Jewish Literary and Dramatic Society, that it offered space to clubs with names like Halevi, Maccabi, Young Judea, and Zion, all Zionist, attested to Rosenwald's broad and expansive view of Jewish culture. He wanted American Jewish culture to blossom, and despite his own negative stance towards Zionism, he did nothing to keep these groups out of CHI and imposed no limitations upon the project of sustaining Jewish life.

He embraced undertakings large and small. As an example of the latter Rosenwald made possible the exploration of local Jewish history, an undertaking that helped Chicago Jews, most of them newcomers, feel at home. Along with a number of east European–born Zionists, Rosenwald in 1918 founded the Jewish Historical Society of Illinois, serving as its president. Through the society, the city's Jews, and its non-Jews, could see evidence that Jews had been present in the city and state since frontier days. Rosenwald provided much of the funding for the society, and he underwrote the publication of Hyman Meites's massive *History of the Jews of Chicago* (1924). His money made it possible for the society to place plaques around the city highlighting the places where Jews had lived as far back as the 1850s. Such work tied in with that of other wealthy and well-connected Jews around the country. In fostering the study of

American Jewish history, both local and national, these sponsors had two goals. They intended to tell their people's story to the majority population, showing how Jews, who, even with the immigration from eastern Europe still in full strength, had been part of the city, state, or nation from its beginning, had helped create it. The sponsors also saw the work of the historical society as a way of building Jewish identity and loyalty, and urged Jews to take pride in their people's impact on the larger society as well as in the depth of their roots in local soil. While they may have come as immigrants, the Jews who showed up in the pages of Meites's book and whose names and deeds had been engraved in the bronze markers around the city had grown up with the city, enriching it with their cultural and religious institutions.

Rosenwald's commitment to fostering Jewish culture included much more than celebrating the local Jewish past. He provided substantial contributions to Hebrew Union College (HUC) in Cincinnati, the Reform rabbinical seminary, as well as to the work of the Union of American Hebrew Congregations, serving on their executive boards, donating money, using his contacts to help raise funds from others, and speaking publicly about the virtues of the two Reform institutions. In the 1920s the chair of the board of HUC acknowledged that Rosenwald had funded the school more generously than any other donor. Given the wealth of the donors who aligned with Reform, his munificent contribution is particularly impressive. He had given substantial sums for the library, recognizing the value of having a rabbinate with access to the best scholarly resources, and in 1928 offered the college $500,000 as the cornerstone for its $4 million campaign, which the institution successfully completed on the eve of the crash of the stock market.

Rosenwald not only gave money for Reform causes. He served as a kind of pitchman for the movement, describing movingly his own experiences as a Reform Jew to inspire others to give as well. In a 1920 address in Cleveland, for example, he explained why he had made a handsome contribution to Union of American Hebrew Congregations' extension work in education. After stating that he felt "deeply concerned with the future of the Jew," he expressed a deep hope that "he shall take his place among the best in every community." He went on to sketch in personal terms how Judaism had shaped his life and, conversely, how his civic involvement had enhanced his sense of Jewishness. "I have a strong conviction that if we desire to retain our self-respect," he told the assembled Reform Jewish leaders and wealthy notables, "and the respect of our fellow citizens we must strive to keep alive the spirit that can only come from what is taught in Sabbath schools and the synagogue." He described the religiosity of his upbringing, the way his mother had "benched" him, using the Yiddish term for "bless," before he went to sleep, and he determined that although his parents "were not Orthodox as we understand that term," still, as he recalled, "they were staunch in their Jewish faith," and they built their lives around the "new Reform Temple." As an adult in Chicago he "naturally affiliated" with the Sinai congregation of Rabbi Hirsch. Speaking as a disciple, JR declared about Hirsch, "I have sat at his feet every Sunday when he held services." Not at all disconcerted by the fact that Sinai held its major religious service of the week on Sunday instead of the Jewish Sabbath, Rosenwald asserted that, "never once in all that time have I left the temple without feeling that I carried away some helpful or inspiring lesson which would not have come to me except for having placed myself under such influence."[17]

The influence of Hirsch cannot be understated. Hirsch had introduced him to Jane Addams and ushered him into the world of Chicago social reform. He later engineered JR's meeting with Booker T. Washington, and he raised JR's consciousness on the issue of race in America and the subjugation of African Americans. Hirsch and the Reform movement more generally showed JR how to live his life as a Jew. But Rosenwald's commitment to synagogues extended beyond Hirsch's own temple. Rosenwald responded positively to requests, small and large, from other congregations and Jewish religious institutions facing financial difficulties. He did not distinguish among synagogues on the basis of denomination and did not favor Reform congregations over others that appealed to him, in both senses of the word.

An episode in 1910 demonstrates his catholicity. JR donated $100 to Morris Shanedling to benefit the tiny traditional congregation B'nai Abraham in Virginia, Minnesota, a minuscule Jewish community on the Mesabi Iron Range. Rosenwald promised Shanedling that if the Orthodox congregation could rid itself of all its debts through small contributions from members, he would make another, larger donation. Nine years later Shanedling returned to Rosenwald's office at Sears armed with "a soiled and tattered subscription list which Mr. Rosenwald had signed in two places. He also brought the mortgage release and four cancelled mortgage notes for $500 each, representing the $2000 debt," now paid off. Congregants had struggled for nine years to pay it, and "many of the payments endorsed on the backs of the notes were as small as $20." According to the memorandum from Rosenwald's secretary, William Graves, the multimillionaire who ordinarily gave gifts in the millions, upon hearing of "such an act of fidelity to a trust," invited Shanedling into his office, shook his hand, and rewarded him with $150.[18]

A tiny amount of money to Rosenwald, that $150 no doubt meant a great deal to the thousand or so Jewish residents of the mining town who could now have a synagogue building in which to worship and gather as a community. In his view synagogue life lay at the heart of Judaism, and he wanted to help. In the late 1920s he gave New York's Jewish Theological Seminary of America (JTS) one of the largest gifts it had ever received. The $500,000 given to the Conservative movement's rabbinical institution, also donated just before Black Friday, 1929, made it possible for the school to weather the ensuing Depression. Rosenwald had pledged this amount to a special fund in memory of the recently deceased Louis Marshall, a communal activist with whom Rosenwald had collaborated in numerous endeavors.

The fact that JR, the committed Reform Jew, chose to give money to JTS, bastion of the Conservative movement, reflected not only his respect for the memory of Marshall, also a Reform Jew, but his vision of Judaism in America. JTS differed from Hebrew Union College, as the Conservative movement did from Reform. Conservative Judaism considered Jews bound by tradition to ritual practices, liturgies, and observance of Jewish law inherited from the past. While not all members of Conservative congregations, a movement that grew slowly starting in the late 1880s with the founding of the Seminary, followed Jewish law, Conservative rabbis used their synagogues and classrooms to expound on the binding nature of halacha.

JTS owed its origins to the disgust a group of traditionalist rabbis had felt when attending the first graduation of Hebrew Union College in 1883. At the celebratory meal which followed the ordination ceremony, plates of profoundly unkosher food showed up on the tables, and the outraged rabbis objected strenuously at the violation of the dietary laws. By the 1910s the movement had attracted some of the better off of the east European Jewish immigrants to America. Unlike Reform Jews, many who belonged to synagogues aligned with JTS embraced Zionism, emphasizing the peoplehood of the Jews and their shared sense of nationhood.

The school's backers, a more diverse group than either the faculty or students since it included Reform Jews like Marshall and JR, believed that JTS could help create a distinctively American form of Judaism. They envisioned this Judaism as

a refined version of Orthodoxy: following tradition but recognizing American standards of synagogue decorum, something that they considered the immigrant traditional congregations lacked. They hoped that this more traditional Judaism
would offer the children of the new immigrants an alternative
to both the old world synagogues of the immigrant enclaves,
with their roots and liturgy in foreign lands, and the alien,
more secular Reform temples, with their organ music and
mixed seating. Marshall had been trying to interest Rosenwald
in JTS since the second decade of the twentieth century. Rosenwald's resistance to the seminary came not, however, because of
its mission to rescue traditional Judaism from his own Reform
style. The problem lay rather in JTS's difficulty finding donors
willing to fund it, an argument Marshall used in trying to enlist
Rosenwald's support. But Rosenwald countered as he did with
nearly all institutions which appealed to him, that if true, the
Seminary had failed to create a constituency who cared about
its survival. And Rosenwald would not give to an organization
that could not raise matching funds.

By the late 1920s, when Rosenwald changed his mind, much
had changed. JTS and the Conservative movement had experienced substantial growth in membership. The decade's prosperity, the rapid movement of immigrant Jews out of their original neighborhoods into more comfortable, wealthier areas, and
the increased educational opportunities for their children had
drawn more Jews to Conservatism, making it more attractive
to Rosenwald. After Marshall's death, he saw support of JTS as
a fitting way to memorialize his friend.

That Rosenwald gave a half million dollars to sustain and
expand JTS in 1929 reflected much about how he saw Judaism
as a religious system in America. Religion, he believed, provided the foundation for Jewish life. He liked synagogues as
Jewish sites for fostering community, and at least as measured
by his giving, he espoused a very American idea of religion,

seeing it as a good that served people by providing them with a moral compass and basis for social life. It offered a communal identity through attachment to a specific denomination and house of worship. Yet by focusing on moral imperatives it instilled compassion for others and engagement with the larger society. With regard to Judaism specifically, Rosenwald hardly concerned himself with punctilious observance of Jewish law but rather saw Judaism as a social force which brought Jews together, serving as Jewish anchors of particularity in a diverse and complex world.

But though he benefited both Hebrew Union College and the Jewish Theological Seminary individually, he saw this support as leading to an eventual union of the denominations. A bit tone-deaf to the ideological differences which divided the two schools from each other and also from the liberal, nondenominational Jewish Institute of Religion founded in New York in 1922 by Rabbi Stephen Wise, he believed that American Jews would benefit from, and Judaism in America would be strengthened by, unity and the nonduplication of efforts. Like his goal of uniting Jewish philanthropies in Chicago under one roof, he looked to American Jews to overcome their differences and shed their denominational individuality. In 1925 he wrote to Adolph Ochs, chair of the board of HUC, that "our aim should be to bring about a consolidation of the three main 'rabbi factories' of this country. The Reformed and Orthodox groups," by "Orthodox" he meant JTS, "are I think, coming nearer and nearer together and the trite saying, 'United we stand,' etc. might be applicable." No school needed to dominate, in Rosenwald's merger scheme, but rather he predicted that all three together "might be able to find a common meeting ground and, by a system of exchange professorships, get together a faculty which would be representative."[19]

Rosenwald's ideal of Judaism being the means for Jews to unite their Jewish culture and traditions with engagement with the larger American world helps explain why he refused when asked to contribute to Yeshiva College, the institution of higher learning of American Orthodoxy. The school grew out of an east European–style institution, the Etz Chayim Yeshiva, founded in 1886 on New York's Lower East Side, reorganized in the early twentieth century into the rabbinical school the Rabbi Isaac Elchanan Theological Seminary. In the first decade of the century it began to offer general courses for study along with rabbinical learning, and in 1928 it transformed yet again into Yeshiva College to provide both rabbinical training and a standard American bachelor's degree. Harry Fischel, a wealthy supporter of Yeshiva College, solicited funds from Rosenwald after a meeting with Lessing, JR's oldest son, in Atlantic City. Fischel reminded Rosenwald that he had given "$500,000 to Hebrew Union College in Cincinnati, which is Reform, and he had then given the same amount to the Jewish Theological Seminary in New York, which is Conservative." It would be only logical, Fischel suggested, for Rosenwald to contribute to Yeshiva, "which is Orthodox." Fischel had a specific amount in mind, $600,000, as a naming opportunity for "an auditorium to be the Mr. and Mrs. Julius Rosenwald Auditorium."[20]

Fischel erred in trying to lure Rosenwald with an edifice bearing his name. He should have known that Rosenwald abhorred having his name plastered on buildings. But more profoundly, the college deviated from the Rosenwald ideal for American Judaism. He did not begrudge his support for Orthodox projects, and consistently encouraged and gave money to Orthodox communal undertakings in Chicago. By lending his name and his funds to the Federated Orthodox Jewish Charities he counted himself as a stakeholder in the city's Orthodox community. Even his tiny gift to the Orthodox congregation on the Mesabi Iron Range demonstrated his positive view of an Orthodoxy that he did not practice but supported in order to assist those who did.

Rather, he objected to Yeshiva College's assertion of the value of being "really a Jewish university," an institution of American higher learning where Jews learned only with other Jews." He would not give his money to an institution of higher learning that offered university degrees only to Jewish students in a setting where Jews studied exclusively with others just like themselves. Education, he believed, in the broadest sense, unlike religion, should foster Jewish integration into American society, bringing Jews and other Americans together. In JR's vision, Jewish institutions which prepared Jews for the rabbinate and for service in the Jewish religious world deserved his support, but a Jewish institution that educated Jews apart from other students did not.[21]

Rosenwald's commitment to Judaism and Jewish education did not stop with the Reform and Conservative movements, nor did he limit it to the United States, or even to synagogues. He gave, indeed the largest contribution ever made, to fund a chair in Rabbinics at the University of Cambridge. Rosenwald's gift surpassed even that of Lionel Rothschild, himself a generous donor to Jewish educational causes.[22] Rosenwald also funded a position for Dr. Nathaniel Reich, an Egyptologist, at Dropsie College for Hebrew Cognate Learning in Philadelphia, and embraced the work of YIVO in Vilna. With regard to YIVO, he offered a rare insight in his letter of support as to why a Yiddish-language, east European, Orthodox institution would attract him. The letter, written by Edward Embree, who ran the Rosenwald Foundation and generally put into words JR's thoughts, encapsulated why he, a wealthy American Jew of Bavarian origin, would find this Yiddish institution to his liking. Embree realized that Rosenwald believed that all aspects of the history and culture of the Jews should be studied systematically, and "removed from emotion and prejudice to the realm of intelligence." In his contention that "facts . . . will not completely remove prejudice—but that they are the best start toward it," Rosenwald made the case for knowledge as a defense of Jews and Judaism. He also considered it important for "an institute of high standing" in Europe to function purely "under Jewish control and with Jewish professors and schools"—something he opposed in the United States. Rosenwald understood that the experience of Jews in America differed from that in eastern Europe. Finally, support for YIVO was part of his ongoing opposition to Zionism; as he noted, "To my mind Eastern Europe means much more in the life of Judaism during the past thousand years than Palestine does."[23]

The Chicago Hebrew Institute, Jewish Theological Seminary, and Hebrew Union College offered Rosenwald major local and national outlets for his project of reconstructing the Jewish world. The Cambridge position and YIVO gave him an opportunity to enhance Jewish culture overseas. For these goals he offered his name, his organizational time, and especially his money. He did not provide the intellectual ideas behind these projects, never claiming any expertise other than how to run a business or spearhead a fundraising campaign. But in the same way that he conducted his civic philanthropy, when he heard of a plan that he liked that addressed a problem that needed to be solved, he stepped forward, using his name to inspire others to do so as well.

His name surfaced repeatedly, and almost randomly, in the American Jewish world in conjunction with projects aimed at enhancing Jewish education, fostering Jewish culture, and supporting a variety of institutions and initiatives. In 1929, for example, the New York Bureau of Jewish Education published a study guide for adolescents by Israel Goldberg and Samson Benderly, titled *Outline of Jewish Knowledge, Being a History of the Jewish People and an Anthology of Jewish Literature from the Earliest Times to the Present.* The copyright page carried the words of appreciation, "The publication of this volume was rendered possible by the generosity of Mr. Julius Rosenwald," evidence of his willingness to help, in a wide variety of formats, in the transmission of Jewish learning, which he saw as a hedge against assimilation.[24]

This overall Rosenwald approach could also be seen in the late 1920s in his contribution to the publication of arguably the most important book in the history of American Judaism, and indeed in all of American Jewish history, Mordecai Kaplan's *Judaism as a Civilization: Toward a Reconstruction of American-Jewish Life*. The book, published in 1934, after JR's death, by Macmillan, one of the nation's largest and most prestigious publishing houses, had been in the works since the late 1920s, when the Wall Street banker Elisha Friedman published an article in *Union Tidings*, a Reform magazine, calling upon some wealthy American Jew to fund a contest for the best piece of writing to explore the condition of Judaism in modern times. Friedman's article followed an earlier piece by Roger W. Straus, president of the National Federation of Temple Brotherhoods, concerning what "Jewish laity can do to further Judaism in America." According to Friedman, the ideal funder of the project should be "long of cash and not short of ideals, and the will to serve," someone who could "set thousands of scholars the world over, thinking on the problem how Judaism" might "be made to function and serve effectively in society?" Friedman listed a few more specific questions, all of which focused on how "the distinctive values of Judaism might be preserved for the next generation of American Jewry."

Almost immediately following the appearance of Friedman's article Julius Rosenwald—surely "long of cash and not short of ideals"—responded, offering ten thousand dollars, an amount he eventually increased so that more than one entry could be honored. As a mark of how much the project meant to him, he allowed the contest to be advertised as the Julius Rosenwald Essay Contest.

The context of the contest offers a peek into Jewish denominational life of the 1920s. Discussion about it began in the pages of a Reform publication, and its guidelines clearly emphasized its Reform origins. The rules stipulated that the best essay explore the question "How can the experiences of the Reform Movement—its contributions and its deficiencies—be brought to bear" on the project of reinvigorating Judaism in America? So too the essays should address "What minimum of ceremonial and institutional life is required to maintain Jewish spiritual values?"—a question that resonated with the Reform worldview. Yet the committee which oversaw the contest, meeting initially in April 1929 at the City Club in New York, included not only Reform Jews, but Orthodox rabbis like Leo Jung of New York's Jewish Center and Sephardic rabbi David da Sola Pool, as well as Jewish educators Samson Benderly and Alexander Dushkin, both deeply associated with Zionism. JR's friend Julian Mack also served on the committee, as did the Zionist leader Harry Friedenwald from Baltimore.[25]

The contest sponsors hoped for an insightful essay, but instead they found themselves with a far lengthier piece of writing. Mordecai Kaplan's *Judaism as a Civilization* ran to six hundred pages and transcended the contest's original mission of measuring the impact of Reform Judaism. Kaplan asserted that American Jews, perhaps Rosenwald among them, had narrowed their concept of Judaism to a religion, and that this had contributed to its decline. In a world in which Judaism had shrunk to symbolic ritual in synagogues, Jewish culture could not compete with American culture. To Kaplan, himself the child of observant Lithuanian Jewish immigrants, a graduate of JTS, a disciple of the American educator John Dewey, and a Zionist, this debased definition of Judaism violated Judaism's essence. To be a living entity, Judaism had to be experienced as a civilization, encompassing culture, language, literature, and social organizations, fostering intense interaction among Jews as Jews. Kaplan, who along with a band of followers would use this book as the foundation of a fourth Jewish denomination, Reconstructionism, warned that for Judaism to survive in America it had to rebuild, to reconstruct itself as a living organism of Jewish peoplehood, a far cry from the words expressed by Reform rabbis in Pittsburgh. Kaplan emphasized that the Jews for most of their history had inhabited simultaneously two civilizations, their Jewish civilization and that of their town or country of residence. In the past, he wrote, Jews had found ways to harmonize their two civilizations. They needed to do so in America as well.

No evidence exists that JR ever plowed through the entire book in manuscript form. Ironically, Kaplan expressed unbridled disdain for wealthy American Jews like Rosenwald who, as the author saw it, concentrated their expressions of Jewishness on philanthropy. Without naming his benefactor, Kaplan considered that those who funded institutions like the Associated Jewish Philanthropies did so only for defensive purposes, having little, or no, interest in Jewish community life. Kaplan owed the successful publication of the book to Rosenwald's money, but he saw JR and his cohort as Jews with an "assimilationist turn of mind." No communalists, they simply did "not want to have it said that their poor are a burden to other groups or to the state." Whether JR agreed with Kaplan mattered less in terms of the appearance of the book and its transformative impact on American Jewish life, than his stewardship of the essay contest.[26]

Rosenwald's commitment to Judaism and to sustaining Jewish culture in America revealed a deep personal belief in Judaism and the Jewish people, Kaplan's future condemnation aside. In 1928 he granted a lengthy interview to the *Jewish Daily Bulletin* in which he declared, "I am no assimilator and I do not believe in the theory of assimilation. The Jews as a people, as an ethnic group, have existed for thousands of years." He predicted with optimism that Jews would "continue to exist . . . in this country in the future." But his commitment grew out of concern with rising anti-Semitism as well.[27]

His awareness of the growth of anti-Jewish sentiment in America and elsewhere did not drive him to the Zionist camp, which essentially argued that anti-Semitism would disappear only when the Jews had a state of their own. No assimilationist either, he did not believe that the best solution to the ever-growing problem of anti-Semitism in America and the world lay in the disappearance of the Jews as a distinct people or the diminution of Jewish culture.

COMBATING ANTI-SEMITISM

In his local, national, and global work for Jews Rosenwald swung between optimism and pessimism. In the same speech or article he would both bemoan the spreading anti-Jewish rhetoric and actions in America and simultaneously minimize their venom. He consistently asserted that people steeped in evil and ignorance could come to see their errors, that through philanthropic social engineering those who harbored prejudices could learn how wrong they had been. Naive, perhaps, but Rosenwald operated out of an instinctive sense of right and wrong. He consulted experts like Louis Marshall about the extent of American anti-Semitism and asked their advice on how he could help combat it. He monitored anti-Jewish initiatives in the United States and globally, and directed his wealth and the power of his name to address the problems.

In a 1912 speech he predicted that anti-Semitism would "ever play a large role in" America, rightly identifying the most extensive form of anti-Semitic discrimination as "social discrimination." Yet in the same speech he asserted that such discrimination "little interests the best Jews and is laughed at by the best non-Jews." Whatever he meant by *best*, he laid out a solution that hearkened back to the eighteenth century and the campaign for Jewish Emancipation, declaiming, "If the Jew fails in the discharge of his civic duty, he does not demonstrate to the nation that it acted wisely when it gave the Jew shelter and liberty and freedom." He might have been describing himself when he continued: "The Jew must be a pillar of civic well-being and moral capacity. He must be the one who in every crisis will be right, militant for the right, the ethical, the spiritual." Rosenwald charged Jews to be the "best in national life." Jews had to display their "usefulness in the highest sense of the term." He held up the jurists Louis Brandeis and Julian Mack "and others of their type," who "will do more for the position of the Jew in America, in countering anti-Jewish prejudice, by creating confidence . . . than all the money in Wall Street and all the wire-pulling in Washington."[28]

He retained his confidence in the necessity and effectiveness of such exemplary conduct by Jews in public life throughout his active decades, which coincided with the enactment of quotas in American universities and professional schools, the Leo Frank case, and the journalistic vitriol of Henry Ford. In a 1928 letter he suggested that Jews not "judge all Americans by the anti-Semitism of some," maintaining that "all persons of the religion to which they belong are likely to be judged by their conduct and that therefore it is important that young Jewish men and Jewish women at colleges conduct themselves well." He advised Jewish students to "demean themselves favorably and participate in college activities."[29]

Rosenwald in the main veered toward optimism, recognizing that American Jews benefited from the rights of citizenship and access to ample economic opportunities. In this, he judged correctly. Jews, whether native-born or naturalized, faced no state-instituted disenfranchisement and had no reason to question the degree to which they could enjoy the state's protections. No laws named them, worked against them, or targeted them.

As to private anti-Jewish practices, which Rosenwald also

recognized and tried to address, they too seem to have placed no barrier to the economic and social mobility and comfort of the majority of American Jews in any substantial or meaningful way. His active years of philanthropy and activism took place at a time when Jews, particularly the children of immigrants, gained increasing entry to the educational, economic, and cultural opportunities available to other white native-born Americans. Yet he heard the voices around him describing escalating discrimination, and he sought to learn the truth about its extent and character. In 1931 he asked Edwin Embree, his hand-picked director of the Rosenwald Fund, to gather information about discrimination against Jewish applicants to medical schools, a particularly vexing matter, as large numbers of Jewish men and women considered medicine an attractive career. Far from discriminating against Jews, Embree learned, medical schools seemed to welcome them. He reported to Rosenwald that "of the students admitted to medical schools [the previous year], 18% are Jewish, roughly six times the proportion of Jews to the population of the country." These data showed that "medical admissions today represent not a discrimination against, but rather in favor of, Jewish students."

American anti-Semitism, unlike the the widespread and systematic subjugation of blacks or the more virulent measures against Jews in eastern Europe, in Rosenwald's view constituted less a systemic problem than a situational concern, to be addressed but kept in perspective. He did not hesitate to speak out or to act when confronted with anti-Jewish practices. He knew full well that anti-Jewish sentiment existed in America, and he founded and funded organizations to combat it. He monitored instances of such sentiment and wrote discreet but firm letters to employers and institutions whose behavior he deemed harmful to Jews. In a 1923 speech, he shared his sense of both foreboding and confidence concerning the future of Jews in America as he described a campaign, mostly rhetorical, "of hatred waged against us daily and weekly." He commented on "the tendency toward restrictions of the Jewish population at universities and elsewhere, and other similar symptoms of discrimination and ill-will," which, he went on, "though they need not occasion despair, nevertheless must fill us with grave concern."[30]

Rosenwald acted on that concern. In 1928, he wrote to the John B. Wiggins Company, a Chicago publishing house, to protest letters it had sent out to young people, soliciting employment applications and promising "an exceptional opportunity for clean-cut young hustlers—Gentiles, etc." Rosenwald explained to Arthur Wiggins, the letter's author, that such phrases must "cast reflection upon and tend to injure to a greater or lesser extent every Jew, regardless of his ability and character." Certainly Wiggins, he noted, had the right of any employer in 1928 not to "employ anyone who is not Christian," as the law did not forbid it; but "to send . . . a letter over your signature which places a stigma upon an entire race, must appear to fair-minded people as unjust and surely not in accordance with the Golden Rule." Rosenwald asked Wiggins whether "it would be too much to ask that in the future your Company discontinue this method of securing help, which I am sure unintentionally discredits thousands of reputable American citizens."[31]

One of the organizations Rosenwald worked with to combat anti-Jewish discrimination in America was the American Jewish Committee (AJC), which sought to "prevent infringement of the civil and religious rights of Jews and to alleviate the consequences of persecution." As a founding member, Rosenwald assumed a leadership position in the Committee, representing, with Julian Mack, Chicago on the founding board and chairing the finance committee. Although he did not devote much of his time to the AJC, he believed in its premise that a small group of well-placed Jews could serve the millions of Jews of America who lacked their extensive political connections and resources to affect public policy. The AJC never intended itself as a membership organization for the masses. Rather, the Committee saw itself as a small knot of elite stewards of the Jewish people in America and, increasingly, abroad. As elites, they believed that they best knew what all Jews needed. The AJC never called for legislation specifically to benefit Jews but rather chose to make its case to people in power, pointing out to them that certain policies or practices harmed Jews and equally harmed America. In the 1910s and 1920s, the AJC vigorously, but unsuccessfully, worked against immigration restrictions, stating its objection as a matter of general policy, not exclusively a Jewish matter.

Rosenwald agreed with the AJC that government action had little role to play in solving the problems facing Jews in America. Discrimination mainly emanated from private sources, and American law tolerated discriminatory practices if they involved private employers, schools, and other kinds of institutions. Whether the discrimination appeared in college admissions offices or in the employment division of the Wiggins Company, Rosenwald believed that he and other Jews in a similar position bore the responsibility of pointing out the errors and harm inflicted by the discriminator, while simultaneously counseling Jews to make every effort to shine whenever given an opportunity at a discriminatory institution.

Even so, Rosenwald did support efforts to redress Jewish grievances in the civic or legal sectors when circumstances arose which called for such action. In 1911, for example, Rosenwald, in conjunction with the American Jewish Committee, attempted to use his influence with President William Howard Taft in the matter of the relationship between the United States and tsarist Russia. In 1832 the United States had entered into a bilateral arrangement with Russia, the Russian-American Commercial Treaty, in which the two governments extended to each other most-favored-nation status. American Jews, regardless of where they or the parents had come from, considered the tsarist regime a perpetrator of violence and an incubator of anti-Jewish policies. As a protest against the pogroms of the first decade of the twentieth century, they hoped to enlist the resources of the American government to pressure the Russian authorities. But rather than cite directly acts against Russian Jews, whether the pogroms or the existence of residential segregation of Jews into the Pale of Settlement, as the reason for America to take action, the AJC delegation that met with Taft, consisting of Rosenwald, Mack, and Marshall, focused on discrimination against American citizens. They pointed out that Jews carrying American passports had been denied entry to Russia, and that this violated the earlier agreement between the two countries. They appealed to the president not to renew the treaty, and instead to support pending legislation, the Sulzer Act, aimed against the Russian government. The bill had been introduced by William Sulzer, representative of New York's Tenth Congressional District with a large Jewish and immigrant constituency, and chair of the House Committee on Foreign Affairs. Rosenwald, Mack, and Marshall argued that the Russian government had violated the terms of the long-standing 1832 treaty by harming American citizens, and therefore the United States should remove the most-favored-nation privileges which Russia enjoyed. In their emphasis on the injury to Americans, and not Jews, Rosenwald and his fellow AJC leaders attempted to deflect attention from the purely Jewish mission which they had embarked upon. Their representations proved successful, and Taft did not sign the treaty.

During World War I, Rosenwald used his political contacts to help the Yiddish press in a dispute with the government. Under the terms of the Espionage Act, a wartime measure, the United States Post Office moved to revoke the mailing privileges of *Forverts*, a socialist Yiddish newspaper and America's largest circulating foreign-language newspaper. The newspaper's editor, Abraham Cahan, had declared in print his support of the recently launched Russian Revolution, an action that brought the paper into conflict with the federal government. Louis Marshall successfully engineered a compromise between Cahan and Postmaster General A. S. Burleson and persuaded Rosenwald to join them at the meeting.

In such encounters with top government officials Rosenwald took on the role of the *shtadlan*, the court Jew who used his personal connections to plead for his co-religionists. Rosenwald seems to have accepted the premise that when a Jew like himself had powerful connections, he had an obligation to use them for the benefit of other Jews, whether at home or abroad. Such a role differed little from that of the philanthropist, who used his economic capital to effectuate social change.

Rosenwald employed his Jewish political capital locally as well. In 1903 a Jewish immigrant from Russia, Lazarus Averbuch, accused of being an anarchist, had been shot and killed by the chief of the Chicago police department, George Shippy. The police initially claimed that Averbuch had attempted to assassinate Shippy as part of an anarchist plot against public officials, a first step toward a revolution. While that version of the story commanded press attention, some Chicagoans, including Jane Addams and Rosenwald, found Shippy's account inconsistent and believed that Averbuch's killing had been in actuality a crime perpetrated by the police. Rosenwald, spurred on by Addams and the Chicago Yiddish-language press, paid for a private investigator. When the details emerged, casting serious doubt on Shippy's story, Rosenwald underwrote the cost of a lawyer, hiring Harold Ickes, the future secretary of the interior, to represent the Averbuch family at the inquest. Although the proceedings failed to condemn the police action, and Shippy emerged unscathed, Rosenwald and the Chicago *Kurier* had joined together to defend a Jewish anarchist, boldly indicting what they saw as local anti-Semitism.

On a grander scale, Rosenwald engaged himself deeply in the case of Leo Frank, a New York Jewish businessman who had moved to Atlanta to manage a pencil factory. In 1913 the police arrested him for the murder of a young white girl, Mary Phagan, an employee of his company. Several trials ensued over the course of two years, and several juries found Frank guilty despite a lack of real evidence. Sentenced to death, Frank faced execution, but the governor of Georgia commuted his sentence to life in prison, in part because of pressure from around the country and in part because he felt that the evidence had not convincingly established Frank's guilt. On August 17, 1915, an angry mob broke into the prison, dragged Frank out, and lynched him.

Julius Rosenwald participated vigorously in the many unsuccessful efforts to free Leo Frank, responding quickly to an appeal by his friend Albert Lasker, considered the founder of American advertising. JR agreed to match every dollar Lasker gave for Frank's legal representation; over the course of Frank's ordeal, Rosenwald contributed thousands of dollars for his defense. Frank expressed his gratitude, as well as his faith in American justice, in a letter written from his prison cell to JR in Chicago: "Allow me to assure you how profoundly grateful I am for the interest you have taken in my cause. I am cognizant of the fact that you have given unselfishly and so largely of yourself to the end that my preservation and vindication become actualities. . . . Surely the day cannot be far distant when Right and Justice holding complete sway, my vindication and acknowledgment of my absolute innocence, will of necessity result!"[32]

Rosenwald also participated in a letter-writing campaign on Frank's behalf, appealing to such notables as former president William Howard Taft, now a professor at Yale Law School, for whom JR had campaigned in 1912, as well as to other prominent non-Jews. In his letter-writing campaign, Rosenwald, who often took his cues from Louis Marshall, made the case for Frank but avoided putting the Jewish issue in his appeals. As he wanted to find the best way to arouse public sympathy for the falsely convicted Frank, Marshall had urged Rosenwald to limit his appeals to other Jews. Marshall had warned that appeals to non-Jews might be seen as tampering with justice. He noted that an accusation "has been made that the Jews, in seeking commutation [of the death penalty], are attempting to save one of their faith irrespective of his guilt or innocence," and admonished Rosenwald, who seemed eager to raise the specter of anti-Semitism, "I believe that it is very unwise to raise the cry of anti-Semitism. No good can come of it. If agitated, it may inspire that feeling among people who are today entirely free from it and do not know what it means."[33] Rosenwald wrote to numerous individuals to press Frank's case, but saying nothing about the Jewish issue. In a letter to Judge Walter Fisher, a fellow Chicago Jew, he begged, "In view of this really tragic situation," and "to help prevent what the future will undoubtedly prove to have been a great calamity in the judicial taking of innocent life, I ask you, in the interest of justice, to write at once in behalf of Mr. Frank to the governor and also to the board of the Prison Commissioners at Atlanta, Georgia."[34]

The arrest, trials, and murder of Leo Frank rattled American Jews across the political, ideological, and class spectrum. They knew about lynching as an American form of "justice" meted out primarily to African Americans. Now a Jew endured this kind of violence as well. The newspapers, speeches, and sermons about the crime made a point of identifying Frank as a Jew, an identification that threatened their sense of security in a land where they believed they enjoyed the state's protections.

In the next decade Henry Ford's viciously anti-Semitic writings in the *Dearborn Independent*, including the infamous *Protocols of the Elders of Zion*, a virulently anti-Semitic forgery that had first been published in Russia, increased Jewish anxieties, and Rosenwald once more entered the fray. Ford launched a two-pronged attack in print on Rosenwald, claiming that because of his involvement with African Americans, JR had deliberately set in motion the great migration from the South. He, according to Ford, had purposely lured blacks to Chicago with promises of work and cheap housing, from which he profited. But Ford's attack also charged that Rosenwald's "Jewish money" had let loose a "tide of white dispossession" in Chicago. He noted as well that Rosenwald controlled gambling operations among the new migrants to Chicago.

The usually reticent Rosenwald retorted with a five-page single-spaced defense, taking on Ford point by point.[35] Ford, undeterred, wrote in a set of four booklets, *The International Jew*, that Rosenwald, along with Aaron Sapiro, a leader in the farm cooperative movement, had been plotting to take over the Boys' and Girls' Clubs as part of a diabolic Jewish scheme to undermine basic American institutions. In 1920, after a clamor of protest from nearly all American Jewish organizations, Rosenwald, as vice president of the American Jewish Committee, headed a massive publicity campaign, sending out via the mail and telegrams the AJC's response, "The 'Protocols,' Bolshevism and the Jews: An Address to Their Fellow Citizens by American Jewish Organizations." Ford continued his anti-Semitic campaign into the latter part of the 1920s, but after threats of lawsuits and loss of business from potential boycotts, he retracted his previous statements, issuing something of an apology. Rosenwald, when asked by the press about the apology, remarked, "Mr. Ford's statement is greatly belated. It would have been much greater to his credit had it been written five years ago," but an apology nonetheless deserved to be accepted in "'the spirit of forgiveness,' which is not entirely a Christian virtue."[36]

How seriously did Rosenwald take Ford's words and to what degree did he see them as harbingers of bad times for American

Jews? Speaking at a banquet in New York after a savage attack in the *Dearborn Independent*, Rosenwald offered a tempered assessment. The threat existed, he agreed, but as a nation, America offered Jews the best environment in which to live. Despite Ford's vitriol and other episodes of anti-Jewish rhetoric and behavior, the United States was fundamentally good to the Jews and despite its shortcomings, likely to remain so. He expressed a less sanguine view of the situation of Jews elsewhere in the world and what the future portended for them. The majority of the world's Jews faced real danger, whether in Russia, the newly independent Poland, or, by the late 1920s, Germany, with its growing Nazi Party. Jews there, JR feared, had no such guarantee of safety and security as they did in America.

ZIONISM

Given Rosenwald's global perspective on matters Jewish and his sense of foreboding about the future for his people, Zionism might have attracted him. Particularly as the campaign to close America's doors to unrestricted European immigration gained momentum, the idea of a Jewish homeland in Palestine might have seemed a viable alternative. So too his interest in stimulating new and vibrant Jewish cultural forms might logically have led him to Zionism, with its vision of a fresh, vigorous Jewish life.

But despite pressures to declare himself a Zionist, a campaign mounted by movement leaders during the 1910s and the 1920s, he hewed to his position, writing to the philanthropist Jacob Schiff, "I am not one bit more of a Zionist than I believe you to be," though he went on, "nor am I Anti-Zionist." He repeatedly justified his position with the logic that the movement could never succeed. "I consider," he continued to Schiff, "their Nationalistic idea a wild scheme." *Wild* was a word he used not only in this letter but in numerous articles, and it represented his belief that Palestine could not support the number of Jews the Zionists envisioned settling there. Its minimal agricultural and industrial infrastructures would never make settlement a practical response to the difficulties faced by millions of Jews in eastern Europe.[37]

JR's wife, Augusta, disagreed, giving generously to Zionist causes, particularly to Hadassah, the women's Zionist organization founded by the American Henrietta Szold. Gussie also attempted to bring the National Federation of Temple Sisterhoods, the women's arm of the Reform movement, to the Zionist cause. Szold frequently stayed in the Rosenwald home when in Chicago, and Gussie would confer with her and other local Zionists, such as Alexander Dushkin, on "how to talk to Julius about Palestine."[38] Szold appreciated Gussie's efforts, praising her for the work she had undertaken in advancing the Zionist cause with the women of the Reform movement through the Federation of Temple Sisterhoods: "You are advancing the cause of Palestine," she wrote.[39] Szold thought that she might win him over by reminding Augusta, who she reasoned would then tell her husband, that Hadassah did not limit its work to Jews, but served the Arab population as well. In describing to both Rosenwalds the cornerstone-laying ceremony for her Health and Welfare center in Jerusalem, Szold emphasized that the event, the first of its kind in Palestine, took place "in the presence of thousands of Christians, Arabs [presumably Muslim] and Jews."[40]

Szold's argument might have inspired Augusta, but it did not budge Julius. He remained convinced of his position, despite his wife's pressure, as well as that of Julian Mack, Louis Brandeis, and others. Jewish newspapers, both English-language and Yiddish, repeatedly claimed to have seen signs of a shift in his views. One Chicago Yiddish newspaper trumpeted news of the November 1914 assembly at Temple Sinai at which Rosenwald announced a massive gift for Jewish war sufferers as a step toward his conversion, declaring in its headline "Zion Triumphs in Chicago."[41] The general press watched the dance between JR and Zionism as well. An article in the New York *Herald Examiner* in 1930 claimed that "Julius Rosenwald made his first appearance at any meeting sponsored by Zionists." JR responded immediately in a telegram to Raymond Rubinow, a Rosenwald Fund staff member, declaring that although he had been present at the Madison Square Garden event, the claim that while in attendance he announced support of Zionism had been printed "without foundation."[42]

His rejection of Zionism put him at odds with many of his peers. In July 1929, for example, Zionists, along with some notable non-Zionists, including several of JR's closest friends and advisers, agreed to collaborate on projects of mutual concern. As the umbrella organization for their work, they proposed to expand the Jewish Agency, a body created by the League of Nations in 1922. JR's good friend Louis Marshall agreed to assist in the expansion. This threw Rosenwald into a personal and ideological dilemma. He confessed to Alexander Dushkin that he could not "sleep nights. My good friends, Louis Marshall and [the banker] Felix Warburg, have joined the Jewish Agency and are urging me to join them." His friends, particularly Marshall, to whom JR usually deferred, were "courting calamity," Rosenwald worried, "and I cannot get myself to join them." He did not.[43]

Despite the barrage of requests, Julius Rosenwald still would not endorse the movement. Ironically, his insistence that its goals could not be achieved could have been applied equally to many other projects Rosenwald did embrace. Several might as easily have been dismissed as impractical, having little chance of success. The intensity of his resistance to Zionism demands other explanations. His being an assimilated, wealthy Reform Jew cannot adequately explain his adamant and public refusal to affiliate with the movement. After all, many in his elite circle, nearly all offspring of German-Jewish migrants, did commit to Zionism, as had Mack, Brandeis, and his wife. Gustav Gotthiel, Samuel Freehof, Stephen Wise, James Heller, Judah Magnes, and Abba Hillel Silver, all Reform rabbis who overlapped chronologically with Rosenwald, helped lead the American Zionist movement, while he refused to support it.

Nor did he ever suggest, in public or private, that he feared that American Jews would be accused of dual loyalty if they embraced a Jewish homeland in Palestine. For one, nearly all Americans whose parents or grandparents had immigrated from abroad participated in and supported homeland causes. Rosenwald generally did not hesitate to take unpopular positions when he thought them right, nor did he expend much time fretting over public opinion. He did not worry that southern Jews might suffer if he poured millions of dollars into the education of African Americans, something their states refused to do. Likewise, at a time when Chicagoans, like many Americans, feared the anarchist threat, he took up the cause of Lazarus Averbuch, aligning himself in this with the anarchist Emma Goldman, dubbed "the most dangerous woman in America."

His aversion to Zionism emerged from sources deeper than these. In the letter he wrote to Schiff in which he called Zionists "wild," he hinted at what most troubled him about Zionism. A Jewish homeland, Rosenwald wrote, "even if they could accomplish what they are after along that line," he doubted "would be in the best interests of the Jews." Why? A few possibilities suggest themselves. Although he did not refer directly to the potential reaction of the Arab population of Palestine to a flood of Jewish immigrants, his enthusiasm for Jewish projects in Palestine, which he had previously supported, had soured by the end of the 1920s in the face of the riots of 1921 and 1929 that swept the land, pitting the two communities against each other. After the 1929 riots he referred to the suffering of people in Palestine, "regardless of religion," and asserted that "part of this trouble is due to the actions of the Jews."[44] He sent numerous letters to Dushkin, asking him why the kibbutzim, the Zionist collective farms in Palestine, did not employ Arab labor, hinting that he saw Zionism as a force pitting Jews against Arabs, to the disadvantage of the latter.[45] Further evidence might suggest itself in the argument of the ever sensitive Szold, who seemed to intuit that to lure Rosenwald to the cause via Hadassah, she had to emphasize its good work for Arabs.

Rosenwald perceived that Zionism emphasized the separateness of the two populations and put Jews above Arabs. Felix Warburg, with whom Rosenwald worked in the vast fundraising effort of the Joint Distribution Committee, would point this out in his eulogy of JR at a memorial sponsored by the Joint. He noted that from "the very first shipment of medicine and food," which Rosenwald himself paid for, he had insisted that it be "distributed in equal parts among the Arab and Jewish population in Palestine." A brief reference, but Warburg's words indicated something of Rosenwald's uneasiness with a movement that sought to serve Jewish needs to the detriment of others in the same land. The prospect of a Jewish state in which many non-Jews lived may have disturbed him.[46]

Rosenwald's decision to abjure Zionism did not keep him from funding projects in Palestine to benefit the long-time residents of the old *yishuv*, the pre-Zionist Jewish residents of Palestine, as well as recent newcomers. A large portion of his donations he understood as relief for Jews in distress, and this he gave willingly. During World War I, he also allowed his name to appear prominently on the letterhead of stationery for the Palestine Emergency Fund as "Honorary Chairman," but he explained at meetings and community gatherings that he did this to help Jews in need, not to further Zionism. In 1914, at the outbreak of the war overseas, he, through his secretary Wil-

JULIUS ROSENWALD

liam Graves, wrote to Mack that his donation, a hefty thousand
dollars a month for the duration of the hostilities, to a fund
earmarked for the Palestinian War Sufferers did not include
assistance to any "specifically . . . Zionist organizations." Lest
Mack think that he had succumbed, Rosenwald continued, "I
reserve the right to apportion, from time to time, the money
partly among educational and other institutions, whether here-
tofore supported by Zionists or not, and partly for purposes of
general relief."⁴⁷ Despite his sense that Jews shared blame for
the 1929 riots, Rosenwald also provided a sizable amount to
an Emergency Fund for the Relief of Palestine Sufferers afterward, allowing himself to be named honorary chairman of the
group.

At times in the 1920s he gave tacit, if lukewarm, approval
to limited Zionist political ventures. In 1922, he had informed
friends and associates that he did not support the Lodge-Fish
Resolution, an act of the U.S. Congress affirming Britain's 1917
Balfour Declaration, in support of the "establishment in Palestine of a national home for the Jewish people." The Jewish
press reported his opposition, but after pressure from Louis
Marshall, also a non-Zionist, Rosenwald changed his mind and
called for passage of the bill. Claiming that journalists had mis-
quoted him, JR compromised, although his muted approval indicated his ambivalence.⁴⁸

He did support ventures in Palestine that he believed would
advance Jewish culture and the welfare of humankind more
generally, and that he deemed did not function as part of nationalist politics. He donated in 1906 to help found the Bezalel
School of Arts and Crafts (now the Belzalel Academy of Art and
Design), in Jerusalem, and contributed to Technikum, later renamed Technion, the Israeli Institute of Technology, in Haifa
that same decade. He considered these and other such Palestinian institutions, such as David Yellin's teachers seminary, the
Palestine Orange Planters, the Palestine Wine Growers, and

the Habima Players, not nationalist undertakings but institutions of potential value to all people, Jews and non-Jews, in Palestine and elsewhere. When making his hundred-thousand-dollar donation to Yellin's Hebrew Institute for Teachers, Rosenwald quoted his friend Schiff, who had given the Technikum its first serious contribution, lauding it with the claim that "it is wedded to no 'ism,' save Judaism."[49]

Rosenwald heavily subsidized, and served as a host for, the Palestinian agronomist Aaron Aaronsohn, who in 1906 discovered and successfully cultivated an ancient wild wheat, *Triticum dicoccoides* (Emmer wheat). Cyrus Adler, an AJC colleague of Rosenwald's and also a non-Zionist, had introduced Aaronsohn first to Mack and then to JR, who for several years underwrote Aaronsohn's work, putting him in touch with other well-connected American Jews. Along with Schiff, Marshall, Adler, Warburg, Szold, and Judah Magnes, Rosenwald also served on the board of Aaronsohn's agricultural colony in Athlit, the Jewish Agricultural Experiment Station. He appreciated that Aaronsohn had worked for the U.S. Department of Agriculture, and regarded him as a Palestinian Jew who had made a contribution, new agricultural techniques, not as a Zionist bent on a nationalistic project but as a scientist seeking to improve the world. On the eve of World War I the Rosenwalds visited Palestine, and their trip to the agricultural station proved a high point. After the war began, however, Rosenwald withdrew his support after he learned that Aaronsohn had helped organize a spy ring, Nili, that assisted the British in their conquest of Palestine. Rosenwald did not like the Ottomans, but he considered this an act of nationalism on behalf of the Jews alone. At that he drew the line.

But despite his opposition to Zionism, he maintained positive personal relationships with Zionists, not only Mack and Dushkin, but also Shmaryahu Levin, the Jewish representative to the Russian Duma and a Zionist leader, whom he hosted. In

1908, when Levin came to Chicago, Rosenwald honored him with a grand lunch, to which he invited several wealthy Chicago Jews, some rabbis, and other notables. Levin successfully enlisted JR's support for the Technikum. Although Levin repeatedly tried to attract JR to the larger cause, and JR consistently refused, the two remained friends. Levin noted that JR had once quipped humorously, "The most I'll do for you in a personal way is to build myself a villa in Chicago and call it Tel Aviv." Levin claimed to have retorted, "We want you to build a villa in Tel Aviv and call it Chicago."[50]

Rosenwald even donated to projects that were clearly Zionist in origin; for example, in 1928 he contributed money to a fund to honor Henrietta Szold. In this and his other contributions to Palestinian causes and institutions, Rosenwald seems not to have fully understood the Zionist process of state building. Perhaps he could not see that any investment in enterprises other than aid to poor religious Jews whose ancestors had lived in the land for centuries constituted planning for a future Jewish commonwealth. Jewish schools and theaters, vineyards and agricultural stations under Jewish auspices, functioned as paving stones to an eventual political reality. Even Szold's medical program, to which JR donated and which served Arabs, created Jewish institutions that would be used by Jewish immigrants who would settle the land.

He made his distinction between supporting Jewish institutions in Palestine and supporting a Jewish homeland in Palestine, erroneously or not, because he believed in Jewish integration, not to foster assimilation or the disappearance of the Jews as a distinctive people, but rather from a deep-seated belief that Jews thrived when they engaged with others. When in workplaces and schools, they met people from other traditions and religions. Zionism, as he saw it, clashed with his vision of an ideal society that accepted and welcomed cultural differences. He believed that Jews needed to find ways to settle internal differences but also prepare to live in a complex world on an equal footing with the non-Jews around them. He saw the Chicago Hebrew Institute, for example, as an ideal institution because it recognized the reality that Jews lived and worked in a diverse society, but used the institution for leisure time pursuits alone.

Rosenwald considered that Zionism, as an ideology and as a political movement, had sown discord and division within the Jewish world. Zionism, he declared in 1926 at a gathering at the Standard Club launching the annual United Jewish Campaign, split Jews apart. "It is tragic," he noted as he kicked off the fundraising effort, "that Palestine, the land which gave birth to our Bible, the land of the Jewish past, and the hope of the future should . . . have provided a divisive element in Jewry."[51]

WORLD WAR I AND THE JOINT

World War I provided Julius Rosenwald with unsurpassed opportunities to act in the interest of Jews, building Jewish unity, boosting the image of Jews in America, and even touting his beloved Chicago. A crisis of mammoth humanitarian proportions, the war found American Jewry in an unusual position. Most of the world's Jews, with the exception of those in the new world, found themselves on the battlefields, trapped in the middle of the conflagration, often as civilians caught between warring armies. The Jewries of the Russian, Austro-Hungarian, and Ottoman Empires faced grave dangers. The war displaced millions of them, as warring armies overran their communities. Jews, who lacked resources to work and feed themselves, found themselves accused of disloyalty, as traitors to the opposing force, and subjected to mass brutality.

Like other American Jews, Rosenwald first turned his attention to the Jews of Palestine, Ottoman subjects who literally starved because of a British blockade. JR responded to the crisis, and at a meeting called by Rabbi Hirsch and held at Temple Sinai in November 1914, Rosenwald exhorted wealthy Chicago Jews to donate aid immediately. He warned that no matter how generous their initial contributions might be, they needed to keep them up until the war ended, however long that took. The Palestinian Jews "will again be faced with extinction unless we Jews make provisions for the future," he declaimed. His words launched a campaign, as did his pledge to send the sufferers a thousand dollars a month until hostilities ceased. He inspired Chicago Jews to participate despite internal divisions of Orthodox versus Reform, new immigrants from eastern Europe versus American, Zionists or not.[52]

The needs of Jewish war victims rapidly spread from Palestine to central and eastern Europe, the lands between the Austro-Hungarian and Russian forces. In December 1915, after American Jews had been galvanized around local fundraising efforts, they sprang into national action. On December 21, a mass meeting took place at New York's Carnegie Hall, chaired by Marshall, that called for a mighty financial relief effort. It would be national in scope but organized city by city, each assigned a quota to fill. The next day the *New York Times* reported that Nathan Straus of Macy's, Jacob Schiff, the Guggenheim brothers, and Julius Rosenwald had each pledged a hundred thousand dollars.

The meeting represented the efforts of three recently formed relief bodies, the Orthodox-sponsored Central Committee for the Relief of Jews, the People's Relief Committee, a socialist project, and the American Jewish Relief Committee, made up of individuals like Rosenwald and Marshall, associated with the AJC. They came together, presumably only for the duration of the war, to form the Joint, formally, the American Jewish Joint Distribution Committee—which sponsored the Carnegie Hall meeting.

The Joint, in which JR participated actively, holding office, attending meetings, and campaigning for around the country, set a goal of $10 million for 1916. Rosenwald agreed to give a hundred thousand for every million raised. In fact, over the next two years he donated $10 million. Rosenwald had initially worried about earmarking humanitarian relief for Jews by Jews, but he took solace in the positive publicity the Joint garnered in non-Jewish sources. Inspired by the Joint's creation and fundraising effort, President Wilson named January 27, 1916, "Jewish Relief Day."

Indefatigable on behalf of the Joint, JR traveled widely, particularly around the Midwest. In each community he studied the lists, tallying the names and donations of Jews and non-Jews. He chided communities which had not met their quotas, lauded those which did. He worked most assiduously in Chicago, and by June 1917 figures showed that New York Jews, despite their much greater numbers, had been bested in their donations by Chicago Jews. The efforts of one person, through donations and fundraising campaigning, had brought this about. One New York–based Jewish newspaper ran a photograph of him with the caption "Must Julius Rosenwald Carry the Burden Alone?"[53]

Rosenwald took the adulation in stride and kept plugging for the Joint. In Chicago he tapped his wealthy non-Jewish peers William Wrigley of chewing gum fame and Cyrus McCormick, Jr. They in turn solicited their rich friends, who had probably never before given to a Jewish cause. Rosenwald must surely have been thrilled when these notable non-Jews contributed to Jewish relief in Europe and when Woodrow Wilson, whose candidacy he had not supported, wrote, "Your contribution . . . serves democracy as well as humanity."[54]

He made himself available for the Joint. When Jacob Billikopf, manager of the Joint's national campaign, asked him to visit wealthy individuals to ask for contributions, he usually succeeded in persuading the hesitant to give and the already generous to redouble their efforts. He took tremendous pride in the fact that, as he noted in a 1917 speech at a banquet in his honor, "it has been brought to my notice that the great success of the Red Cross fund was due in part to the . . . contribution from our fund . . . and that without that start, it would not have been possible for that fund to reach $100,000,000." He used *our* in this sentence, not *my*, as the operative pronoun. That the work of the Joint, which he in no small part made possible, inspired non-Jews to give to an analogous cause, the Red Cross, demonstrated the power of Jews to do good for others as well as themselves, benefiting all humankind.[55]

The work of the Joint, a body transcending the deep fault lines among American Jews, had inspired such warm words from the president, had facilitated Red Cross war relief, had prompted wealthy non-Jews to assist Jews, and had provided millions of dollars to ameliorate the acute needs of the Jews. In many ways the Joint and its war relief effort embodied everything Rosenwald cared about: promoting Jewish unity, gaining the respect of non-Jews, and addressing human suffering.

GAMBLING ON THE SOVIET UNION

Rosenwald could look back on the World War I experience and the Joint's vast work with satisfaction. His involvement in the 1920s with the Agro-Joint, a project to settle Jews in the Soviet Union on farms in Ukraine and the Crimea, brought much less gratification, although he embraced it with equal zeal and optimism. Probably no aspect of his career in Jewish philanthropy provoked as much anger, generated as much hostility, or made him such a reviled figure among some Jews as this one.

The idea of transforming Jews, petty merchants in the main, into farmers did not come out of nowhere, and the vision of Jewish farming long predated the Agro-Joint. Not limited to thinking about Russia, believers in the romance of a

Jewish embrace of agrarianism had for over a century predicted a double benefit if Jews abandoned commerce in favor of agriculture. By working the soil, advocates of the agricultural movement asserted, Jews would transform themselves and dispel negative images of them as nonproductive parasites, eternal money men. The proposition extended back to the late eighteenth century and endured into the twentieth, growing out of various philanthropic schemes. Whether it had ever been practical, it reflected the sense of crisis pervading the Jewish world in the modern era. One advocate for Jewish agricultural colonies in late-nineteenth-century America declared: "Jewish agriculture in whatever part of the globe . . . has a special interest and is of a particular importance, not common to agriculture as such, namely, it is living proof of the falsehood of the assertion of the political anti-semites . . . that the . . . Jew avoids productive work, especially the noble vocation of the tiller of the soil. It further proves that whenever and wherever the . . . Jew enjoys political freedom and freedom of selection of a calling, he does not neglect agriculture as well."[56]

Rosenwald had been smitten by the promise of farming. In 1905 he made a sizable donation to the Agricultural Aid Society, pledging $4,000 to a Jewish agricultural undertaking in Michigan if the colony raised $20,000. His fascination with Aaron Aaronsohn's agricultural research station in Palestine blinded him to the reality that Jewish farming in Palestine served the cause of nationalism. In 1916 he busied himself with Jewish agrarianism in America, offering, with Jacob Schiff, $150,000 to the Baron de Hirsch Jewish Agricultural College in Woodbine, New Jersey.

Rosenwald kept faith in his agricultural vision after the end of the war as part of his continued participation in global Jewish matters. With Louis Marshall, Oscar Straus, Stephen Wise, and others, he had been in contact with the leaders of the newly independent Poland, Ignacy Jan Paderewski and Roman

Dmowski, pressing them to promise that the 4 million Jews who lived in the recently formed state would enjoy equal rights. So, too, the leaders of the Joint stepped in when one of the tectonic shifts in modern history, the Russian Revolution and the emergence of the Soviet Union, ended the restriction of Jews to the Pale of Settlement and abolished other anti-Jewish legislation, but also abolished commerce, an act of tremendous significance to 3 million Jews now Soviet citizens. These Jews had benefited from the first change, but they found themselves uprooted by the second. Most had operated at the lowest level of business, as peddlers, market stall owners, and tax farmers. But such occupations contravened new Soviet policies. The Soviet government's plan to establish cooperatives to produce clothing, textiles, furniture, and other goods handicapped Jews who had eked out their living as artisans. They could not compete with the proposed state enterprises.

In 1924, the Joint entered into an agreement with Soviet authorities. Under the leadership of Joseph Rosen, a Russian-born agronomist who had resided in the United States since the early twentieth century but returned to his native land in 1921 with the American Relief Administration, the Joint began to negotiate with the Soviet government on behalf of the Jews, purchasing land cheaply from the state in Ukraine and the Crimea. In exchange for United States currency, the authorities allowed the Joint to sponsor a project of Jewish colonization, Agro-Joint, which Rosen and his American backers hoped would bring tens of thousands of Jews back to the soil.

Agro-Joint operated in tandem with the Soviet agency KOMZET, the Commission for the Rural Placement of Jewish Toilers. Jews would be encouraged to move to Ukrainian or Crimean colonies at a cost per household of $750–$1,000. Initially the colonies would function as self-governing collectives. Because the colonies existed on the geographic margins of Soviet lands, the state allowed the colonists relatively wide latitude in organizing their enterprise. Children studied in Yiddish, rather than Russian, in the primary schools well into the 1930s. In the early years, when JR first became engaged in the project, the Jewish colonists managed their own affairs and benefited from programs like those which trained nurses, allowing the colonists to enjoy a degree of self-sufficiency. They maintained a vibrant Jewish life, staging Hebrew and Yiddish plays. Reports from the settlements emphasized the positive interactions between the Jewish colonists and their non-Jewish neighbors, demonstrating that the Jews' shift to farming, the common way of life for the rest of the community, had had the hoped-for effect of lessening the long-held animosity of local residents toward Jews.

Rosenwald embraced this plan enthusiastically. He had learned about the project from Felix Warburg, another donor to the Jewish Theological Seminary, the Joint, and many of JR's other causes. Warburg passed along Rosen's report, a glowing document spelling out the prospects for the undertaking. Rosenwald approved of the seemingly practical, straightforward, agricultural, empowering scheme. It would enable the Jews to help themselves, leading to self-supporting productivity. JR presumed that such a result would reduce the centuries-long animosity felt by the majority population toward the Jews, facilitating their integration into the new Soviet state and setting them on an equal footing with their neighbors, farmers too. He described the plan, known as Agro-Joint, as "constructive work," the implication being that other proposals for the post-war future of the Jews, such as Zionism, portended discord and disruption.

Rosenwald read Rosen's report and offered to donate a million dollars, to be matched by other donors. He had heard from other supporters of the Soviet farming plan such as Jacob Billikopf, who considered that Agro-Joint would be able to work well with Soviet authorities, as the government in 1922 had embarked on Lenin's New Economic Policy (NEP), creating a mixed economy in which small private businesses would be allowed. Pleased to learn that Soviet officials now supported cooperation between the public sector and some private enterprises, JR offered to donate a million dollars, to be matched by other donors. Herbert Hoover, who had supervised the earlier American Relief Commission's efforts in the Soviet Union during the 1920–21 famine, praised Rosenwald for his generosity toward Agro-Joint, heralding his "princely benefaction," his "great heart and . . . [the] willing hand with which it is given." Hoover had warm words for JR's "dedication of [his] wealth to make it possible for a people who have been starving as petty tradesmen to return to their ancient calling and become producers."[57]

Billikopf encouraged Rosenwald to attend an upcoming Joint meeting in Philadelphia, scheduled for September 1925, to add his voice to those who wanted the Joint to formally endorse the Soviet scheme. Rosenwald agreed, and though he claimed that he had no plans to speak at the meeting, he brought with him a prepared text, with which he hoped to persuade the assembled group, some of whom, like Stephen Wise and other Zionists, opposed any investment of money in the reconstruction of Jewish life in eastern Europe. Following a number of speeches Rosenwald arose and publicly endorsed the Soviet farming work, declaring that never before had Jews been presented with such an opportunity to perform constructive work for their "co-religionists." The Jews, he said, had previously only engaged in "palliative relief," but now Jews, no matter how poor, would be "in a position to help themselves." He then declared the financial bottom line. He would offer his million dollars only if the Joint could raise another $9 million.

So excited by the scheme, despite ill health JR announced that he wanted to join the delegation and travel to the Soviet Union in 1926 on a mission headed by the journalist Sherwood

Eddy. His doctors forbade him to make the arduous journey, so in his stead he sent his son William, who accompanied Billikopf to see how the colonies, by then involving over a hundred thousand Jews, had progressed and whether the money had been well spent. William and the others sent JR enthusiastic reports. One letter described a colony that had named itself Rosenwald, in tribute to its American benefactor. These reports spurred JR to increase his gifts to the colonies, and although dealings with the Soviets did not proceed smoothly, Rosenwald seemed undaunted. Indeed, in 1929, just before the collapse of the stock market and Stalin's liquidation of the NEP, he contemplated donating money to another Soviet project, retraining Jews to fill positions in industry, in "establishments for the manufacture of raw materials," another new venture for them. By early 1930, Rosenwald was funding both the agricultural and industrial projects, despite difficulties with Soviet authorities and the Joint board. He believed that the two Agro-Joint ventures would benefit Jews in the long term, making a better way of life for millions.[58]

How ironic that Rosenwald, the merchant-prince capitalist, and Warburg, the banker, dealt comfortably with the Soviet government, doing so despite the fact that the United States still refused to establish diplomatic relations with the Communist regime. During the civil war which followed the Bolshevik Revolution, the United States, in fact, assisted the anti-Bolshevik forces, the White Army, against the new regime. Americans generally expressed antipathy toward communism and the Soviets, and anti-Semites such as Henry Ford condemned Jews for their proclivity toward what was considered an un-American ideology. Even Rosenwald, who had little use for central government and revered the free-market system, embraced the chance to work with the Soviet government. As a Jew, concerned with the needs of Jewish women and men, he responded to the agricultural projects, as well as to Rosen's argument concerning the "eugenic value of having a large number of our co-religionists get out into God's sunshine once more to earn their bread by the sweat of their brow."[59]

Not all Jews appreciated Rosenwald's investment in Agro-Joint. Indeed, few projects he undertook engendered such vituperative responses. Even the Joint, knowing how many American Jews, Zionists in particular, hated the plan, felt compelled to separate the funds for the farming project from its general budget. To Zionists every penny spent in the Soviet Union constituted a penny not spent in Palestine, and to have Rosenwald, whose name carried such positive weight in America, hitch his wagon to the Crimean-Ukrainian star undercut their work.

Zionists launched an all-out attack on Rosenwald. Reacting to Rosenwald's claim that the Crimea project cost less than the Palestine scheme and had fewer negative consequences, Rabbi Stephen Wise stormed that although the first "may be cheaper . . . the Jewish people will not stoop to bargain at the counter of Redemption." Wise predicted that the money Rosenwald gave to the Soviet Jewish agrarian project would result in "the utter breakdown of the Jewish nation." The Chicago *Jewish Chronicle*, which usually lionized JR, published a headline asking whether Rosenwald's donation to the Soviet Union constituted a "Blessing or a Curse." Answering its own question, the writer declared, "With one scratch of his pen on a check," the multimillionaire "blasts the hopes of millions of Jews, living and dead."[60]

A war of words raged in the Jewish and American press. Partisans argued over the benefits of Agro-Joint versus Zionism, and over whether Rosenwald, Rosen, and the others had helped bring forth a productive new venture in Jewish life or if they had helped destroy the dream of Jewish self-determination in a homeland of their own. One of JR's allies in the Crimea-Ukraine farming scheme, David Brown, predicted in 1926 that "the barrage attack will now be aimed at J.R. and the whole Rosenwald family. . . . There is going to be hell to pay in this country someday if this whole rotten business of attacking everybody just because they don't see with the eyes of the Zionists is continued."[61] But Rosenwald retained his faith in the project, hoping to convince the Jewish public. He gave a lengthy interview in 1928 to the journalist S. M. Melamed for a Yiddish newspaper with strong Zionist sympathies, *Der Tog*. Melamed did not incline toward Rosenwald's views, and he sneered at JR's claim that he was "not an anti Zionist; I am what may be termed a non Zionist," describing him as a "vehement opponent of Jewish colonization in Palestine and almost a rabid anti-Zionist." Melamed alleged that Rosenwald "is probably the only remaining enemy of Zionism that survived the anti Zionist period." Rosenwald had chosen to give the interview despite Melamed's reputation as a Zionist, hoping the paper's readers would appreciate, even if they did not agree with, his support of the Soviet colonization scheme, and why he preferred it to trying to make a homeland in Palestine.[62]

Supporters of Agro-Joint went on the defensive, justifying their work and hoping to defuse the Zionists' attacks. Rosenwald used his contacts with the Chicago *Tribune* to offer positive accounts of the Soviet Jewish farming projects, while pamphlets and books appeared such as *Founding a New Life for Suffering Thousands: Report of Dr. Joseph A. Rosen on Jewish Colonization Work in Russia* (1925), with an introduction by the highly respected Louis Marshall; David Brown's *The New Exodus: Back to the Soil; The Story of the Historic Movement of Russian Jews* (1925), published by the Joint; and Joseph Rosen's *The Present Status of Russian Jewish Agricultural Colonization and the Outlook* (1926), a report of the trip JR had been unable to join. These publications boasted of Rosenwald's contributions, which were enabling the "historic" work. His efforts gave "new life" to thousands of "suffering" Jews. In 1937, five years after

Rosenwald's death, Evelyn Morrisey, the treasurer of Agro-Joint, dedicated her laudatory *Jewish Workers and Farmers in the Crimea and Ukraine* "To the Memory of Julius Rosenwald."

Others also commented positively on Agro-Joint. The Yiddish press, particularly the anti-Communist *Forverts*, extolled the great opportunity the farming project offered Jews in the Soviet Union. Editor Abraham Cahan published a raft of laudatory articles predicting that the colonies would be harbingers of a bright future for Jews living under Soviet rule. Cahan went to the Soviet Union in 1927 and reported back to his readers on the colonists' economic productivity, healthful lives, and vibrant cultural activities. In the English pages of the newspaper, Cahan described former Jewish businessmen who, thanks to Rosenwald money, now thrived as artisans and farmers. Cahan, a socialist, advocate of trade unions, and self-appointed spokesman for east European Jewish immigrants in America, shared little with Julius Rosenwald, but support for the Jewish farming colonies brought them together.

During this period in which Rosenwald donated his millions to so many projects, American Jewish organizations and institutions depended upon the contributions of a few individuals. Without donors like Rosenwald, no Jewish schools, synagogues, charitable societies, magazines, textbooks, or community centers could exist. American Jewish life consisted of an array of voluntary institutions which depended upon philanthropy for support.

Rosenwald created none of the projects to which he contributed. The Chicago Hebrew Institute owed its origins to young immigrant Zionists. Hebrew Union College and the prize which eventuated in *Judaism as a Civilization* emerged from the rabbis and laity of a movement eager to update Judaism to fit America. The Jewish Theological Seminary had been founded by observant rabbis as a compromise between

Reform and Orthodoxy. The Joint combined the efforts of a mass of American Jews across class and ideology united by the realization that they alone among the world's Jewries enjoyed the blessing of isolation from the devastation of World War I. Agro-Joint had been hatched by a handful of Jewish activists and millionaires who objected to creating a Jewish homeland in Palestine. Rosenwald responded to these visionaries' ideas. He dipped his hand into his very deep pocket to translate their visions into reality.

Like all philanthropists and communal activists, Rosenwald gave his time and money only to undertakings that resonated with him. His upbringing in Reform Judaism had trained him to believe that as a Jew he had to right the wrongs of the world. He gravitated toward projects that promised to enrich Jewish culture, bring Jews into positive contact with non-Jews, and improve Jews' lives. He sought to direct Jewish culture toward the general good, never making donations to benefit only Jews. His Jewishness underlay nearly all his actions, whether obviously "Jewish" or not.

American Jews responded to Rosenwald as a Jew. Although he had his critics, mostly among Zionists who considered him ignorant of the Jewish people's true needs, for most American Jews he offered a public face to be proud of. Jewish publications lauded him, describing his work as exemplifying the best of Judaism, as the Jews' gift to America. He, a Jew, made America better, and by benefiting all Americans he benefited Jews. Editorials, articles, and personal letters praised him, and by association validated American Jewry.

Abraham Sepenuk of Jersey City, New Jersey, an immigrant who had recently graduated from Fordham University School of Law, wrote to Rosenwald in 1929, after seeing the Movietone in which JR had commented on his success being the result of luck, not intellect. Sepenuk marveled at Rosenwald's willingness to say that "your success or any success is not based exclusively upon hard work, effort, etc., but that the element of luck or 'mazel' as I call it plays a very important part." With that word, Sepenuk highlighted the Jewish bond between himself and the multimillionaire, continuing, "It took a lot of courage on your part to speak as candidly as you did for the other so called 'wealthy' gentlemen attribute their success to their wisdom, for[e]sight, intelligence and other such flap-doodle." He closed the letter by stating that he counted himself among "a group of your unknown admirers." Sepenuk recognized the deeply Jewish underpinnings of Rosenwald's life. Here was a public figure who made his Jewishness central to his life and work and emphasized humility and the common good.[63]

4

A Jew Steps In

In 1924, the *American Israelite* challenged Henry Ford's anti-Semitic and xenophobic outpourings with a small piece. "Here's an item for Ford's Folly," it mocked: "a group of Nordics in the South—white 100 percent, American money-lenders—were about to stop Herman E. Perry, Negro financier of Atlanta . . . when a JEW by the name of Julius Rosenwald stepped in." Rosenwald offered to rescue Perry's business, the Atlanta Life Insurance Company, from certain death. The *American Israelite*'s designations "Nordics" and "100 percent" Americans took aim at a common 1920s anti-immigrant trope, and when it then identified them as "money-lenders," it subverted the centuries-old condemnation of Jews as usurers. After all, a "JEW" had demonstrated to the white Georgia Christians the meaning of generosity.[1]

The piece highlighted the prominence of Julius Rosenwald, the one who "stepped in" to assist Perry's business, in initiatives aimed at ameliorating the dire economic conditions endured by black Americans. Rosenwald knew Perry and admired him. He also felt that if the bank failed, black people in Atlanta and elsewhere would suffer. Much of Rosenwald's philanthropic and civic activism revealed a disposition to step in and act for and with America's black population, who were largely living in extreme poverty, lacking access to basic services offered by private institutions and denied the basic rights guaranteed by governments, local, state, and federal, to American citizens.

Julius Rosenwald's name had been linked to black causes since the early twentieth century, and many Americans knew of his dedication to lessening inequalities between blacks and whites and addressing the nation's deliberate failures. In his work for "the Negro," his Jewish self-image and worldview played a large role.

Shortly after Rosenwald's death in 1932, the philosopher Alain Locke, a leading voice of the Harlem Renaissance and author of the pathbreaking anthology *The New Negro* (1925), eulogized the philanthropist's life and work. In a few pages, Locke summarized charitable giving in general, American democracy, the status of African Americans, Jewishness, and the bonds connecting Jews and blacks, as he contemplated the "benefactions of Julius Rosenwald . . . a man who discovered a new social and spiritual dimension for the philanthropist's dollar." Rosenwald, with his distinctive brand of charitable giving and his focus on "the Negro," had become, according to Locke, a "patron of democracy."[2]

Why did Locke, the chair of the Philosophy Department at Howard University, a beneficiary of Rosenwald's philanthropic work, equate JR's philanthropy with working for democracy? Locke noted that much of American philanthropy contained within it "un-American elements," given the "bureaucratic trend of the self-perpetuating foundation and the enfeebling effect of private giving to social objectives that should be recognized clearly as public or state responsibilities." This predominant form of American philanthropy did not alter social realities, but perpetuated them while alleviating some immediate problems temporarily.

But JR's insistence that beneficiaries of philanthropy, such as the millions of southern blacks who lived in communities which housed "Rosenwald schools" or African American men around the country who spent leisure time at the YMCAs he funded, contribute to these organizations as well transformed those beneficiaries into partners in their own advancement rather than objects of charity. To Locke, this difference mattered. Most white initiatives to help blacks were "enfeebling . . . patronizing at best," but JR had offered "a constructive gift that requires effort on the part of the beneficiary." Rosenwald's work "steadfastly refused to pauperize, to dominate and control . . . or to act as a palliative."

Locke declared that because Rosenwald had insisted that "the state or some agency of the community" be involved, he had fostered "shrewd and common sense humanity," demonstrating to whites that the "Negro situation" did not exist as "a separate or special issue, but as part and parcel of the working problems of practical social democracy in America." Rosenwald's efforts on behalf of, and with, African Americans far transcended "Negro welfare work." They fit into a project of "spiritual development" that recognized the "common denominator . . . beyond the material benefactions . . . the unequivocal recognition that seen far-sightedly," as Rosenwald did, demonstrated that "the cause and best interests of any and all minorities is really the cause and best interests of the majority."

During his career Rosenwald gave generously to projects serving "any and all" of America's minorities. Hull House and the Immigrants' Protective League provide examples of thinking and giving to institutions which serve diverse populations. But he directed special efforts toward only two minority groups, African Americans and Jews. He did not exclude other minorities from his vision of a better, progressive society, but only for these two groups did he connect himself publicly and directly. They represented his greatest interest, and Locke, like many other contemporary commentators, considered this notable, inspiring, and in need of an explanation.

The "patron of democracy," Locke declared, "was a Jew." In his lifetime JR expended much time and fortune on "the many causes of modern Jewry," a focus the philosopher described as "pardonable partisanship." A rich Jew had bestowed millions on his own people, and regardless of whether all Jews appreciated his particular choices, no one questioned that his giving reflected his Jewish concerns. To Locke, that Rosenwald, "the most conspicuous contemporary benefactor of the Negro," had directed more money to African American than to Jewish endeavors made him not "less Jewish" but "all the more American." Rosenwald, by his actions, lived by American democracy's unfulfilled ideal of "equality and full state responsibility." By directing his work toward creating greater equality between blacks and whites, by investing millions in the welfare of African Americans and forcing the nation to address their needs, the Jewish Rosenwald helped America become more American. In a curious rhetorical twist, commentators repeatedly said of Rosenwald that he prodded the nation to become "more Christian," more "spiritual."

Locke ended his tribute with a theme commonly raised by those, white gentiles, blacks, and Jews, who speculated on the relation between Rosenwald's African American work and his Jewishness. Assuming, Locke wrote, "that this spiritual dimension" would some day "enter the body of American philanthropy, it will largely as a result of the spiritual fusion of two minority experiences, the Jewish and the Negro, meeting unselfishly and fruitfully in an American environment and issuing in a shining example through the spirit and good works of Julius Rosenwald."

From 1911 on, Julius Rosenwald directed both philanthropic energy and his public reputation toward the needs of black Americans, defining this work as an imperative for him as a wealthy, white American Jew. His resources, race, citizenship, and cultural heritage alike goaded him to work to create greater equality for black Americans, underwriting programs, organizations, and other undertakings to expand their opportunities by improving American society.

Little in his background prepared him for such a focus. He left no reminiscences about any awareness of the inequities based on skin color which existed around him during his boyhood in Springfield. He never asserted that growing up in Lincoln's shadow inspired him. In 1908 a bloody race riot roiled his city, but no evidence indicates that JR, his parents, his siblings, or his friends and family commented on it.

He might, however, have learned that in the riot's aftermath a new organization came into being, the National Association for the Advancement of Colored People. The signers of the 1909 "Call" that launched it included several familiar Jewish names, most important for him his rabbi, Emil Hirsch of Sinai congregation, the institution Rosenwald cited as having defined his moral life as a Jew. But if this had been the case, he never mentioned it. Even after he reached adulthood, he could refer privately in a letter to his wife to "darkies," "culled" (colored), and "niggers," although he put quotation marks around the latter two words, suggesting that he recognized their inappropriateness.

JR's interest in African Americans seems to have begun in the summer of 1910 when he read John Graham Brooks's biography of William H. Baldwin, a white executive of the Southern Railway who, under the spell of Booker T. Washington's uplifting autobiography, *Up from Slavery*, decided to dedicate time and money toward improving education for African American children in the South. Rosenwald received the book from his friend Paul Sachs. The biography extolled Baldwin's efforts to help black people in the South, and the tale gripped JR. The book, he wrote to his daughters, provided a "glorious . . . story of a man . . . whom I shall endeavor to imitate or follow as nearly as I can." Rosenwald learned from it that Washington, who had so inspired Baldwin, "made a great study of the Negro problem along common sense, helpful lines."[3]

Washington's approach appealed to Rosenwald. Born in 1856, the educator could not recall his own enslaved childhood, but painfully recognized the resemblance between the conditions of servitude and the difficulties African Americans in the post–Civil War South endured. Educated at the Hampton Institute in Virginia, Washington became the first teacher and later president of Tuskegee Normal School (now Tuskegee University), founded in 1881 in Alabama. Aiming to equip students with basic literacy and artisanal skills, he wanted them to achieve economic independence as farmers, artisans, and domestic workers. Some Tuskegee graduates would become teachers and pass on these skills to others. Washington hoped that a skilled southern black population, women and men who could support themselves, could become more self-sufficient and less dependent on white landowners and employers who considered themselves superior and entitled to exploit black people. Those who passed through Tuskegee would prove themselves invaluable by the excellence of their work.

Washington articulated this most clearly in the speech he delivered at Atlanta's Cotton States and International Exposition in 1895. He made two points. The first, "Cast down your buckets where you are," Washington directed at black listeners, while the second, "In all things purely social we can be separate as the fingers, yet one as the hand in all things essential to mutual progress," he pitched to white people, architects of and adherents to Jim Crow, the regnant system of racial segregation in public accommodations, schools, hospitals, and transportation, as well as the near-total disenfranchisement of African Americans.

Rosenwald found Washington's life story, retold in *Up from Slavery*, compelling. He responded to the educator's charismatic personality and to the economically driven mission pursued by the "wizard of Tuskegee." Both JR and Washington believed that if minority groups hoped to change dominant attitudes against them, they had to compile sterling records of achievement. Rosenwald agreed with Washington's prescription that to foster the region and nation's "mutual progress," black people had to develop and showcase their own economic and material progress. Rosenwald, the man of commerce, saw in Washington's message a way to remake American society, lessening inequality and dissolving prejudice.

Rosenwald first met Washington when the principal of Tuskegee came to Chicago to address a ceremony marking the fifty-third anniversary of the city's YMCA, an institution that excluded black patrons. Wilbur Messer, a YMCA official and ally of JR's, asked him to host a dinner to introduce Washington to other Chicago businesspeople and reformers. Rosenwald agreed, the dinner went off well, and the Alabama educator invited JR to join Tuskegee's board. JR declined but indicated that he wanted to see the Alabama school made famous by *Up from Slavery*, and he later became both a large donor and a member of Tuskegee's board of directors.

The depth of Rosenwald's admiration for Washington, and his willingness to follow the Tuskegeean's lead, complicates stock ideas about givers and takers. Rosenwald had the money and contacts. As a rich Jew, he had access to his own funds and those of a wide network of rich friends and associates. As a white man, he could go wherever he wanted unhindered and maintain contacts with powerful individuals. He could use his political influence and financial resources far more easily than could Washington. But the satisfaction JR derived from participating in the undertaking of serving black people, the nation, and the Jews depended on Washington's guidance. Rosenwald took his cues from Washington on how to apply his political influence and wealth, to whom he should give, and how much. For the most part, in the four years between JR's first entry into African American matters and Washington's death in 1915, Rosenwald would first seek Washington's approval before responding to requests involving black people. If Washington said yes, JR usually agreed, and if Washington said no, Rosenwald tended to refuse.

Rosenwald assisted Washington in other ways. Beyond his bounteous contributions to Tuskegee and his board service, JR introduced Washington to other whites, Jews and non-Jews, with means. Washington saw Rosenwald as a conduit to powerful men and women who could further his cause. The two respected each other, collaborating in a complicated dance of race and racial etiquette in segregated America.

After the 1912 election, for example, Washington learned that the newly elected president, Woodrow Wilson, would be in Chicago and asked Rosenwald to meet with Wilson and talk to him about Tuskegee. Rosenwald jumped at the chance, and with his typical exuberance suggested doing more, proposing that Washington travel from Alabama to Chicago at JR's expense, as usual. He would host a lunch for the three of them. Washington, however, thought this a bad idea, reasoning that if the first southern president elected since Zachary Taylor in 1848 sat down to dine with a black man, the press would explode, and charge that Washington wanted to foster "social equality." This, Washington said, would "embarrass Governor

Wilson and would certainly furnish the newspapers with a basis for some rather sensational reports" that would not help the people whom he served and would do little to further the cause of the black people with the Virginia-born president, a Democrat who believed in segregation as the natural order of things. Rosenwald deferred to Washington's judgment.[4]

But most of Rosenwald's involvement in the cause of black Americans transpired after Washington's death, and Rosenwald then asked advice from others or, when need be, relied on his own counsel. While he rarely departed from Washington's vision of economic development, self-help, and education, neither did he follow it single-mindedly or blindly.

THE BLACK YMCA CAMPAIGN

Rosenwald's inauguration into the affairs of African Americans slightly predated his first meeting with Washington. A few months after he had written to his daughters about Brooks's biography of Baldwin, an opportunity to put his resolve to follow Baldwin's example into action presented itself. Wilbur Messer solicited Rosenwald to help a campaign to fund a facility for "the colored men of Chicago." No YMCA, north or south, admitted African Americans. In January 1911, at a meeting launching the project, Rosenwald pledged twenty-five thousand dollars, on condition that Messer and his associates raised an additional hundred thousand.

Then, with no forewarning, Rosenwald announced that he would make the same offer to any city that would rise to the challenge.[5] Between 1913 and his death, the Rosenwald challenge grant, considered the first of its kind in fundraising history, resulted in twenty-five YMCAs and two YWCAs for African American women. Rosenwald's black YMCA campaign went forward, with JR vigorously involved in the effort to raise the money to build and staff the facilities.

Exclusion from the YMCA had been a serious problem for African Americans, as the years Rosenwald busied himself with this project coincided with the great African American urban-bound migration. Millions of men left the rural South for northern cities, but when they got there they could find no lodgings or leisure centers. Most hotels would not rent them rooms, and even the ones that did charged more than these men, migrants in search of work, could afford. Even non-migrant black male residents of Chicago, Atlanta, Philadelphia, Kansas City, Washington, D.C., and other cities had few venues for exercise, swimming, or taking classes.

Better-off African American urbanites perhaps benefited from the Rosenwald YMCA project more than the newcomers since they could pay the fees. Rosenwald stipulated that the Ys charge people something, however nominal, to belong, and that individuals and institutions in the local black community contribute to their funding. He had already come to abhor charity per se, preferring to support institutions in which users collaborated with donors. The black residents, many professionals, business owners, and skilled workers troubled by the massive influx of rural, poor southern blacks, also sought respectable places to gather among themselves, away from the newcomers. Sometimes referred to as the "old settlers," they saw the YMCA as a place where middle-class urban blacks could teach respectability to the newcomers by their example and thus fight racism. The black YMCA movement reached out to migrants in hope of weaning them from cafés, street corners, taverns, pool halls, and other places defined by the middle class as disreputable.

Regardless of which segment of the African American population benefited most from the YMCA project, Rosenwald saw it as an important first step in emulating Baldwin. By pledging a mammoth sum of money and then raising even more, he demonstrated his selflessness even as he became a player in the city's and the nation's philanthropic elite on be-half of a downtrodden group. His efforts evoked praise from the rich and the important, like President William Howard Taft, who wrote about JR that his donation "makes one re-joice that a man of his heart and soul and generosity has had the genius—for he has wonderful business genius—and execu-tive force to build up a fortune that enables him to do what he would with his money for the betterment of mankind." The YMCA project gave Rosenwald his first big platform from which to articulate publicly his philosophy, to declare "no to alms giving, which tends to pauperization and degradation," and rather to offer "the colored young men of the land those opportunities of self-improvement for education and recre-ation, for the acquisition of spiritual, moral, mental, and physi-cal strength, that makes for manhood and self-reliance"; thus, he argued, "can we of the white race be of the greatest aid in furthering this progress."[6]

Rosenwald attended the dedications of Ys around the coun-try, relishing the opportunity. He spoke at many, making a point of lauding the institution and what it offered. He also tried to articulate the project's deeper meaning through his thoughts about race, prejudice, and the relationship between blacks and whites. In one typical address in 1913, after thanking contribu-tors, touting their good work, and praising the YMCA staff, he outlined a message that would endure. The black YMCA of Chicago would give "the negro," he declaimed, a place "not to be worked *for* but to be worked *with*." It would not be an insti-tution where "the white race" did something "for the benefit of the negro" and might "hand it to him, let him take it away and blame him, if he fails to make the best use of the benefac-tion." Rather, as a dynamic venue to effectuate change, it would launch "the unfinished work . . . the great task before us of re-moving prejudice against negroes, of bringing about a univer-sal acceptance that the man and not the color counts." Beyond gym, pool, restaurant, library, and meeting rooms, the YMCA offered black men a setting from which to demonstrate their abilities to the antagonistic white people of the city. Speaking directly to this constituency, Rosenwald declared, "You are organizing the force to operate the plant. You're going to run it, too. What a chance for you to make good! . . . What an efficient help to dissipate prejudice!" This, the core of his vision, matured and sharpened over time as he increasingly defined "help" as not just giving money but giving it in a way that allowed the beneficiaries to shape their own institutions.[7]

The campaign also put Rosenwald in touch with African Americans for the first time. During the Chicago launch and those in other cities, he met with black professionals and community activists, individuals such as Jesse Moorland, an official of the national YMCA. While he, Rosenwald, held the project's purse strings, the national organization could kill the endeavor. He needed its support. These African American community workers confronted the abhorrence expressed by some in their ranks at accepting anything that smacked of segregation. The black professionals with whom Rosenwald worked and on whom he depended came with their own agendas, representing constituents who might, like a writer for a Cleveland black newspaper, lambaste the YMCA project as a "Magnificent Monument to Race Prejudice, Intolerance, Inhumanity, and White American Christian Hypocrisy." Despite Rosenwald's not being a Christian, such scathing comments surfaced regularly. Whether involving the YMCAs, schools, or hospitals, this criticism mattered to black professionals and community activists who embraced Rosenwald's projects despite their segregated structure. They wanted to ensure that such sentiments did not deter the masses from using the institutions or contributing funds to them.[8]

The novelty of a Jew, a white man, supporting a black Christian institution generated much commentary in the black, the Jewish, and the general white press, most of it glowing. The *Chicago Defender*, one of the nation's premier African American newspapers, likened his actions to the Emancipation Proclamation. Such praise enabled JR and other Jews to bask in the aura of his beneficence, demonstrating the Jews' goodness and broad-mindedness. As Julius Stern, a Chicago attorney, wrote to JR, "Some remarks . . . made in my hearing yesterday among non-Jews, showed such keen appreciation by them of your actions as an individual and as a representative member of our Jewish community." Rosenwald, Stern said, "brought credit upon [himself] and upon the Jewish people," a sentiment echoed by Alfred Decker, another Chicago Jew, who noted, "What impresses me . . . [is] your . . . assisting a race that is discriminated against like our own."[9]

IN THE SHADOW OF TUSKEGEE

The massive project JR conceived and undertook for the education of southern black children, his boldest, most far-reaching and visible undertaking in America, made his name nearly synonymous with white support for African Americans. Although other of the nation's white philanthropists, including other Jews, contributed to this cause, the scope and nature of his work put it in a class by itself. And while Rosenwald's involvement in black American causes extended well beyond schools, his educational work defined him for the nation at large. In the course of his twenty years of involvement, first with money from his personal accounts and then with grants from the Rosenwald Fund, JR's money and vision created some 4,977 elementary schools as well as over 200 homes for teachers, establishing these in every state that had joined the Confederacy during the Civil War, as well as in states like Maryland, Oklahoma, Missouri, and Kentucky that ignored or marginalized the educational needs of black children. By the year of his death, over one-third of all southern black children attended a "Rosenwald school," a term which resonated deeply in the black rural communities, where the schools were not viewed as charities but operated as cooperative ventures, as sources of collective pride linking them to the man in Chicago.

Had Rosenwald simply given money for the schools, his generosity would surely have earned him a place of honor in the history of American philanthropy and in African American history. When in 1913 he launched his first six schools in rural Alabama, most southern states provided little or no education for black children, assuming that children inevitably bound to be future agricultural laborers or domestic servants did not need education. What formal schooling these children received took place during the few months of the growing season, when planters could spare their hands from fieldwork. Come planting, tending, and picking seasons, the children joined their parents, nearly all of whom made a living as sharecroppers or tenant farmers, tightly controlled by white employers, whose authority over the workers enjoyed the protection of the law. Black schools received meager state funding even though black workers paid state taxes at the same rate as the white people whose children received whatever constituted publicly supported education. But the money of African American taxpayers went to finance the education of white youngsters, at whatever level the states mandated. State-supported black schools had few textbooks, and those they did have had been hopelessly out of date for years, having been discarded by the white schools. Facilities rarely met minimal standards. The majority of the teachers, often dedicated African American women and men assisted by contributions from local churches, earned paltry salaries, and few had the highest level of training. A few black schoolchildren attended private institutions, supported by white philanthropists or church bodies, but the states gave these schools no support.

Rosenwald's engagement with African American education began in 1911, at his first encounter with Booker T. Washington, who invited him to visit Tuskegee. Later that year, Rosenwald assembled an entourage for the journey that included family members, business associates, and Rabbi Hirsch. The visitors approved of what they saw after touring the campus, attending chapel, and meeting faculty, staff, and students. "I was astonished at the progressiveness in the school," Rosenwald wrote; "I don't believe there is a white industrial school in America anywhere that compares to Mr. Washington's at Tuskegee." Washington exulted in the fact that Rosenwald agreed to join the board, writing to former president Theodore Roosevelt, also a Tuskegee supporter, that he had snagged "that Jew who gave so much money for colored YMCAs. . . . I think he is one of the strongest men we have ever gotten on our board."[10]

Washington's characterization of Rosenwald as "that Jew" in his letter to Roosevelt would be repeated not just with regard to Rosenwald's interest in this institution, but for all his eventual massive investments in the institutional life of black America. Rosenwald's association with Washington allowed him to accomplish several goals, to be able do good in the world, to illustrate to other prominent Americans, such as Theodore Roosevelt, his role as a promoter of civic improvement, and prominently to serve the Jewish people. Rosenwald's generosity to African American causes would be seen as an outgrowth of his Jewish upbringing and worldview.

For the rest of his life, JR committed himself to Tuskegee, contributing to the college even after Washington's death, though he had little confidence in Washington's successor, Robert Russa Moton. JR's first small gifts to Tuskegee, beyond his service on the board and solicitations among wealthy white associates, offered no hint of the millions he would eventually give. He began by sending the students, most very poor, hats and shoes from Sears, and according to his general principle he insisted that they pay a portion of the cost of these items. He never lost his conviction that outright charity demeaned both giver and recipient. Soon the gifts of hats and shoes multiplied, and he also started distributing handsome cash bonuses to teachers and staff as thanks for their work. Finally he began giving larger gifts, freeing Washington, who suffered from ill health, from having to travel around the country to court donors.

In addition to the considerable sums Rosenwald gave to Tuskegee, he solicited gifts from both Jewish and gentile white donors. He introduced Washington to notable and influential journalists, jurists, and reformers. As vice president of Temple Sinai, Rosenwald invited Washington to speak at the dedication of the synagogue's new grand edifice in 1912, giving the educator an excellent forum from which to solicit for his school and on behalf of other African American causes. The congregation attracted an affluent membership, primed to contribute handsomely to causes that appealed to them as Jews in America. The Chicago press gave the dedication ceremony detailed coverage, which enabled the congregation to bask in the glory of having secured such a notable speaker, while Washington could be assured that his message would be heard widely by the right people.

Rosenwald looked to Washington for guidance as he fielded an avalanche of requests from many African American schools and other educational projects. By accepting Washington's assessments, he bolstered Tuskegee's power base in the black community. Rosenwald funded six small schools in rural Alabama, run and administered by Washington from Tuskegee, as extensions of the institute. All operated as private schools, with no state involvement or funding. By giving money to support black schools, JR joined a small but influential group of northern white philanthropists and philanthropic foundations that considered the vast gap between African American and white literacy rates and the inadequate schooling opportunities for black children a serious moral issue.

This interest soared in 1912, the year he turned fifty, and it changed its scope and direction. He named Tuskegee among the philanthropic projects he earmarked as birthday presents to himself. He specifically designated an African American elementary school program which Tuskegee ran as a beneficiary.

But he did not stop there; as part of the birthday bonanza, JR offered to fund a school in any southern black community designated by Washington. He sketched out a general outline of the plan in a letter to Washington, explaining that the educator could veto any of the provisions. The letter began with the proviso, "providing you concurred." He went on, suggesting, "You select such schools as in your judgment would participate, naming the amount for each and the purpose for which the money is to be used, if you so desire, and as soon as any school which you have named has raised an equal amount, I will pay to it such an amount as you have designated. I will agree to pay a total of $25,000 to such schools as soon as they furnish a list of bona fide subscriptions equal to the amount you have designated."[11] Working with Jane Addams, Judge Julian Mack, and the editor of the *Chicago Record-Herald*, H. H. Kohlsaat, JR and Washington drafted a press release to launch their endeavor.

The project differed from other educational contributions from white philanthropists to black schools in requiring the local African American population to join the effort. While Rosenwald gave the bulk of the money, the black community involved had to chip in as well, providing money, labor, and materials. African Americans, community by community, devised fundraising campaigns, including bake sales and donations of goods and services, as well as dipping into their pockets to meet Rosenwald's challenge. A consummate businessman, JR never forgot the bottom line, advising Washington in his proposal letter that the schools be built "at the lowest possible cost without sacrificing quality." That, he wrote, did not "mean a cheap building, of course, but a good building at a low cost," one in which the largest number of children could be educated in a solid structure.

At one point Rosenwald suggested that local groups which took up his challenge use supplies purchased at discount from Sears. Washington immediately counseled against this, convincing Rosenwald that the schools should be constructed from lumber prepared at local, black-owned sawmills and bricks from black-owned kilns, ensuring that all African American residents would see themselves as beneficiaries of the school campaign. As he almost always did, Rosenwald jettisoned his own ideas in favor of Washington's.[12]

Where communities could not raise the cash, the men and women would literally build the buildings, offering their labor as their share of the cost. The Rosenwald schools, some five thousand of them, emerged as central institutions of black community life, embraced by all across lines of difference. African Americans even in small towns splintered into multiple religious denominations, each with its own church. The Rosenwald schools represented common space. Campaigns to build these schools brought black people together, town by town, cutting across fissures of class, age, social status, occupation, and religion. After they completed the school buildings, JR envisioned them as a physical statement about community unity, testifying to the common purpose that had brought the community together. This had been one of Rosenwald's goals.

In keeping with Rosenwald's overarching vision of philanthropy, he did not want the schools to be known by his name. Although the moniker "Rosenwald school" surfaced immediately, informally and universally, it reflected common usage, not an official name. Each school, JR felt, should bear the name of its town. By requesting that the schools not carry his name, he was denying that he alone was responsible for building or staffing them. Rather, he wanted Americans to know that the schools had come into being through the efforts of their communities, each member contributing as he or she could. The schools would not have existed without his money, but neither would they have done so without broad communal efforts.

Rosenwald's schools differed from the others launched by northern white philanthropic efforts on a second front. He required that the states, whether Mississippi or Georgia, Texas or Virginia, all run by white people to serve white people, had to participate in the schools' operations. Because southern states did educate their white children, Rosenwald took a principled stand, refusing to contribute to any white school, public or private, however worthy. In response to a request from the School for Organic Education in Stanhope, Alabama, an experimental Montessori-inspired school, Rosenwald wrote, "I am of necessity compelled to confine myself to a given policy and while I am interested in Southern Schools, my activity is confined almost entirely to work for the colored people." He rejected the request "not because the whites are not equally deserving, but [because] they already get so much larger a share of the money that is expended for school purposes in proportion to the population and in addition have many other advantages which blacks do not have."[13]

Other northern white philanthropists funded private schools for black children, circumventing the apathetic, or even hostile, state education officials. As Mary McLeod Bethune, a formidable African American educator, put it about her state, though she could have been speaking of any of them, "The state of Florida does, as you know, nothing to help us." But Rosenwald insisted that his schools function as public entities, endorsed by white bureaucrats and elected officials.[14]

Rosenwald mandated that states provide public oversight in such matters as standards of instruction, curriculum, and teacher qualifications. They had to inspect the buildings to ensure they met health and safety standards, and monitor the number of days of instruction so that they equaled those white students received. Rosenwald stipulated that his money "be used in a way to encourage public school officers" to take responsibility for educating black children. Communities needed to convince their states to appoint agents, government officials, to join in their school building campaigns and then continue to be involved in running the school. Most states initially appointed white men as agents for the Rosenwald schools, but over time added African American staff, whose salaries Rosenwald moneys initially covered, but states eventually assumed.

The resultant state involvement in the education of black children can be considered a turning point in the relation between black communities and the state, a moment when tax money began to flow back to black communities. White and black state officials began working together for a common purpose. While they did not take up the issue of segregation, white officials did start to make equity in education an issue to be addressed across racial lines.

Rosenwald's requirement that southern states incorporate the black schools into their jurisdictions might be read as acceding to the white government more control over black lives. It gave the white people in authority powers they did not have over private schools, which in the main had been paid for by philanthropists or funded by churches. Since the states had to agree to Rosenwald's terms, a state government could kill a project, denying again the black residents' efforts to educate their children. A determined band of white residents in any community could wield veto power.

But substantial opposition failed to materialize. Individual incidents probably took place, and some white southerners complained that Rosenwald's gift ought to be seen as a Trojan horse, threatening the system that served them so well. The sociologist John Dollard, who conducted a months-long ethnographic study in Indianola, Mississippi, in the 1930s, reported in *Caste and Class in a Southern Town* that local white residents expressed anxiety over possible "northern interference" with their "natural right to conduct race relations as they saw fit." Several planters he interviewed boasted that that they had "refused to accept Rosenwald money . . . because they feared the money would be followed by attempts at outside influence."[15]

But as the almost five thousand schools came into being, few acts of violence flared in this ever violent region. The historian Carter Woodson, founder of the Association for the Study of Negro Life and History and a one-time visitor to the Wabash Avenue YMCA, noted that the schools flourished because in every town "an enthusiastic minority" of white people "could grasp the new idea of democratic education." Rosenwald and others had worried that antagonism among white residents "might result . . . in the burning of the schoolhouses after they had been completed," but Woodson marveled at how few cases of incendiarism took place, occurring "much less than one might expect." Implying that some schools had been torched, Woodson asserted that the scattered acts of arson did not halt the projects. Every state in the South became home to multiple Rosenwald schools and every state agreed to the terms. No massive white resistance, organized and systematic, coalesced, blocking the proliferation of the Rosenwald schools. Woodson, a self-described radical affiliated with the NAACP, commented in his "Story of the [Rosenwald] Fund," that through its work, "there are in the South . . . certain changes of attitude which indicate that the Fund has been instrumental in effecting a revolution in Southern sentiment." That change, he predicted, would allow the Fund to "withdraw from this field, as the states would finally take up their responsibility to provide education." In response to criticism from some African Americans, mostly northern activists who disparaged the schools as institutions based on segregation and inequality, Woodson argued, "The Julius Rosenwald movement, laying the foundation for the super-structure upon which these new forces have had to build[,] deserves more credit than we can at this time appreciate."[16]

Advocates of the racial status quo had good reason to fear that an increasingly educated black population would sooner rather than later refuse to accept things as they existed. White southerners who feared Rosenwald's undertaking might have been correct in thinking it subversive. Even after Rosenwald's death, the Rosenwald schools galvanized southern racists, who resented their intrusion into the white southern way of life. In 1942 supporters of Eugene Talmadge, the governor of Georgia and an archetypical southern politician who defended segregation and fanned the flames of racism, added a verse to his campaign theme song:

Gene saved our college system
From all the Rosenwalds
Who sought to end traditions
Which we know are dear to all.

We don't want all their millions
And neither their advice
On how to educate our youth.
We Southerners think twice.[17]

Talmadge supporters accurately understood the destructive power of educating African Americans and resented Rosenwald's strategy of recruiting state officials and sympathetic local whites to the schools cause. As they saw it, he and his money shook up local customs, cracking the solidity of white hegemony. They wanted to preserve this system and he did not. Likewise, Hortense Powdermaker, a Jewish anthropologist who also went to Indianola, under the auspices of Yale University's Institute for Human Relations, in the 1930s to study race relations, recalled in her autobiography that she met Indianola's only white liberal, the superintendent of schools. Other white people confided their suspicions of him, believing that the time he had spent at a northern school on a Rosenwald scholarship had corrupted him.

Step by step, by means of his schools and other publicly supported facilities, Rosenwald pushed state policy makers toward providing more equitable resources for black citizens. In 1929, for example, the Charlotte, North Carolina, Public Library, a whites-only system, applied for a grant. The Rosenwald Fund, always operating according to Rosenwald's principles, approved the grant but stipulated that the city must assume responsibility for the private Library for Negroes. Black and white readers still would patronize separate buildings, but the Charlotte library system now had to make African American readers its responsibility.

Starting in 1928 the Rosenwald Fund began using this strategy for medical care, pressuring state boards of health and local public health departments to hire African Americans, though facilities would remain segregated. The Fund paid the salaries of the African American doctors and nurses, but insisted that the states contribute toward their salaries and recognize them as agents of the state health system. Jurisdictions had to agree to support their African American medical personnel if they received Rosenwald money. They also had to promise to employ black medical personnel when the Fund ceased, which it inevitably would, as stipulated by its charter, twenty-five years after Rosenwald's death. By the 1930s, Louisville, Kentucky, Birmingham, Alabama, and Baltimore, Maryland had hired black public health workers through the Rosenwald challenge, and while they served only black clients, they functioned as state employees. In a 1930 speech in New Orleans to the American Hospital Association to celebrate the opening of a hospital there for African Americans, paid for in part by the Fund, Rosenwald asserted that "charity cannot do it all. Either the state will have to take responsibility for the medical needs of its citizens . . . or else physicians, hospital managers and representatives of the general public must unite to find the best methods whereby people will get good medical care at a fair price." Rosenwald enunciated a classic Progressive-era formulation, that "disease is not a thing that can be segregated. The germs of tuberculosis and typhoid fever and measles do not obey Jim Crow laws," and he charged state governments to care for all the people who lived within their jurisdictions, since "a community is in serious danger with only half protected against disease."[18]

At the same time, JR said little about the federal government and its responsibilities toward African Americans. The fate of African Americans as a federal concern had been sealed by the Compromise of 1877, labeled by the historian Rayford Logan "the betrayal of the Negro." To resolve the disputed presidential election of 1876, Republicans and Democrats forged an unwritten but strictly observed pact that promised the South freedom to pursue its race policies with no threat of interference from Washington, D.C. Yet Rosenwald did begin, slowly, to challenge this policy as well through his philanthropy.

The cataclysmic flood of the Mississippi River in 1927 devastated a swath of about thirty thousand square miles, killing nearly 250 people, displacing millions of others in seven southern states, and creating a crisis no state could address alone. Rosenwald became involved after calls for federal action, directed at Secretary of Commerce Herbert Hoover, led to a plan for the government to coordinate a mass philanthropic effort, but to do so without spending any federal money. Southern planters embraced the idea on condition that their work force, African American sharecroppers, not use the funding to flee the region and join the Great Migration to the north.

Hoover had worked with Rosenwald through the Joint after World War I. He saw the flood as an opportunity to propose a land-redistribution scheme. Since a great deal of arable land had now become available in the flood's wake, as owners of small and medium-size farms left, JR saw this as a moment when a large-scale plan could assist homeless black families to purchase land at low cost. But since the federal government had no intention of paying for the program, he approached Rosenwald, who would in 1928 actively campaign for his presidential bid, as the obvious person to finance the project.

Rosenwald refused. A project of such monumental scope, affecting the most distressed and vulnerable element of the southern population, displaced African American sharecroppers, in his opinion had to be the responsibility of the federal government, not individual philanthropists. The needs of African Americans, Rosenwald told Hoover in 1929 after he had moved into the White House, had to be systematically addressed by the national government, not left to good-hearted individuals like himself or to states eager to maintain the oppressive status quo. Rather, the federal government had to take a lead and accept its responsibility toward these "12 million colored people."

Rosenwald's refusal to finance the land program reflected his growing sense that the problem, national and urgent, defied philanthropy.[19] As he wrote to Hoover, "The measures to be adopted" by the nation with regard to African Americans "are many, but three stand out conspicuously. First educational programs should be accelerated, with particular reference to the elimination of illiteracy. Second, health activities should be restudied to make sure that this group of people, whose conditions of life are in many ways different from those of whites, receive the aid in the elimination of disease that is desirable for their health and for the protection of the rest of the population." Rosenwald advised Hoover that "the improvement of opportunities for employment should be made the serious concern of government. . . . When employment can be given to the colored man . . . the national welfare and prosperity are promoted since on the whole the opportunities for employment for the Negro are much more restricted than for the white."[20]

Rosenwald's statement came at a time when the federal government did little for its citizens. Education fell under the purview of the individual states, each free to set its own standards, to do what it wanted. Health care functioned as a purely private matter, and for issues involving employment and labor standards, the government had no role, as employers zealously claimed this as their prerogative. Extensive involvement of the federal government on these three issues would have to wait until Franklin Roosevelt's New Deal of the 1930s, Lyndon Johnson's Great Society programs of the 1960s, and Barack Obama's Affordable Health Care Act of 2010.

Rosenwald's assertion that the nation, through the federal government and individual states, owed something to black people constituted an innovation in the role of the state. The Rosenwald schools, libraries, and public health initiatives forced white and black administrators, teachers, librarians, doctors, and nurses to take their first tentative steps toward working together. By calling upon southern states to intervene on behalf of *all* living within their borders, he helped reconfigure southern racial policies. Segregation remained fixed in place, but the nature of Rosenwald's donations generated change. By never directly challenging Jim Crow, Rosenwald's gifts appeared benign and unthreatening, other than perhaps to the Talmadges of the world. But indirectly they chipped away at it.

By forcing state governments to fulfill their obligation toward their African American residents, Rosenwald launched a quiet revolution. With money as the lure, he cajoled state governments to end their near-total neglect of the millions of black residents who contributed to the wealth of the state through their labor and taxes. Rosenwald set a precedent for other state engagements, and while he continued to accept segregation as a reality, he altered southern racial dynamics. This work escalated with the creation of the Rosenwald Fund in 1917 and the transfer of the schools project from Tuskegee to the Fund's southern headquarters in Nashville.

MORE THAN A TALENTED TENTH

Feared or not, the Rosenwald schools became part of regional life. But after Booker T. Washington's death and Robert Russa Moton's appointment as president of Tuskegee, Rosenwald began to rethink the administration of the schools project. Rosenwald had supported Booker T. Washington, Jr., as the ideal candidate to replace his father, but the board did not agree, preferring Moton, previously an administrator at Hampton. At the same time, JR began to fret over increasingly frequent criticisms detailing shortcomings of Tuskegee's administration of the program, pointing to a lack of uniformity among the schools, instances of slipshod construction, and teachers who lacked appropriate educational credentials.

Rosenwald moved the program to Fisk University in Nashville, headquarters of the Rosenwald Fund, and from here, under the direction of Samuel L. Smith, the former superintendent of Negro education for Tennessee, the massive program took off in earnest. The Fund committed itself to building modern facilities, equipped with excellent lighting, efficient heating for the winter months, good ventilation, the highest sanitary standards, and commodious space for large communal gatherings. The Fund required all schools to designate two acres of land outside the school house for gardens and playgrounds.

During the 1920s the schools project, which initially focused on elementary education, expanded to high schools and teacher training institutes. By extending its scope, Rosenwald made a statement that belied his apparent acceptance of elementary education as the desired outcome of his philanthropy, and segregation as the norm in America. He declared that black young people need not receive the minimum education available, nor did they have to be limited to the country's lowest economic rungs. Rather, at a time when only a minority of white American teenagers attended high school, the Rosenwald Fund declared that black youth should be prepared for increasingly higher levels of accomplishment. Why, the Fund essentially asked, should black Americans not have a chance to partake of the most advanced education available?

The impact of the Rosenwald schools could be measured by the millions of children who during JR's lifetime and beyond attended them. One 1930s estimate concluded that 89 percent of all buildings in which Mississippi's black youngsters received schooling came into being as Rosenwald schools, with similar data coming from other states. The schools' impact manifested itself in the legions of boys and girls who grew up to become teachers, nurses, social workers, and ministers, within a society that considered them unworthy to benefit from its resources. One study undertaken in the early twenty-first century by two economists at the Federal Reserve Bank of Chicago estimated that 30 percent of the educational gains achieved by African Americans in the 1910s and 1920s could be attributed directly to the Rosenwald schools, asserting that, according to evidence from the "Army General Classification Test . . . access to the [Rosenwald] schools raised the AGCT scores of rural blacks by about 0.2–0.45 standard deviations." Statistically significant, these figures indicate the seriousness of the impact.[21]

Rosenwald's funding of black higher and professional education in law, medicine, teaching, social work, the social and natural sciences, and the humanities began in the 1920s and also made a difference. These undertakings, along with the yearly fellowships the Fund awarded to African American artists, musicians, and writers, created a post–World War I black leadership cadre with expertise, advanced education, and accomplishments in keenly competitive endeavors. Despite JR's devotion to Booker T. Washington, he increasingly favored an outlook more akin that of W. E. B. Du Bois, who in 1903 called for the creation of an African American "talented tenth," which would provide leadership to the community. The Rosenwald Fund embraced the idea that academically able black students be supported in higher education and other intellectual and artistic pursuits.

Rosenwald expected that the black college graduates supported either directly from his pocket or through Fund programs would use their education to benefit their communities. Starting in 1915 he gave substantial amounts to Howard, Fisk, Dillard, and Atlanta Universities, as well as to Meharry Medical School, which constituted the premier institutions of higher learning for African Americans and which produced the majority of the doctors, lawyers, teachers, librarians, academicians, and other professionals whose work transformed America. The alumni of these schools and of the fifteen other black private colleges and the seven black state colleges Rosenwald supported provided the human energy needed to challenge the nation's seemingly unshakable racial system.

Rosenwald's contribution to each school had its own history. A contribution might make possible the construction of new buildings, expand and upgrade a library, modernize science laboratories, or facilitate the acquisition of larger and better trained faculty. The gifts enabled more black students to attend college, receive professional training, and go out into the world to serve their communities. They also fulfilled another of his missions, to demonstrate to the white world the untruth inherent in the widely accepted belief, held by nearly all white Americans, that whites and blacks had been endowed with fundamentally different and unequal abilities. Whites certainly believed in their own innate superiority and in the truth of African Americans' inferiority.

Rosenwald's involvement with Howard University in Washington, D.C., offers a good example of how his programs operated, but the details of his relationship with Howard differed little from those of his involvement with other black colleges. Rosenwald considered Howard an important institution. He served on its board of trustees and communicated often with its president. In 1925 Rosenwald learned from two of Howard University's other Jewish donors and supporters, Julian Mack and Felix Frankfurter, that the school's law library had become outmoded, lacking the volumes mandated by the Association of American Law Schools for accreditation. Had Howard's law school lost its accreditation because of the library's inadequately stocked bookshelves, its graduates would not have been admitted to the bar and consequently been able to argue in court. Without the law school, black Americans would have had fewer legal advocates. Thurgood Marshall, who received his law degree from Howard in 1933, might never have been able to successfully argue in 1954 in front of the U.S. Supreme Court the case of *Brown v. Board of Education*. Rosenwald offered the school $2,500 on condition that Howard raise an equal amount from other donors. The school raised the money, and two years later Rosenwald came to the rescue of Howard's school of medicine, providing $25,000, which was matched by Abraham Flexner, a key figure in American medical education.

Rosenwald also assisted black students to attend white schools. He concentrated on graduate and professional students, although he sometimes helped individual undergraduates. He provided money to some young people so they could attend northern schools that admitted few or no African American students. After all, segregation and discrimination knew no regional boundaries. In the South, such exclusion enjoyed the protection of the law, but it prevailed in the North as well, and Rosenwald's efforts to send black students to such institutions might be considered his first, tentative steps toward thinking about how to break down barriers between whites and blacks, although, obviously, most of those barriers persisted long beyond JR's lifetime.

Rosenwald often had to cajole officials at white schools, directly or through surrogates, to accept his scholarship students. In 1919, for example, Abraham Flexner informed Dr. V. C. Vaughan of the University of Michigan Medical School that "Mr. Julius Rosenwald of Chicago contemplates the establishment next year of a certain number of fellowships to be awarded to promising Negro graduates in medicine for the purpose of establishing them to pursue advanced work." The burden fell on the University of Michigan to admit the students if it wanted the money. Rosenwald had thrown down the gauntlet.[22]

For the most part, Rosenwald concentrated on educating black undergraduates and professionals at black institutions. He envisioned these colleges and universities as symbols of group pride and accomplishment for a people whose parents or grandparents, as slaves, had been denied the right to learn to read. The schools, as community institutions in their home cities, served a broader purpose and population than just providing education to the matriculated students. By helping fund Howard University, for example, he indirectly facilitated the flowering of an artistic renaissance in Washington, D.C. The writers, musicians, poets, journalists, and civil rights activists who pivoted around Howard, used its facilities, and lived in the LeDroit Park neighborhood shaped the city and the nation's intellectual and creative life.

One African American scholar in particular captured Rosenwald's interest. Ernest Everett Just had graduated Phi Beta Kappa from Dartmouth College in 1903, and with his bachelor's degree had accepted a position teaching English, rhetoric, and his real subject, biology, at Howard University. He spent numerous summers at the Marine Biological Laboratory at Woods Hole, Massachusetts, where he took courses in marine invertebrate eggs and embryos, and completed a doctorate in 1916 at the University of Chicago. By 1919, Rosenwald had become involved with Just's career, following and funding his research, largely at Howard University. In Just, Rosenwald saw an exemplar of a talented black man, someone who could help disprove racial stereotypes.

Just encouraged JR's assistance, cultivating and flattering his benefactor, and sending him his publications, which JR no doubt could not comprehend. Just shared news of the national and international honors bestowed upon him. Like any supplicant coming to a donor for more support, Just laid in front of Rosenwald the extent of his gratitude, writing in 1925, "You will never know how much you have meant to me and what an abiding light you and your life have meant to me. . . . As I write these lines my heart is full. I do so want in some way to measure up to something . . . you have done not for me alone but for the Negro race." Just proposed that he identify himself on his letterhead as the "Julius Rosenwald Fellow in Biology," a risky suggestion to an individual who turned down most requests involving use of his name. Rosenwald agreed, allowing the "black Apollo of science" to be known by the rare Rosenwald designation.[23]

The year Rosenwald met Just, he also inaugurated his fellowship program for individual African Americans whose work he judged potentially important. The first six fellowships went to medical researchers, but starting in the mid-1920s they expanded to create a diverse cadre of "Negro creative workers of unusual ability."[24] The list of beneficiaries of Rosenwald fellowships during JR's lifetime included nearly every African American who achieved renown in the nation's artistic, literary, intellectual, academic, educational, or civic life. They include the civil rights activist and historian W. E. B. Du Bois, the diplomat Ralph Bunche, the first African American to win the Nobel Prize, the poets Langston Hughes, James Weldon Johnson, and Countee Cullen, the educator Horace Mann Bond, the sociologists E. Franklin Frazier and Charles Johnson, the sculptor Augusta Savage, and the opera singer Marion Anderson, whose Rosenwald money enabled her to study lieder in Germany. Her 1939 performance at the Lincoln Memorial symbolized for that era the absurdity and injustice of the nation's racial divide.

This list of Rosenwald winners could have included many more, some less well known nationally, but these women and men achieved much in their fields, whether education, medicine, the arts, or the academy. Many changed their local communities, while some attained national and international prominence. Together they told a powerful story about JR's belief in the importance of investing in African Americans who individually and as an aggregate would advance his mission.[25]

Rosenwald's view of the world, whether profoundly naive or uncannily prescient, valued individual achievement and held that inequality existed because of prejudice, which itself followed ignorance. Black Americans, he believed, whether talented sculptors, brilliant scientists, or among the millions of hardworking women and men who sacrificed for the education of their children, sustained communities and served the nation. They demonstrated the untruth of conventional thinking among white people which held that African Americans lacked white people's moral and mental abilities. At the same time, he did not underestimate the impact of structural inequality.

He showed his awareness of its power in his principle of never giving to white schools, as they already received more than their fair share. By building five thousand schools to educate millions of African American children whom their states considered either uneducable or undeserving of education he showed his recognition that the American system distributed resources inequitably based on skin color and that that inequity, if unaddressed, would persist. Those who benefited from the system had no incentive to give up their privileges. He decided to use his money to fulfill a self-imposed responsibility to level the playing field.

Almost the entirety of JR's philanthropic engagement with the causes of African Americans, particularly for education and the fellowship program, reflected his wish to create a more equitable society.[26] But in the constant process of decision making, the weighing and balancing of requests, most from worthy causes and institutions, he set priorities, and education triumphed. Yet he did not neglect other difficulties endured by African Americans. His involvement in the issue of African American health care deserves a brief treatment.

In the early twentieth century, African Americans had access to far fewer health services than white people, experienced higher mortality rates, and found most medical facilities closed to them. Rosenwald expended millions on creating, staffing, and sustaining hospitals and other medical facilities to care for black patients. He invested in medical schools to train black doctors and in rural health projects for black nurses. Provident Hospital in Chicago's African American neighborhood drew his attention as early as 1912. Even in Chicago, he learned, black people had little access to care. Most of the city's hospitals refused to admit them. He used his clout as a member of the board of trustees of the University of Chicago to press its medical school to provide doctors and nurses for Provident's patients. He supported the work of black medical professionals at Provident and used his experiences there to create similar facilities in New Orleans, Nashville, and rural Alabama, among other places. As with the Rosenwald schools, he set up his medical care gifts as challenge grants, asking local African Americans to aid in these campaigns, and he and the Fund staff used their political influence to get state departments of public health to recognize their obligation to ensure the health of all their citizens.

But education continued to be the centerpiece of his vision. Rosenwald saw in education the key to the future. Well-educated students would be able to support themselves, sustain their communities, and demonstrate to the prejudiced white people that their prejudices had no basis in fact. Every African American teacher, nurse, doctor, librarian, or social worker working within his or her community exposed the falsehood of the nearly universally held truth among white people that black people accepted their relegation by white society to work as field hands and domestic servants. Every penny he gave to black causes he understood as offering a lesson for white people as well as blacks.

This put a burden on African Americans. White people did not, as a group, have to prove anything to other races, although Rosenwald recognized that this exemption did not apply to Jews. For white people, entitlements flowed from their skin color, and they enjoyed their privileges as a birthright. Whites who did not send their children to school or who drank, gambled, and engaged in disreputable behaviors did not stigmatize their "group," for whiteness constituted America's norm. Black people, as Rosenwald understood, had no such luxury. Each African American had to prove not only his or her own worth but the worth of black people in general. As a consequence, JR held that white Americans would never change unless African Americans demonstrated their abilities and thus exposed the falsity of prejudice.

Black Americans, therefore, had to comport themselves with dignity, sobriety, and order. They had to be above reproach. They had to teach white people, north and south, the truth about their people. They had to show the white public that they deserved better as a collectivity and as individuals than the limited opportunities America provided. Rosenwald considered his money a tool in this effort, and he shouldered his responsibility to use it as one, with little hesitation or soul-searching.

Rosenwald articulated this vision in a speech in which he discussed the record of the African American soldiers had who served in World War I. Before Rosenwald left on his government service trip to France in May 1918 Emmett Scott, Booker T. Washington's former secretary, asked him to pay a call on the black troops serving abroad, bringing greetings from home and seeing how they fared in their segregated units. JR visited the men, but he also addressed white soldiers about their obligation to give their African American comrades-in-arms "a square deal."[27]

Rosenwald used his encounters with the African American soldiers in the speech, lecturing to his white audience about their need to rethink their ideas and to mend their ways. The speech, "Reconstruction and the Negro," encapsulated his positive view of the future and of white Americans' responsibility to change the status quo. After noting that the war had made the United States "a leading nation in the world," he shifted tone, pointing out to his white audience that "approximately ten percent of our present population is colored." Whites needed to recognize that "every man, woman, and child of this ten percent should be given the opportunity to utilize whatever ability he has in the struggle for the maintenance of the world leadership we now face." "We" meant Americans, but "insofar as we refuse to give this part of our population an opportunity to lend its strength . . . we weaken the total strength of the nation"; "we" and "our" now meant whites. The first-person plural continued to run through Rosenwald's speech, as he declared, "We can either give our colored population the right and the opportunity to do the best work of which it is capable and increase our efficiency, or we can deny them their rights and opportunities, as we have done in [so] many instances, and decrease our efficiency."[28]

JR then described what he had seen in France, noting that he had had the "privilege . . . to visit colored troops in France during hostilities." He witnessed the exemplary actions of these "gallant warriors."

> There is no question that the Negro has given a splendid account of himself both as an exceptionally fearless fighting man and as a member of non-combatant troops. . . . It is much easier for a man to become lax in his conduct there [behind the lines] than in actual fighting. Without exception every officer I questioned stated he could not ask for . . . more obedient, willing, harder working or more patriotic troops than the Negro regiments had proven themselves to be. Every account I have read . . . and every case in which I had the opportunity to inquire personally . . . led me to believe our colored men were as good soldiers as could be found in either our own army or the armies of our allies, regardless of color.

He also documented the service "rendered by colored persons in civil life both in doing war work and in the purchase of Liberty Bonds and War Savings Stamps."

After reciting these accomplishments and lauding their good behavior on the battlefields, in the army bases, and on the home front, Rosenwald chided the white population for "asking the impossible of the colored man and the colored woman." He pointed out that "we have demanded that they be honest, self-respecting citizens, and at the same time we have forced them into surroundings which . . . make this result almost impossible. In many places they are deprived of a fair opportunity to obtain education or amusement in a decent environment. Only the most menial positions are offered them. An educated girl particularly has practically no opportunity to earn a livelihood in the manner for which her education fits her." He informed them of the structural discrimination African Americans endured, pointing out that labor unions refused to admit them, and that "the north is especially neglectful in not providing openings for the colored men in trades." "*We, therefore must help the Negro to rise*" (emphasis in the original), he admonished his white audience. Whites, and he included himself, had a responsibility to ensure that African Americans "be rewarded with an equal chance with the white man to climb as high in the industrial and professional world as their individual capacity warrants."

RACIAL PROGRESS THROUGH BUSINESS

Rosenwald's support for black businesses offered him another way he hoped to help African Americans overcome racism. Rosenwald, a businessman who had achieved enormous success, could see how entrepreneurs helped shape collective economic mobility. He celebrated the beneficence of American capitalism and embraced opportunities to invest in black businesses.

But help to stimulate business, as in his other endeavors, did not mean charity. Entrepreneurs always turned to one another for start-up capital and expansion funds. Richard Sears had sought out Aaron Nusbaum to capitalize his company; he, JR, had to turn to his father and his cousin to buy into Nusbaum's scheme; and later on he turned to Henry Goldman for a loan. For Rosenwald, extending credit to black business ventures and giving advice on best commercial practices made sense. He realized, though, that African Americans had nearly no access to bank loans, and few individuals in their own communities had enough capital to launch new ventures. Most lacked family or kinship credit networks, all of which made it nearly impossible for them to get ahead through business. So when he learned about black businesses in need, Rosenwald would step in. His interest in fostering African American businesses conformed with Booker T. Washington's agenda and dovetailed neatly with his own belief in the positive value of commerce and the ability of people of humble means to become rich through capitalism. Washington had launched Tuskegee with the hope that its graduates would become the South's best carpenters, masons, and the like, and that by the excellence of their crafts they would be able to set up businesses that would allow them to become self-supporting, no longer dependent upon planters who owned their labor. With training, they could sell their products and services at a good price and raise their standard of living, liberating themselves from the hopeless cycle of tenancy, sharecropping, and debt peonage which most endured.

Washington helped form the National Negro Business League in 1901, before he met Rosenwald. Later Rosenwald provided the bulk of the funds to sustain its work. The league would, Washington envisioned, "promote the commercial and financial development of the Negro." This resonated with Rosenwald, who considered matters economic fundamental to social realities. Black business ownership could, in the Washington formula endorsed by Rosenwald, bring about a new emancipation.

Take the matter of Mound Bayou, Mississippi, a black enterprise that engaged both Washington and Rosenwald. Begun before the Civil War by Joseph E. Davis, the brother of Jefferson Davis, the future president of the Confederacy, it was envisioned as a model plantation, nearly utopian, to be based on the writings of Robert Owen, the Scottish reformer and founder of the cooperative movement. There the slaves would receive excellent nutrition and medical care. Some could become merchants. At the end of the war, Davis sold the land to Benjamin Montgomery, a former slave and town shopkeeper, who renamed it Davis Bend, and it functioned for a time as an autonomous black community.

Davis Bend failed during a serious agricultural depression, but Montgomery's son Isaiah established a new community in 1887, Mound Bayou, carved out of undeveloped Delta bottomlands in northwestern Mississippi. By 1900, black farmers constituted more than half of Mound Bayou's landowners, an unprecedented statistic. Community leaders, spearheaded by Charles Banks, a successful African American entrepreneur from Clarksdale, Mississippi, and associate of Washington, decided that the town should diversify its economic base as a hedge against the ups and downs of cotton prices. In 1911, Banks conceived the Mound Bayou Cotton Oil Mill, which he wagered might provide cotton farmers with a different way of profiting from their crops, by marketing the plant's oil. But the mill needed more cash than the townspeople could invest.

In stepped Julius Rosenwald after he learned that Andrew Carnegie had refused to help. Isaiah Montgomery met JR in New York in 1912 and sparked his interest in the project. Rosenwald endorsed Mound Bayou and its cotton oil mill, liking the fact that it had secured a huge base of small shareholders, a perfect embodiment of entrepreneurship and community involvement. Mound Bayou families had bought shares costing one dollar each, and the majority of the townspeople invested in it, whether smaller or larger amounts. Montgomery easily convinced JR to buy bonds and also to invest in the local Bank of Mound Bayou. Rosenwald, at Montgomery's suggestion, alone provided the needed capital, making him the only investor from outside the small tight-knit community.

Rosenwald saw his investment as having two advantages.

It would benefit black people and, since only he from the out-side had invested in the project, he expected to reap a nice profit. He did not consider such goals incompatible. Rather, they complemented each other. But the Mound Bayou Cotton Oil Mill and the Bank of Mound Bayou failed dismally in 1915. Local white bankers and landowners helped hasten their demise, and another economic depression ravaged the South. Additionally, infighting within Mound Bayou's African American leadership and between them and Washington weakened the enterprise. As a business venture in which Rosenwald had expected to make money, it could not have been a more disastrous failure. But it demonstrated his belief in business and his hope that capitalism would help black Americans achieve economic independence and wealth, potent weapons in the struggle for a different kind of America. Despite Mound Bayou's failure, he repeatedly assisted black entrepreneurs, individuals who asked for help to start or sustain businesses, as he had done for Herman Perry and his Atlanta insurance company.

THE URBAN LEAGUE AND THE NAACP

Rosenwald's view of the world through an economic lens makes it unsurprising that of the two enduring organizations founded in the early twentieth century dedicated to altering race relations, the Urban League and the NAACP, he leaned toward the former, formally the League on Urban Conditions Among Negroes, founded in New York in 1910, rather than toward the National Association for the Advancement of Colored People, established a year earlier. The Urban League brought together three existing young organizations, all tied to Booker T. Washington. They included the National League for the Protection of Colored Women (established in 1905), the Committee for Improving the Industrial Conditions of Negroes in New York (1906), and the Committee on Urban Conditions Among Negroes (1910). Chicagoans organized their Urban League branch in 1915, and Rosenwald supported both the national and the local organization, not only because they carried Washington's blessing but also because they conformed to his bias toward solving social problems through economic means.

The league focused on expanding economic opportunities for black people, particularly the masses who in the early twentieth century streamed out of the rural South, converging in northern cities in search of a livelihood. In good Progressive style, the league investigated the labor conditions awaiting the migrants and explored potential opportunities for them. The league trained women and men to help address the "industrial, economic, social and spiritual conditions among Negroes." An elastic and flexible project, the Urban League identified securing well-paying jobs, fostering the migrants' economic advancement, and smoothing out conflicts between black and white laborers as its goals. It tried to connect local employers with the migrants from the South, encouraging them to hire African Americans, at the same time that the League sought ways to soothe the seething resentment of white laborers, many of whom viewed the newcomers as threatening. Black workers often got their first factory jobs as strikebreakers, which hardly helped ease tensions, and the Urban League sought to calm unrest while also securing jobs for black men and women. White workers, mostly immigrants, generally considered their whiteness a symbol of superiority, further poisoning the toxic atmosphere in cities like Chicago.[29]

The Urban League attracted Jewish donors and activists from the start, and when Rosenwald lent his name and money to it he was joining many co-religionists. Paul Sachs, who had steered him to Washington and Tuskegee, also connected him with the newly formed league. Jews alone did not sustain the Urban League; the national organization's single largest contributor, John D. Rockefeller, donated about three thousand dollars a year. Rosenwald, the second-largest donor, contributed approximately two thousand annually. After the founding of the Chicago branch, JR began concentrating on the local organization. In Chicago, though other Jews and white gentiles gave generously, JR ranked as the league's biggest supporter. He agreed to provide a hundred dollars for every two dollars raised by the branch, and in its first years he provided one-third of its operating budget. As contributions from others, mostly local African Americans, both individuals and associations, flowed into the league's treasury, its staff members, particularly T. Arnold Hill, the executive director as of 1917, reported regularly to Rosenwald, telling him, down to the last dollar, how much had been raised. Hill thanked JR for his support in 1918, writing, "We all feel that, but for your countenance and help, the substantial service our League has been able to render to our colored fellow-citizens would have been quite impossible." He meant what he said.[30]

Although Rosenwald distinguished between the Urban League, whose work he considered practical and likely to yield measurable results, and the NAACP, which tackled broader, more political issues, focused particularly on securing equal rights through legal challenges to segregation, he belonged to the Chicago branches of both organizations. In the 1920s Rosenwald and his son-in-law Edgar Stern tried to broker a merger of the NAACP and the Urban League because, as in business, he abhorred duplication of efforts. He considered that the organizations' goals overlapped. That he perceived similarity rather than difference in the two reveals much about him. Both associations, he believed, hoped to obliterate inequality based on color. How they attacked the problem mattered less to him than their shared aims.

As Rosenwald and Stern pursued their campaign to fold the two into a unified body, they also hoped that the bigger, combined organization would be headed not by Eugene

Kinckle Jones, the executive director of the national Urban League, but by James Weldon Johnson, the executive secretary and de facto chief officer of the NAACP. Both southern-born black men had earned good college educations, but Rosenwald considered Johnson best suited to helm the enlarged organization he hoped to bring about. Ironically, Johnson might have appeared likely to be less attractive to Rosenwald than Jones. An author, poet, musician, and leading light of the Harlem Renaissance, Johnson favored a highly political agenda vis-à-vis the needs of black Americans, advocating for anti-lynching legislation and supporting the NAACP's legal campaign against disenfranchisement. Jones, whom JR hoped to push out, fit more closely the Washingtonian model. Trained first in engineering and then sociology, he knew the world of black education and social work and had written a master's thesis which examined "the evidence of progress of the American Negro since emancipation." In his thesis and his public activities Jones asserted and held the view that while much work still needed to be done for black Americans, progress had been made, and change would come through economic advancement.

The merger never happened, despite Rosenwald and Stern's lobbying, demonstrating that large sums of money did not always put the power into the hands of the largest donor. But although Rosenwald withdrew his active support of the Urban League after his defeat, the other Jewish activists did not leave with him. Jews continued to provide a substantial portion of the board membership, including the new rabbi of the Sinai Congregation, Louis I. Mann, who had replaced Emil Hirsch, and they continued to make up much of the donor base.

Rosenwald's early close association with the Urban League overshadowed his significant involvement with the NAACP. He contributed money to that organization as well, benefiting both the national office and the Chicago branch. His comparatively modest gifts represented sporadic rather than systematic support, but most years he found some cause taken up by the association that caught his attention and that he contributed to. In 1910 he provided funds for an early NAACP court case, that of Pink Franklin, a black man accused of killing a white constable in Orangeburg, South Carolina. He underwrote and helped arrange the association's 1912 meeting, held at the Sinai Congregation, putting up half the money to cover expenses. He spoke at that convention, as did Du Bois, and the Rosenwald Fund, during JR's lifetime, helped underwrite Du Bois's work, making possible the publication of the *Crisis*, the NAACP magazine, which Du Bois edited. In 1913 Rosenwald paid most of the costs associated with an NAACP pageant in Chicago to mark the jubilee of the Emancipation Proclamation.

Just as Zionists sought out his wealth and the power of his name, so too the NAACP showered him with information about its activities, bluntly detailing its poor financial situation and appealing for help. In 1923, Johnson, in one of a stream of missives to JR, cataloged the association's important work, and without subtlety listed the Jews who supported it. He pointed out to Rosenwald, who had been consumed with the Leo Frank case, that the NAACP had just scored a great success in the U.S. Supreme Court case, *Moore v. Dempsey*, which ruled that an Arkansas court must grant a retrial to a group of African American defendants because of the highly prejudicial nature of their original trial. Because of the NAACP's actions, Johnson declared, the court had "laid down a principle which . . . might have saved Leo Frank from being lynched."[31] Such appeals did not fall on deaf ears. When in 1928 Edwin Embree, the Fund's president, Rosenwald's guide to giving, and his confidant, recommended in a written report that money be earmarked for the NAACP and its "great work" in the field of "legal defense in order to prevent the hardening of injustice into custom," JR scrawled a note on the margin, "If you recommend it—you may write that I will cont. $1000 for this year."[32]

Though the amount hardly equaled what he gave to other African American projects, he could not be considered an enemy of the NAACP or an opponent of its assertive, politically oriented strategy. In 1914 he commented, "There is no doubt in my mind that the work [of the NAACP] is doing extremely valuable" service, but "other phases of service for individuals of that race are of greater personal interest to me."[33]

THE RED SUMMER OF 1919

In nearly all his endeavors, Rosenwald did not initiate projects, but when asked to donate his money, his time, or his name to matters that concerned him, he did so with dedication. Standing back when he saw something wrong, letting others act when he had the power to do so, or declaring himself too busy did not fit the Rosenwald style.

The events which gripped Chicago in the summer of 1919 provided such an opportunity for JR to demonstrate his proclivity for action and use his resources to take on ugly realities at home. During that summer, specifically on July 27, an oppressively hot day, a black teenager, Eugene Williams, accidentally swam over to the de facto whites-only beach on the shores of Lake Michigan. An outraged white gang hurled rocks at him, killing him. A police officer nearby refused to arrest the assailants, instead arresting a black man in the vicinity.

This event sparked a riot that lasted five days and resulted in thirty-eight deaths, mostly of black people. The riot caused a great deal of property destruction and the press reported hundreds of bodily injuries. Bands of young white men roamed the city, pulling African Americans off streetcars and beating them, some to death, while African Americans, some returned soldiers transformed by wartime service, responded in kind, refusing to passively accept the violence.

Chicago's racial conflagration coincided with increasing racial animus, national in scope, with race battles flaring in over three dozen cities. In Chicago as elsewhere, a single event, like the tragic death of Eugene Williams, catalyzed into widespread mayhem. But deep seething tensions generated by the panic felt by whites at the great black migration, which brought the threat of labor competition at a time of postwar unemployment, along with allegations of Bolshevik and other radical activity and the racism embedded in American life, underlay the the frenzy. The police often collaborated with the white rioters, and the white press presented sensationalistic accounts of crime, labeling perpetrators as black.

The Chicago fires had barely subsided when the Illinois governor, Frank Lowden, approached Rosenwald to join a commission to investigate the riot's underlying causes. Despite juggling multiple demands, JR did not hesitate for a moment. He suggested names of black community leaders to serve as members of the Chicago Commission on Race Relations and enlisted Graham Romyn Taylor, son of the Progressive reformer Graham Taylor of the Chicago Commons, to chair it. Rosenwald demanded that African American activists play a key role, particularly in the fact-finding phase of the commission's work, in the preparation of the report, and in the framing of recommendations. He made sure that T. Arnold Hill of the Chicago Urban League occupied a central position, and personally recruited Charles S. Johnson to the commission. An African American sociologist and holder of a doctorate from the University of Chicago, whose education JR had helped finance, Johnson later became president of Fisk University and produced such crucial scholarly works as *Shadow of the Plantation*, *Growing Up in the Black Belt*, and *The Collapse of Cotton Tenancy*. Johnson wrote the report based on the commission's findings. Published by the University of Chicago Press, *The Negro in Chicago: A Study of Race Relations and a Race Riot* became the gold standard of early-twentieth-century writing about race relations in an American city.

Rosenwald actively served on one of the commission's six committees, on housing and public opinion, and attended meetings of the racial contacts committee. He sat on the executive committee and, not coincidentally, provided its financing, giving more than any other who contributed money to make possible the commission's work. Although he realized that the governor had little real interest in the work of the commission or indeed of the situation of blacks in Chicago, JR continued to urge on the project, despite official apathy, hoping to advance its mission of understanding why the violence had broken out and thinking of ways to prevent future tragedies. While the latter goal clearly failed, the commission's vision represented an important stage in political engagement on the issue of race, particularly by social scientists, who would recognize race as their central concern by the mid-twentieth century.

In the early years of the century, as Rosenwald worked at his many projects focused on African Americans, and in later years, when scholars looked back at them, his commitment to this cause inspired much discussion. Why, people asked, should Rosenwald have elevated the concerns of black people above nearly all other social issues? Why did he define as personally important the needs—educational, medical, recreational, and economic—of the one-tenth of the nation whom white Americans viewed as less worthy by virtue of their color?

Rosenwald's involvement with African American causes could be seen as a steady march from early small gifts to bigger, broader, and more systematic contributions. Over the years, his expenditures of money, time, and influence for and with African Americans touched nearly every aspect of his public life. In time his engagements became less attempts at uplift and more based on partnerships seeking fundamental societal change. In the same way, over the decades of Rosenwald's involvement with the black YMCAs, the Urban League, the NAACP, and black colleges and elementary schools, he came to redefine the appropriate role for the state. His initial focus on serving individuals shifted toward the need for collective, governmental action.

JR AND THE AMERICAN WAY OF LIFE

The history of Rosenwald's involvement in African American affairs cannot sidestep several deep and problematic issues. In nearly all his work he accepted the reality of segregation. He financed Jim Crow elementary schools, Jim Crow YMCAs, Jim Crow hospitals, and Jim Crow colleges and universities. He assumed that the black doctors, lawyers, teachers, social workers, and librarians, women and men whose education he facilitated, would serve black people in a well-funded racially segregated universe of institutions and services. Rosenwald's initiatives embodied the idea of separate but equal, emphasizing the importance of equality, but never suggesting integration. In 1928, for example, impressed by model housing projects he saw in Germany and Austria, he initiated with a gift of $2.7 million the Michigan Boulevard Apartments, a housing complex for black Chicagoans. Built around leafy gardens resembling the quadrangles of the University of Chicago, the "Rosenwalds," as residents called the apartments, boasted supervised playgrounds, meeting rooms, nursery schools, heating, access to nearby shopping, and commodious kitchens equipped with up-to-date appliances. But only African Americans would live there. JR never suggested putting his money toward a model housing project based on integrated living.

With a few exceptions, which became more frequent as his contacts and commitments among African Americans grew, he did not speak out against the durability with which segregation had been woven into the fabric of the American way of life. He supported undertakings in which segregation existed as an undisputed given. He happily gave money to institutions like

Chicago's Frederick Douglass Center that served black people exclusively, congratulating its founder, Celia Parker Wooley, on the fact that "the colored people subscribed" some of the funding for the facility only they would use, which kept them away from the city's white settlement houses, to which he also contributed generously.[34] So too in the last year of his life, Rosenwald donated money to buy land in Chicago's "Black Belt" for a public library. The George Cleveland Hall branch of the Chicago public library, named for a pioneering African American surgeon, whom JR also aided in his work, would serve African Americans. Hall and Vivian Harsh, Chicago's first African American librarian, approached JR with a proposal that he fund a library for black residents. He agreed with enthusiasm, but he never suggested that the city hire Harsh or future black library professionals to serve in the city's "white" libraries. He did not propose that the Special Negro Collection which Harsh organized be placed in an integrated facility, that perhaps it belonged in the central library on Michigan Avenue. It would be situated in the Hall branch, in the African American neighborhood where whites would most likely never venture. JR accepted the reality that black readers would go to this library, and white readers would go elsewhere. In 1929 he announced that he would give money to county libraries in the South, which meant whites-only libraries, but only if "equal service be given to all people of the county (rural and urban, negro and white) and that the services be adapted to the needs of each group."[35]

Some African Americans in Rosenwald's day mobilized their political resources around issues far broader than poverty and educational inequality, and with the exception of the NAACP, Rosenwald did not join them. No record exists that he said or did anything about lynching, either by donating money to advance the work of Jessie Daniels Ames or Chicago's Ida Wells Barnett and their anti-lynching crusades or by exerting political pressure for government action. He could have lobbied for the Dyer Anti-Lynching Bill of 1922, but he did not. He focused relatively little attention on the legal system's vast inequities, although at various times, when asked to help in a specific campaign, he took out his checkbook. Rosenwald expressed "pleasure" in making a contribution in response to attorney Clarence Darrow's request in 1916 that he cover the court costs of Isaac Bond, a black man convicted of rape and murder in Oklahoma. But for the most part he used neither his money nor his clout to aid in such matters.[36]

He also expended no energy on efforts, mostly undertaken by the NAACP, to secure voting rights for African Americans. During his lifetime the association had begun to tackle the ubiquitous denial of black voting rights in the South, securing one of its first victories in 1915 when it successfully argued in front of the United States Supreme Court the case of *Guinn v. United States*, in which the court struck down key elements of Louisiana's "grandfather clause." JR did nothing to make this triumph possible.

He did at times lend his voice to political matters germane to African Americans. In 1915 he led a successful movement in Chicago to persuade city officials to ban the release there of D. W. Griffiths's incendiary and unabashedly racist film *The Birth of a Nation*. JR warned Mayor William "Big Bill" Thompson that allowing it to be seen "would only do harm."[37] But his vast philanthropic enterprise for African Americans usually skirted civil rights and the pursuit of political justice, focusing instead on economic opportunities, perhaps understandable in someone who saw his own status and good fortune, and that of his family and his peers, facilitated by economic means.

It had been the possibility of making a living that had drawn the Rosenwalds, and most European Jews, to America. The success of these migrants through business, peddling, retail and wholesale clothing sales, and manufacturing, facilitated by intra-Jewish networks and their white skin, paved the path for their integration into American society. For someone who had spent his entire life behind a cash register, literally and figuratively, it made sense to consider economic success a civic escalator. How, he must have asked himself from his first meetings with Booker T. Washington in the 1910s until his death, could he use his life's lessons to help promote economic justice for African Americans?

His actions, in particular the schools project, seemed to show an endorsement of the black-white divide, a willingness to underwrite a system in which white children went to their schools and African Americans to theirs. Snippets from his writings, random references that popped up in speeches or notes scrawled by hand, however, offer the possibility that he did envision an integrated future. In 1929 he approved a request for funding from a Charleston museum because it "has opened the Museum to Negroes."[38] Providing scholarships for African American graduate and professional students to attend all-white universities, and leaning on administrators to admit them, also indicated that he might have envisioned a future beyond segregation.

But most of his philanthropic money flowed to schools and other institutions for black people. Rosenwald believed that in such institutions African Americans as individual members of a "race" would not be stuck forever at the bottom. He considered progress for African Americans a real likelihood, but achievable in a segregated context. Optimistic always, he thought improvement inevitable, but contingent on bold present action, and he appointed himself a leader in such action. He never claimed that he did it alone, but he confidently assumed the challenge of leadership. He did not despise other approaches, but he would not give as amply or open-handedly to strategies he deemed inadequate or unrealistic. While he did not hesitate to speak for black people, he did so only when he or his black mentors like Booker T. Washington considered that the voice of a rich white man would get a wider hearing than theirs. He never claimed a monopoly in representing blacks, as witnessed by his underwriting Du Bois's editorship of the *Crisis*, but when it seemed to JR that a white person had a better chance of delivering a particular message, he did so.

His rosy view on most subjects and his belief in the future improvement of the situation of African Americans and Jews rested on a basic assumption that prejudiced people could change their views. White people like himself had a responsibility to ensure that African Americans had the chance to prove their mettle. JR did much of his speaking about African American concerns to whites, pointing out that they too had a stake in helping blacks. Writing in 1930 to J. M. T. Finney, a white doctor who ran Baltimore's Provident Hospital, a black institution, Rosenwald noted: "If colored doctors and nurses are to have the teaching and stimulus which will enable them to reach high standards, white physicians must encourage them by counsel and service: white citizens must help if adequate funds are to be provided for Negro hospitals and health. And it is well to remember that germs recognize no color line and that disease in one group threatens the health of all."[39]

Rosenwald rejoiced when he discerned what seemed to be signs of progress. In his remarks to the 1912 NAACP annual meeting, he commented that amid all the speeches detailing "the struggles and the hardships and the abuses that the colored people of the North and South have to suffer," he found hopeful and notable that Chicago's white newspapers had lavished extensive, positive coverage on the association and its "demand that the colored people have their rights and be given better treatment." That the *Chicago Tribune* and the *Record-Herald*, among others, "have outdone themselves in their liberality and demand for the rights of the colored man," he asserted, warranted optimism.[40] In 1917 he embraced an idea brought to him by Emmett Scott to finance a film that would be a rejoinder to the massively successful *Birth of a Nation*. *The Birth of a Race*, produced by Scott himself, would tell the story of Booker T. Washington and in the process undermine images of black people as wild, brutish beasts, bent on raping white women. Rosenwald loved the idea of a "photoplay designed to help remove misunderstanding between the White and Colored races, to make for more sympathetic and helpful relationships, and to show the best of both races rather than the worst of either." Washington's *Up from Slavery* had so inspired him that he assumed that a film adaptation of it would do the same for the American public. The film, however, proved to be an artistic and financial disaster, but it revealed Rosenwald's commitment to presenting the public with positive images so as to undermine the prejudices which dominated.[41]

GIVING AS A JEW

What made Julius Rosenwald's support of blacks a specifically Jewish action? How does JR's extensive public involvement with the conditions of black Americans constitute an aspect of his life as a Jew? These questions extend beyond Rosenwald and his philanthropy. From the early twentieth century on, individual American Jews, many, like Rosenwald, sons and daughters of mid-nineteenth-century central European immigrants, participated in efforts to overthrow America's racial system. As individuals, many Jews hoped to transform America, as they understood it, into a place which did not assign privileges or liabilities to people based on skin color. Similarly, a striking number of more recent Jewish immigrants from eastern Europe and their children also involved themselves in projects challenging America's racial system.

Of the many early-twentieth-century American Jews who attended to African American affairs, though, none engaged

with them as dramatically as Julius Rosenwald. No revolution-
ary or radical, Rosenwald enjoyed his wealth, believing in the
nation's basic goodness. How could he not? It had benefited
him and his peers greatly. Yet he, like many of them, many
prominent American Jews, expressed self-consciousness about
their place in America, ever nervous that their American
hosts merely tolerated them as guests in the Christian nation.
Whether correctly or not, they feared that the United States
could at any moment reject them. Yet they marshaled their political and economic clout to champion the nation's most despised and disadvantaged people, among other causes.

Such advocacy could easily have backfired. The willingness
of these immigrants and their children to question the American system could have harmed them all. Silence might have
served them better, and they might logically have concluded
that active endorsement of the racial system would win them
American friends. Yet many of these Jews, with Rosenwald
leading the way, stepped forward and did what they considered
right and necessary for and with African Americans.

Jews participated in the effort to create a society that recognized individuals rather than groups. Such efforts grew out
of their desire to validate Judaism, particularly as interpreted
by liberal Jews, and to undermine prevalent images of Jews as
self-serving. It allowed them to claim the mantle of cultural
citizenship, articulated by a group of people who understood
their past and present as shaped by racial hatred and who did
not wish to see others suffer from that same hatred.

Rosenwald's actions and words, echoing those of many
Jews, articulated in their newspapers and by the leaders of their
many organizations, reflected a belief that as a Jew he had a
particular obligation to assist another despised people. Louis
Marshall, JR's associate in the world of organized Jewry, addressed the 1926 annual meeting of the NAACP, on whose
board he sat, as a Jew, a member of "an ancient race which has

had even longer experience of oppression than you have. We came out of bondage nearly thirty centuries ago and we have had trouble ever since."[42]

Beyond showing empathy, Jews' words and actions allowed them to tell white Christian America that they had no monopoly on either American culture or acts of loving-kindness, in Hebrew, *gemillut hasadim*. The *Yiddishe Tageblatt*, an Orthodox newspaper that JR probably never read, expressed his sentiments and those of his cohort when it editorialized in 1917 after the race riot in East Saint Louis, Illinois, and the NAACP's protest march down New York City's Fifth Avenue, "A Jewish heart is more moved by reading the banners which were carried in the East St. Louis Silent Protest, thinking about the injustices being done. . . . Who but a Jew can taste oppression?" These words reflected the norm of American Jewish public discourse on the matter of race and the plight of black people, whether articulated in English or Yiddish.[43]

However explained, Jewish support for black America functioned as a leitmotif of American Jewish life in the early and mid-twentieth century. Jews encountered one another at board meetings, gatherings of donors and supporters, and public events sponsored by Tuskegee, the NAACP, the Urban League, and others. When JR went to Tuskegee he filled his train car with Jewish activists, some wealthy, some not, who he believed had something to learn from the trip or something to contribute. Alexander Dushkin recalled that JR, whom he tried in vain to recruit to Jewish nationalism, brought him along on a trip to Tuskegee for Founders Day. Dushkin, an educator of modest means but interested in youth, education, and minority groups in American society, used the journey to continue cultivating Rosenwald for the Zionist cause. Dushkin invited Rosenwald to his family's upcoming Passover Seder, which "he gladly accepted." The trip to Alabama resounded with the cadences of Jewish culture and politics. So too the many events held at Sinai which brought African American speakers and organizations into the building forged a close bond between the public programs of American Jewish life and the concerns of African Americans. Whenever Rosenwald operated in the world of African American causes he engaged with other Jews, making his work on this issue integral to his life as a Jew, blurring the lines between Jewish and black activism.[44]

Discussions about Rosenwald's African American benefactions emphasized his Jewishness. Those who disliked his actions seized on it, regardless of their particular reason for attacking his work. African Americans who resented Rosenwald's acceptance of segregation, for example, linked that acceptance to his Jewishness. "Why has not Mr. Rosenwald," asked a group of African American doctors in 1931, "established a Jewish medical school for . . . Jewish candidates?"[45] A writer for Pittsburgh's African American newspaper the *Courier* sneered at Rosenwald's medical donations, calling him a "Semitic Santa Claus" who gave "alms not opportunity."[46] Cleveland's African American paper, the *Gazette*, headlined an article, "'Jim Crow' Y.M.C.A. Dedicated . . . Wealthy Jew Gives Money to Aid Establishment of the Color Line," sneering at "the idea of removing race hatred by establishing an institution which draws the color line! How can it be done? The trouble today is that the races are getting further and further apart. Race hatred can only be removed by free racial intermingling in religion as well as business."[47]

Southern whites condemning Rosenwald's work with African Americans also focused on his Jewishness, following the path laid down by Henry Ford in 1923 when he claimed in the *Dearborn Independent* that Rosenwald personally had encouraged the black migration to Chicago and that "Jewish men of wealth" like Rosenwald did so to make a profit both by selling the unsuspecting migrants property and supporting gambling enterprises. Opponents of the schools project alleged that his Jewish background had inspired him to threaten their region. [48]

Jews who derided Rosenwald's choices of Jewish causes, particularly his refusal to endorse Zionism, pointed to his active support of black causes as evidence of his being, put bluntly, a bad Jew. How, they asked, could he champion African Americans but be impervious to the Jews' most basic need, a homeland? Louis Ginzberg, a Talmudist at the Jewish Theological Seminary and an active Zionist, commented on this in 1920 in a letter to Emanuel Neumann, then education director of the Zionist Organization of America. As the two worked on a fundraising campaign for the recently opened Hebrew University in Jerusalem, Ginzberg wrote, "I hear that a rich Jew in Chicago has given a considerable donation in favor of a negroe [*sic*] university." How, he asked Neumann, might the movement "persuade persons that our University will not be much worse than a negroe one"?[49]

Jews who wrote to and about Rosenwald, however, usually expressed excitement and pride in his work, lauding him as Jews for his efforts as a Jew on behalf of African Americans. This too bothered Zionists. The literary critic and Zionist Ludwig Lewisohn deprecated the many accolades Rosenwald garnered among Jews for his work with black people. Lewisohn dismissed JR and his Jewish admirers as assimilated, a pejorative term, denouncing JR's activism for black causes as a surrogate for genuine Jewish loyalty. In a 1925 polemic, he charged that despite distancing themselves from authentic Jewish matters, these Jews hid behind the fact that "Mr. Rosenwald of Chicago has given another magnificent contribution to negro education. These not very Jewish Jews," Lewisohn declared, who celebrated Rosenwald's donations to black causes and expressed pride as Jews in his generosity, did so for bad reasons, and did so without committing to real Jewishness and "the integrity of Israel."[50]

Lewisohn aside, Jews who commented on Rosenwald considered his public activism honorable, important, humane, and "good for the Jews. " Such language ranged widely, whether coming from individuals who wrote to JR or the Jewish press in English or Yiddish. As the *B'nai B'rith Messenger* put it in 1928, "In Mr. Rosenwald's serving the stranger we see the performance of the highest mission of the Jew. The mission of the Jew is to contribute to mankind out of his idealism and enrich the world with his age-old experience as a civilized human being—to serve at the common altar." While the magazine writer could not have been more wrong in labeling African Americans "the stranger" in America, such rhetoric pervaded American Jewish life. One Jewish publication judged Rosenwald "the greatest friend the negro has had since Abraham Lincoln," while yet another, in an obituary, suggested that "in a world that despised the Negro he was his generous protector." Rabbi Louis Mann, at Rosenwald's funeral, encapsulated Jews' understanding of the Jewish roots of this work: "By helping the Negro, Rosenwald was motivated both intellectually and emotionally. . . . Rosenwald's devotion to the cause of uplifting the Negro was, in the light of . . . emotional motivation, one of the most intensely Jewish things that Rosenwald ever did. . . . His passionate interest in helping the black man was a practical application of Hillel's golden rule and an ethical paraphrasing of 'remember the stranger for ye, too, were strangers.'" A white man who accepted the burden of the black man! A Jew who built Young Men's Christian Associations![51] Mann, like most Jews, saw in JR's mighty efforts to address the dire situation faced by African Americans Jewish work, pure and simple.

Though rarely explaining himself, Rosenwald did link his Jewish life with his public life on behalf of black Americans. "As an American and as [a] Jew," he once said, as he mused about his vision, "I appeal to all high-minded men and women to join in a relentless crusade against race prejudice, indulgence in which will result in the blotting out of the highest ideals of our proud nation."[52] He made here a claim about his goals for

America and his understanding of racial hatred toward both his groups.

African Americans, at least those whose words endure, rarely failed to connect his Jewishness with his advocacy for them when they expressed their appreciation of his actions. Horace Mann Bond, the prominent African American educator and a former agent for the Rosenwald schools project, wrote a seminal history of African American education. When introducing Rosenwald and the Rosenwald Fund in his narrative, he pointed in several places to the fact of his being a Jew.[53] Booker T. Washington repeatedly described his Chicago benefactor as "that Jew who gave so much."[54]

The YMCA gift announcement had aroused robust commentary, and black communal figures made much of the religious and racial implications of a Jew supporting an organization with Christian evangelical roots that served black people. Jesse Moorland, executive secretary of the Washington, D.C., black YMCA and founder of the Negro-Americana Museum and Library at Howard University, to which Rosenwald contributed, mused, "I doubt if there is any single gift to any public institution that has brought a greater return to the community than this one single benefaction, which is all the more interesting because it is the gift of a Jew to a Christian religious institution."[55]

African Americans' references to other white philanthropists, supporters of their institutions and endeavors, ignored their benefactors' religion or ethnicity. Andrew Carnegie's birth in Scotland and his Presbyterianism, John D. Rockefeller's devotion to the Baptist denomination, and the German origins of the father of the NAACP founder Oswald Garrison Villard generated no commentary. But reference to Rosenwald's Jewishness ran throughout their discussions. Read in this context, African Americans saw JR as not just another rich white man who helped them. They saw him as a Jew.

PARALLEL VISIONS

How Rosenwald directed black Americans to use his money deviated little from his instructions to Jewish beneficiaries. He required both to match his gifts with contributions from other donors. He insisted that institutions promote efficiency, cost management, and strict financial procedures. He urged agencies, black or Jewish, to consider merging to avoid duplication, and favored practical programs which united different constituencies. He encouraged both black and Jewish recipients to partner with him by contributing to their own causes, and held up the ideal of intra-group harmony, something he believed strengthened them as they faced the outside, hostile world.

He believed that for both blacks and Jews to defuse prejudice they had to comport themselves well. Just as black migrants to Chicago ought to join the YMCA for its clean and wholesome recreation, abjuring street-corner life, so too Jews needed to remember that their enemies always tracked them, ready to expose bad behavior. When he counseled Jewish college students to behave well on campus, he asserted that anti-Semitism existed everywhere. Even when dormant it could awaken. To a Jewish correspondent interested in his opinions on Jews in politics, JR wrote, "I am not in the least anxious to see many Jews in politics or even on the bench." Such prominence carried danger.[56] His investment of millions of dollars in Jewish farms in the Soviet Union followed a script similar to that of his myriad undertakings for southern blacks. Jews had to abandon their old ways to quench old hatreds. Jews had to show hostile non-Jews that they too could get their hands in the soil, a companion to his vision that blacks in the South, by developing their skills, achieving literacy, and learning economic independence, would dissipate prejudice.

His reluctance to join the Zionists, despite the avalanche of appeals, paralleled his lack of support for militant activism among American blacks who advocated a full-on assault on segregation. Both movements, as he saw it, raced too far, too fast, ignoring reality. How, he asked both, could Jews and African Americans make the best of the problematic realities they faced? How could they foster greater equality of circumstance within anti-Semitic and anti-black worlds? Politics would not wipe out prejudice, but investing in the future would. That would disarm prejudice.

His wife, Augusta, gave a revealing speech in a 1915 address to a biracial audience in Alabama, after the couple's visit to Palestine. Although she spoke for herself she also represented him, revealing much about his vision. She related that when they had been in Palestine, they asked how Jews and Arabs got along. She declared that the people they had met had told them that "solving the problem of harmony between the races" could be accomplished by undermining hatreds. The Jew and the black person, she declared, needed to "radiate the dignity and worth of his work in the world," so that "the defenses of prejudice must fall down before him."[57]

Rosenwald's vision for Jews and blacks, beyond class matters, can be seen in his support of African American cultural work and workers, including scholarly bodies like the Association for Negro Life and History, and his analogous concern for a reinvigoration of Jewish culture in America, perhaps best exemplified by his underwriting of Mordecai Kaplan's *Judaism as a Civilization.* Jews and blacks, as they labored to prove themselves, should not forget their cultural distinctiveness. Rather they should seek expressive ways to combine being American with their unique cultures.

The commonalities between the way Rosenwald conceived of his work for blacks and his work for Jews took place in a universe of difference. However much Jews suffered, they did so outside the borders of the United States. Real, violent hatreds germinated far from America. American Jews, Rosenwald included, worried about and worked for their co-religionists abroad, knowing that they, as Americans, lived in safety. In the United States, Jews reaped the full benefits of citizenship, unlike blacks. Their white skin allowed them, immigrants and their children, to partake of the nation's political, legal, and economic bounty. Despite a pinprick here and there, they could tell their story as a successful one.

In higher education some private schools limited Jews by admissions quotas, yet most excluded black students outright. Some Jews encountered difficulties gaining positions in Wall Street law firms, yet African American job-seekers found nearly all of industry, public service, and retail shuttered. Jews might have been unwelcome at some hotels, but in the buildings of the federal government, the physical edifices embodying the nation, African American women and men used restrooms marked "colored." Jewish men served in World War I, never consigned to segregated units. Booker T. Washington had asked JR to speak to Woodrow Wilson on behalf of America's black people. But the president soon afterward segregated the federal service and dismissed many African American employees from jobs they had long held. That same Woodrow Wilson courageously nominated Louis Brandeis to the U.S. Supreme Court.

No schools segregated Jews, no hospitals refused to care for them, and no states denied them rights of citizenship. Their America did not resemble the one occupied by black people. These differences, like the similarities, motivated Julius Rosenwald. Those differences inspired reams of commentary, offered in the context of his immense contributions.

At his death in 1932 the descant of Rosenwald, the Jew who concerned himself with "the Negro Race," as invoked in a memorial tribute by the educator Nannie H. Burroughs, daughter of a slave mother and founder of the National Association of Colored Women, reached a crescendo. Her sentiments typified the torrent of adulation black Americans offered in memory of "a marvelous and matchless humanitarian." Burroughs called Rosenwald a "prince of humanitarians," carrier of a "blazing torch of world service to . . . Jews and gentiles in every nation and in every race under heaven."[58] James Weldon Johnson in his eulogy delivered at a memorial service in the chapel at Fisk University, a school greatly indebted to Rosenwald, looked back to the YMCA episode. "I do not know," he shared with the mourners, "whether Mr. Rosenwald saw, but I am certain the country never saw the irony of one great Jew rebuking a national Christian organization through the teachings of a greater Jew," Jesus, "in whose name it was established. In the death of Julius Rosenwald the world lost a great citizen. . . . The Negro people of America lost, in addition, a great friend and champion."[59]

W. E. B. Du Bois perhaps should get the final word on Rosenwald, African Americans, Jews, and the nation. No two individuals might have seemed farther apart in their efforts to confront "the problem of the color-line." Du Bois, scholar and activist, urged stridency; Rosenwald, practical businessman with little education, invested mainly in projects championed by Du Bois's rival and antagonist, Booker T. Washington. Yet Du Bois in his moving tribute in the *Crisis* noted, "As a Jew, Julius Rosenwald did not have to be initiated into the methods of race prejudice, and his philanthropic work was a crushing arraignment of the American white Christians."[60]

———◆◆◆———

Forgetting Julius Rosenwald

JULIUS ROSENWALD died on January 6, 1932, at the family's residence in Ravinia. Ill health had plagued him for years. Persistent kidney troubles had prevented him from journeying to the Soviet Union to observe the Jewish farming colonies at first hand. His five children, Lessing, Edith, Adele, Marion, and William, as well as his second wife, Addie, with a few close friends alone attended the simple graveside funeral in Rosehill Cemetery. They buried him under a plaque, as he had wished, that read only, "Julius Rosenwald, 1862–1932." While Jewish, African American, and a variety of other organizations, institutions, and publications marked his passing with memorial meetings, obituaries, tributes, and broadcasts, he forbade either a showy funeral or a granite marker listing his accomplishments.

Those accomplishments, which received praise across America and beyond, told the story of the life of, in the words of a resolution passed by the board of the Jewish Joint Distribution Committee and read over the airwaves of the National Broadcast Corporation, "a great Jew, a distinguished American, a beloved leader." Others speaking about Rosenwald at the memorial gathering sponsored by the Joint, lauded him as "a Jew" who "probably did more for the education and elevation of the Negro race in America than any other single man," someone who acted in "the great tradition of his people." The final words, offered by Paul Baerwald, Rosenwald's co-worker in the Joint, predicted, "His memory will never fade from our minds."[1]

If by "our" Baerwald meant the men and women who had worked with JR on his many projects, stretching from Chicago to the rest of the United States, and on to Poland, Palestine, the Crimea, and Ukraine, his prediction came true. Those who had attended a Rosenwald school, a Rosenwald YMCA, or another institution that came to be known by his name, might have said the same.

For some time after his death, Rosenwald's name was invoked by writers who sought to inspire generosity and goodwill. Irving Melbo, an educator in the Oakland, California, public schools' Department of Instruction and Curriculum, wrote *Our America: A Textbook for Elementary School History and Social Studies*, published in 1937. Full of inspiring examples from American history of courageous and good people of the nation's past, the book acquainted students with individuals who shaped the nation and whose lives demonstrated personal traits that marked their greatness. Melbo devoted a chapter to Rosenwald, "whose work lives on." Yes, Melbo wrote, "Julius Rosenwald made a great deal of money from his business. He became one of the richest men in the United States. But he did not care about money for itself. He was not the selfish kind of businessman" a noteworthy trait while the Depression raged. *Our America*, which by 1948 had gone through four printings, depicted Rosenwald, the boy who grew up "across the street from the home of Abraham Lincoln" in a "Jewish family," as someone who cared deeply about the plight of "the negroes." Melbo created a portrait for young readers of the philanthropist who exhibited such a broad set of concerns, Julius Rosenwald.

Melbo's Rosenwald also acted to aid "the Jewish people in eastern Europe," who during World War I "perhaps suffered more than any other group." The book praised the "great gift" Rosenwald made possible to the "suffering Jews of Europe," which inspired Americans in general to give generously. Because Rosenwald had given so much to Jews, he claimed, he enabled the Red Cross "to raise ten times as much for their work." The Jewish Rosenwald in this book spurred other Americans to do good.[2]

But in fact the name of Julius Rosenwald slipped into obscurity after his death and had all but disappeared by 1948. His name, with the passage of time, elicited little recognition. It may be that it faded in public consciousness because his commercial success derived from an enterprise called Sears, Roebuck, though those two men had long departed the scene. Perhaps Henry Ford's name has never disappeared because Americans drive Ford cars, and Thomas Edison's lived on because their local Consolidated Edison generated their electricity.

The demise of the Rosenwald Fund in 1947, a dissolution based on JR's fierce belief that each generation had to decide how to spend the wealth it inherited, meant that future American artists, intellectuals, writers, and musicians did not apply for a "Rosenwald," or submit applications to a foundation named for him. Guggenheim, Rockefeller, and Ford Foundation grants kept the public conscious of their original donors. No student applied to a university named Rosenwald, unlike the case with Cornell, Stanford, Johns Hopkins, and other universities that made the names of the wealthy individuals who founded them part of the common culture. No hospital, museum, or community center exists which perpetually calls attention to the Rosenwald name. Since these absences reflected his wish, he might perhaps have wanted to be remembered only by his children and friends. His good works lived on after him without his name, and that might have been just fine with him.

But his disappearance from the public consciousness might equally be related to the dramatic way the world changed, undergoing tectonic shifts that coincided with his death, making his vision and his projects seem somewhat beside the point. The world, even in the ten years after 1932, witnessed events of such cataclysmic proportions that new realities overshadowed his accomplishments and called his vision into question.

Julius Rosenwald did not live to see the Depression lead to the New Deal, which utterly transformed the federal government's involvement in the lives of Americans. Rosenwald had opposed labor unions, thinking that benign and good employers, like himself, could best address the needs of workers. But the many brutal and violent labor confrontations of the 1930s, such as the sit-down strikes in the automobile industry and the Memorial Day Massacre in Chicago's steel mills, gave urgency and credence to the union vision. The passage of the National Labor Relations Act of 1935 legitimized that which JR had opposed.

At the same time Americans redefined their relationship to the state, seeing themselves as entitled to protection from the vagaries of the economy. The federal government through its relief programs began to fund directly and indirectly many of the enterprises that generous benefactors had supported in Rosenwald's era. Even Jewish institutions, particularly communal welfare agencies, started to receive government money, primarily through Social Security, established in 1935, which blurred the once rigid line between public and private.

Black Americans, perhaps some of them graduates of Rosenwald schools and products of the colleges and universities he funded, began in the decade after 1932 to escalate their demands for equality. In their vociferousness they eschewed Rosenwald's vision of how to address racial realities. The NAACP emerged in the 1930s and 1940s as the dominant voice in that assault. Inspired by the decision its board enunciated in the Margold Report of 1930, it put its energy into dismantling the proposition that "separate but equal" could ever be equal or acceptable. The vision inherent in the Rosenwald schools, hospitals, housing, and recreational undertakings claimed that it could be, and while the status quo might not persist forever, in the short term, however, individuals with means would better serve by concentrating on providing enhanced facilities so that African Americans could go to school, get good medical care, and find employment opportunities, have use of libraries, and the like. By the time of Rosenwald's death, his African American critics had triumphed, seizing the moment.

African American political action began to focus more directly on fighting discrimination, seeing little virtue in doing so quietly. In the early 1930s the NAACP led the successful campaign to block the Senate confirmation of Judge John J. Parker, a North Carolinian nominated by Herbert Hoover who had disparaged the possibility of African Americans ever voting. And as another index of change, in 1941, when the United States entered World War II, black activists from the labor movement, A. Philip Randolph and Bayard Rustin, threatened a march on Washington in the pursuit of equality in government employment, winning a tremendous victory with FDR's Executive Order 8802, which prohibited racial discrimination in defense work. Rosenwald's solutions to the situation of black America withered in the face of such militance.

Voting rights emerged as a sharp demand in the 1940s, as the NAACP began to challenge discriminatory state practices in a string of court cases. Among the most committed workers for this cause, aiding the NAACP with money and contacts, none did more than Julius Rosenwald's daughter Edith, who along with her husband, Edgar Stern, helped fund and coordinate the civil rights effort in New Orleans, focusing on this issue in particular.

Rosenwald passed from the scene just a year before Adolf Hitler's accession to leadership of the land Rosenwald's parents had left. In the face of that threat, and reflecting the demographic changes of American Jewish life, the Reform movement's acceptance in 1938 of the idea of Palestine as the Jews' homeland redefined the internal political world of Julius Rosenwald's people. Ten years after Rosenwald's death, his son Lessing, named for the German Christian advocate of Jewish emancipation, helped found the American Council for Judaism, an organization of the few Reform Jews who rejected their movement's shift to Zionism.

Julius Rosenwald might also have been grievously disappointed with the realization that after 1933 the United States, the nation he considered so hospitable to the Jews, responded to the threat of Nazism and the Nazis' persecution of the Jews and their desperate search for places of refuge, with little sympathy, offering them no meaningful welcome. In the face of the global crisis, American Jews organized to aid their coreligionists, and among other responses created the United Jewish Appeal for Refugees and Overseas Needs (UJA). A dynamo of fundraising, the UJA collected millions through its relentless campaigns; William Rosenwald, the little boy who had loved the Munich technology museum, served as its first president. He, along with his sisters Adele Rosenwald Levy and Marion Rosenwald Ascoli, who during the war and postwar years chaired the women's division, spent the late 1930s and early 1940s raising money to help the millions of Jews trapped in Nazi-dominated Europe.

They managed to save over three hundred of their own relatives and bring them to America. But like all American Jews, they experienced frustration that their money achieved relatively little against a menace so bent on the Jews' destruction. The enormity of their challenge made the one their father faced during World War I mild by comparison, although they built on his legacy.

Nor did Julius Rosenwald, who invested millions in the Soviet Union, particularly for agricultural work in Ukraine, its bread basket, either witness that region's great famine, the Holodomor, which killed millions, or have to deal with Joseph Stalin, who shortly after JR's death revealed himself as a totalitarian dictator, overseer of the great purges that led to the arrest, execution, and exile of millions. No one knows the fate of the Jewish farmers in the Ukrainian and Crimean colonies, including those who lived in "Rosenwald." Probably many ended up as the nameless victims of the great massacres perpetrated by the invading German army and its local allies, who joined in the killings. The Germans and their Ukrainian friends, some probably the farmers JR had believed would come to appreciate their Jewish neighbors, slaughtered approximately 1.5 million Jews in the fields, forests, and ravines of the place Rosenwald envisioned as a potential setting for a model of Jewish integration. Less than a decade after Rosenwald died, war engulfed the world, and in its face, his progressive, optimistic ideas about investing in people and engaging in practical humanitarianism would have seemed quaint and irrelevant at best, even misguided.

But the man who felt lucky that he could venture beyond his father's men's clothing store in Springfield, Illinois, and who aspired to have enough money to be able to give away one-third of his annual earnings to charity, might have considered that he died at the right time. The grim realities he missed might have shattered his ideas about the power of individuals to make a difference and broken his faith in the ability of money given thoughtfully to change people and better their lives.

Julius Rosenwald, the one-time manufacturer of seersucker suits who soared to the pinnacle of wealth, whose life story embodied the essence of the American dream of success, considered that his good luck demanded that he help repair the world, a concept that American Jews decades after his death invoked as *tikun olam*. Without calling it that, he devoted much of his life to this goal, seeking to humanize the city he lived in and to improve the lives of Jews and African Americans, in particular.

These concerns engaged him as a Jew. "Why are you doing so much to help the negro?" an interlocutor once asked him. "I am interested in America," he replied. "I do not see how America can go ahead if part of its people are left behind. That is why I help the negroes." But he did this work in large measure as a Jew who articulated clearly the connection between doing good in the world and doing so in the context of his Jewishness. In 1912, just as he embarked on his massive public works, he noted in a talk that the Jew "must be the one who in every crisis will be right, militant for the right, the ethical, the spiritual, the best in national life. If he falls short of this standard," the individual who held himself to it predicted, "he will himself have brought into being the monster which will one day destroy him and unseat him from his position of safety in America."[3]

And by doing what he did, Julius Rosenwald believed he helped Jews. By remaking the world for others, he made a better place for his own people.

NOTES

Introduction

1. Florence Frank to Adele Levy, March 5, 1929, Rosenwald Fund Papers, 90, 3, Fisk University.

2. "Statement by Julius Rosenwald," December 6, 1929, Rosenwald Papers, 32, 3, University of Chicago Library, Special Collections.

3. Julius Rosenwald, "Principles of Public Giving," *Atlantic Monthly*, May 1929, 3–10.

4. See Leonard Dinnerstein, *Uneasy at Home: Antisemitism and the American Jewish Experience* (New York: Columbia University Press, 1987).

Chapter 1: Taking Advantage of Opportunities and Luck

1. "Statement by Julius Rosenwald," December 6, 1929, Rosenwald Papers, 32, 3, University of Chicago Library, Special Collections (hereafter UCL).

2. "Rosenwald on Millionaires—Outtakes," Fox Movietone News Story, 1-674, filmed on January 2, 1929, http://mirc.sc.edu/is landora/object/usc:32467; see also 26, 8, Rosenwald Papers, UCL.

3. On Jewish migration to America in these years see Hasia R. Diner, *A Time for Gathering: The Second Migration, 1820–1880*, vol. 2 of *The Jewish People in America*, ed. Henry L. Feingold (Baltimore: Johns Hopkins University Press, 1992).

4. See Adam Mendelsohn, *Rag Race: How the Jews Sewed Their Way to Success in America and the British Empire* (New York: New York University Press, 2014).

5. For this American and, indeed, global pattern, see Hasia R. Diner, *Roads Taken: The Great Jewish Migrations to the New World and the Peddlers Who Forged the Way* (New Haven: Yale University Press, 2015).

6. Herman Eliassof, *The Jews of Illinois* (Chicago: Bloch and Newman, 1901), 377.

7. B. C. Forbes, *Men Who Are Making America* (New York: Forbes, 1917), v–vii.

8. JR to C. H. Rammelam, August 30, 1929, Rosenwald Papers, 3, 20, UCL.

9. Much of the material on Julius Rosenwald's life comes from his grandson Peter M. Ascoli's fine and detailed biography, *Julius Rosenwald: The Man Who Built Sears, Roebuck and Advanced the Cause of Black Education in the South* (Bloomington: Indiana University Press, 2006).

10. Ibid., 3.

11. Quoted in Diner, *Time for Gathering*, 228.

12. Ibid., 191.

13. Ibid., 39.

14. The history of race in post–Civil War Springfield can be found in Thomas Bahde, *The Life and Death of Gus Reed: A Story of Race and Justice in Illinois During the Civil War and Reconstruction* (Athens: Ohio University Press, 2014), 79.

15. Quoted in Diner, *Time for Gathering*, 198.

16. See Lee Shai Weissbach, *Jewish Life in Small-Town America: A History* (New Haven: Yale University Press, 2005), 159–60.

17. Quoted in Ascoli, *Julius Rosenwald*, 5.

18. Boris Emmet and John E. Jeuck, *Catalogues and Counters: A History of Sears, Roebuck, and Company* (Chicago: University of Chicago Press, 1950), 129–30; Louis Asher and Edith Heal, *Send No Money* (Chicago: Argus, 1942), 18.

19. Emmet and Jeuck, *Catalogues and Counters*, 51.

20. Cecil C. Hoge, Sr., *The First Hundred Years Are the Toughest: What We Can Learn from the Century of Competition Between Sears and Wards* (Berkeley: Ten Speed Press, 1988), 62.

21. Ascoli, *Julius Rosenwald*, 166.

22. Quoted in Susan Roth Breitzer, "Uneasy Alliances: Hull House, the Garment Workers Strikes and the Jews of Chicago," *Indiana Magazine of History* 106, 1 (2010): 40–70.

23. Julius Rosenwald to William Graves, February 20, 1925, Rosenwald Papers, 28, 19, UCL.

24. Quoted in Ascoli, *Julius Rosenwald*, 170.

25. Arthur W. Burritt, Henry S. Dennison, Edwin F. Gay, Ralph E. Heilman, and Henry P. Kendall, *Profit Sharing, Its Principles and Practice* (New York: Harper, 1920), 185–86.

26. "This Profit Sharing Plan Solves Many Problems: Sears, Roebuck & Co. Have Developed a Profit-Sharing Scheme That Is Attracting Widespread Attention," *New York Times*, December 31, 1916.

27. Quoted in Emmet and Jeuck, *Catalogues and Counters*, 212.

28. Quoted in Ascoli, *Julius Rosenwald*, 223–24.

29. Roy V. Scott, *The Reluctant Farmer: The Rise of Agricultural Extension to 1914* (Urbana: University of Illinois Press, 1970), 267.

30. *Architectural Digest* (July 1905): 27–32.

31. Edward E. Purinton, "Satisfaction or Your Money Back," *Independent*, February 5, 1920, 298–99.

32. Clipping from *The Grain Growers' Guide*, 1913, Julius Rosenwald Papers, 14, 24, UCL.

33. "Statement by Julius Rosenwald," December 6, 1929.

34. Quoted in Ascoli, *Julius Rosenwald*, 172.

35. Quoted in Emmet and Jeuck, *Catalogues and Counters*, 670.

36. David Potter, *People of Plenty: Economic Abundance and the American Character* (Chicago: University of Chicago Press, 1954).

37. Michael Klepper and Robert Gunther, *The Wealthy 100: From Benjamin Franklin to Bill Gates—A Ranking of the Richest Americans, Past and Present* (Secaucus, N. J.: Carol, 1996). Klepper and Gunther based the individual's wealth at the time of his—only men made the list—death and what percentage of the Gross National Product it constituted. Rosenwald's was 1/726 of the GNP while John D. Rockefeller, who stood at the top of the list, had a wealth that was 1/65 of the GNP.

Chapter 2: Not by Bread Alone

1. Quoted in Peter M. Ascoli, *Julius Rosenwald: The Man Who Built Sears, Roebuck and Advanced the Cause of Black Education in the American South* (Bloomington: Indiana University Press, 2006), 54.

2. Julius Rosenwald, "The Burden of Wealth," *Saturday Evening Post*, January 8, 1929, 12.

3. "Philanthropy Hall of Fame: The Philanthropy Roundtable," http://www.philanthropyroundtable.org/almanac/hall_of_fame (accessed February 6, 2017).

4. Quoted in Ascoli, *Julius Rosenwald*, 265.

5. Rosenwald, "Burden of Wealth," 12.

6. Julius Rosenwald, "Charity," *Harper's Weekly*, May 29, 1915, 522.

7. Quoted in Edwin Embree, *Julius Rosenwald Fund, 1917–1936: Review of Two Decades* (Chicago: Julius Rosenwald Fund, 1936), 3–4.

8. Rosenwald, "Burden of Wealth," 12.

9. Quoted in Waldemar A. Nielsen, *Inside American Philanthropy: The Dramas of Donorship* (Norman: University of Oklahoma Press, 1996), 43.

10. Rosenwald, "Burden of Wealth," 12.

11. Ibid.

12. Julius Rosenwald, "Principles of Public Giving," *Atlantic Monthly*, May 1929, 602–3.

13. William Graham Sumner, *What the Social Classes Owe Each Other*, 2nd ed. (New Haven: Yale University Press, 1924), 132–33.

14. Rosenwald, "Charity," 522.

15. Ibid.

16. Quoted in Tobias Brinkman, *Sundays at Sinai: A Jewish Congregation in Chicago* (Chicago: University of Chicago Press, 2012), 156.

17. Ibid.

18. Quoted in Kathleen McCarthy, *Noblesse Oblige: Charity and Cultural Philanthropy in Chicago, 1849–1929* (Chicago: University of Chicago Press, 1982), 120.

19. Julius Rosenwald, untitled speech, May 20, 1912, Rosenwald Papers, 34, 6, University of Chicago Library, Special Collections (hereafter UCL).

20. "Speech with Discussion," November 19, 1912, Rosenwald Papers, 34, 6, UCL.

Chapter 3: Some Little Touch of the Divine

1. Quoted in Irving Cutler, *The Jews of Chicago: From Shtetl to Suburb* (Urbana: University of Illinois Press, 1996), 35–36.

2. *The Sentinel History of Chicago Jewry, 1911–1961* (Chicago: Sentinel Publishing, 1961), 24, 32.

3. Alexander Dushkin, *Living Bridges: Memories of an Educator* (Jerusalem: Keter, 1975), 97–98.

4. Quoted in Peter M. Ascoli, *Julius Rosenwald: The Man Who Built Sears, Roebuck and Advanced the Cause of Black Education in the American South* (Bloomington: Indiana University Press, 2006), 68–69.

5. Minnie Low to Julius Rosenwald, September 17, 1910; Minnie Low to JR, November 20, 1914, both in Rosenwald Papers, 4, 17, University of Chicago Library, Special Collections (hereafter UCL).

6. Memorandum, Kipnis Children, Rosenwald Papers, 32, 14, UCL.

7. Quoted in Ascoli, *Julius Rosenwald*, 97.

8. Associated Jewish Charities of Chicago, *Report of the Annual Meeting, May 17, 1913*, Rosenwald Papers, 34, 5, UCL.

9. Quoted in Ascoli, *Julius Rosenwald*, 251.

10. Hyman L. Meites, *History of the Jews of Chicago* (Chicago: Chicago Jewish Historical Society, 1924), 229.

11. Chicago Hebrew Institute, "Statement," Rosenwald Papers, 6, 15, UCL.

12. Quoted in Rivkah S. Lissak, *Pluralism and Progressives: Hull House and the New Immigrants, 1890–1919* (Chicago: University of Chicago Press, 1989), 87.

13. "Hebrew Oratorio Society," October, 1917, Rosenwald Papers, 76, 15, UCL.

14. Quoted in Meites, *History of the Jews of Chicago*, 224.

15. Quoted in Linda J. Borish, "Jewish Girls, Gender and Sport at the Chicago Hebrew Institute: Athletic Identity in Jewish and Cultural Spaces," *Journal of Jewish Identities* (forthcoming).

16. Quoted in Meites, *History of the Jews of Chicago*, 226.

17. Address, November 26, 1920, Rosenwald Papers, 48, 7, UCL.

18. Memorandum, n.d., Rosenwald Papers, 32, 14, UCL.

19. Julius Rosenwald to Adolph Ochs, January 15, 1925, MS 5, Hebrew Union College Records, 3, 5. My thanks to Kevin Proffitt of the Jacob Rader Marcus Archives for bringing this document to my attention.

20. Harry Fischel to Lessing Rosenwald, January 1, 1932, Rosenwald Papers, 43, 11, UCL.

21. Julius Rosenwald to Henry Fischel, September 27, 1929, Rosenwald Papers, 43, 10, UCL.

22. Julius Rosenwald to Jack Mosseri, July 7, 1929, Rosenwald Papers, 5, 2, UCL.

23. Edward Embree to Julius Rosenwald, October 1, 1930, Rosenwald Papers, 43, 11, UCL.

24. Israel Goldberg and Samson Benderly, *Outline of Jewish Knowledge, Being a History of the Jewish People and an Anthology of Jewish Literature from the Earliest Times to the Present: Including a Brief Account of the History and Civilization of the Nations with Whom the Jews Have Come into Contact, and an Exposition of the Present-day Status and Problems of the Jewries of the World* (New York: Bureau of Jewish Education, 1929). My thanks to Judah Bernstein for making me aware of this document.

25. The Julius Rosenwald Essay Contest, *Statement of the Committee and Rules Governing the Contest* (New York: Julius Rosenwald Essay Contest, 1930).

26. Mordecai Kaplan, *Judaism as a Civilization: Toward a Reconstruction of American-Jewish Life* (New York: Macmillan, 1934), 297.

27. Quoted in Dushkin, *Living Bridges*, 96.

28. Untitled speech, May 20, 1912, Rosenwald Papers, 34, 6, UCL.

29. Julius Rosenwald to Harold Kramer, October 27, 1928, Rosenwald Papers, 31, 1, UCL.

30. Quoted in Ascoli, *Julius Rosenwald*, 253.

31. Julius Rosenwald to Arthur Wiggins, November 1, 1928, Rosenwald Papers, 31, 1, UCL.

32. Leo Frank to Julius Rosenwald, July 11, 1915, Rosenwald Papers, 15, 15, UCL.

33. Louis Marshall to Julius Rosenwald, January 8, 1915, Rosenwald Papers, 31, 1, UCL.

34. Quoted in Ascoli, *Julius Rosenwald*, 175–76.

35. Quoted in Neil Baldwin, *Henry Ford and the Jews: The Mass Production of Hate* (New York: Public Affairs, 2001), 201–2.

36. Ibid.

37. Quoted in Harry Barnard, *The Forging of an American Jew: The Life and Times of Julian W. Mack* (New York: Herzl, 1974), 176.

38. Dushkin, *Living Bridges*, 97.

39. Marvin Lowenthal, *Henrietta Szold: Life and Letters* (New York: Viking, 1942), 84–88.

40. Henrietta Szold to Julius Rosenwald, Herman Bernstein Papers, YIVO Center for Jewish History, New York, RG 713.

41. "Zion Triumphant in Chicago," *Yiddishe Kurier,* November 23, 1914. My thanks to Judah Bernstein for sharing this reference.

42. Julius Rosenwald to Raymond Rubinow, November 3, 1930, Rosenwald Papers, 33, 11, UCL.

43. Dushkin, *Living Bridges*, 97.

44. Julius Rosenwald to Abraham Meyer, September 19, 1929, Rosenwald Papers, 29,12, UCL.

45. Dushkin, *Living Bridges*, 99.

46. *Julius Rosenwald: In Memoriam: The Record of a Memorial Meeting Held on Sunday, March 27, 1932, at twelve o'clock noon. Broadcast Through the Courtesy of the National Broadcasting Company Under the Auspices of the American Jewish Joint Distribution Committee* (New York: American Jewish Joint Distribution Committee, 1932), n.p.

47. Letterhead, Palestine Emergency Fund, Rosenwald Papers, 29, 11, and William Graves to Julian Mack, January 28, 1919, Rosenwald Papers, 29, 15, UCL.

48. "Lodge Palestine Resolution: Its Origins and What It Means to World Jewry," Simon Glazer Papers, 1, 17, American Jewish Archives, Cincinnati, Ohio; "Address delivered by Elihu D. Stone, President of New England Zionist Region on Sunday June 17th, at the Municipal Auditorium, Nashua, New Hampshire," Elihu Stone Papers, American Jewish Historical Society.

49. Quoted in Ascoli, *Julius Rosenwald*, 103.

50. Quoted in Samuel Maurice, *Little Did I Know: Recollections and Reflections* (New York: Knopf, 1963), 213.

51. Quoted in *The Sentinel History of Chicago Jewry*, 24.

52. Quoted in Ascoli, *Julius Rosenwald*, 212.

53. Matthew J. Silver, *Louis Marshall and the Rise of Jewish Ethnicity* (Syracuse: Syracuse University Press, 2013), 263.

54. Quoted in Cutler, *Jews of Chicago*, 110–11.

55. *New York Times*, clipping, Ernest Grunfeld Papers, Leo Baeck Institute, Center for Jewish History, New York, LBI AR 7149, 1.

56. Quoted in Katherine Sabsovich, *Adventures in Idealism: A Personal Record of the Life of Professor Sabsovich* (New York: privately printed, 1922), 169.

57. Quoted in Merle Curti, *American Philanthropy Abroad: A History* (New Brunswick, N.J.: Rutgers University Press, 1963), 369.

58. Quoted in Ascoli, *Julius Rosenwald*, 338.

59. Quoted in Oscar Handlin, *A Continuing Task: The American Jewish Joint Distribution Committee, 1914–1964* (New York: Random House, 1964), 58.

60. Quoted in Jonathan Dekel-Chen, *Farming the Red Land: Jewish Agricultural Colonization and Local Soviet Power, 1924–1941* (New Haven: Yale University Press, 2005), 73, 246nn13 and 17.

61. David Brown to Herman Bernstein, August 14, 1926, Herman Bernstein Papers, folder 593, YIVO Center for Jewish History, New York, RG 713.

62. "From the Day of August 3, 1928," Rosenwald Papers, 32, 5, UCL.

63. Abraham Sepenuk to Julius Rosenwald, February 1, 1929, Rosenwald Papers, 33, 7, UCL.

Chapter 4: A Jew Steps In

1. Quoted in Hasia R. Diner, *In the Almost Promised Land: American Jews and Blacks, 1915–1935* (Baltimore: Johns Hopkins University Press, 1992), 191.

2. "Julius Rosenwald: Patron of Democracy," n.d., Alain Locke Paper 116, 14, Moorland-Spingarn Research Center, Howard University. My thanks to David Weinfeld for bringing this document to my attention.

3. Quoted in Robert Bone and Richard A. Courage, *The Muse in Bronzeville: African American Creative Expression in Chicago, 1932–1950* (New Brunswick, N.J.: Rutgers University Press, 2011), 29.

4. Louis Harlan, *Booker T. Washington: The Wizard of Tuskegee, 1901–1915* (New York: Oxford University Press, 1983), 351–52.

5. W. D. Weatherford, *Present Forces in Negro Progress* (New York: Association Press, 1912), 172.

6. Quoted in Peter M. Ascoli, *Julius Rosenwald: The Man Who Built Sears, Roebuck and Advanced the Cause of Black Education in the American South* (Bloomington: Indiana University Press, 2006), 86.

7. "JR's Remarks at the Dedication of YMCA for Colored Men," Rosenwald Papers, 34, 5, University of Chicago Library, Special Collections (hereafter UCL).

8. Quoted in Diner, *In the Almost Promised Land*, 184.

9. Ibid., 190.

10. Quoted in Ascoli, *Julius Rosenwald*, 89.

11. Ibid., 130.

12. Harlan, *Booker T. Washington*, 196.

13. Quoted in Diner, *In the Almost Promised Land*, 168.

14. Mary McLeod Bethune to Julius Rosenwald, n.d., Rosenwald Papers, 3, 18, UCL.

15. John Dollard, *Caste and Class in a Southern Town* (New Haven: Yale University Institute of Human Relations, 1937), 45.

16. Carter G. Woodson, Manuscript history of Rosenwald schools, Rosenwald Papers, 33, 1, UCL, 1–2.

17. Quoted in Darryl Pinckney, "Writers and the Rosenwald Fund," in *A Force for Change: African American Art and the Julius Rosenwald Fund*, ed. Daniel Schulman (Chicago: Spertus Institute of Jewish Studies, 2009), 38.

18. Speech, American Hospital Association, October 20, 1930, Rosenwald Papers, 34, 8, UCL.

19. Rayford Logan, *The Betrayal of the Negro from Rutherford B. Hayes to Woodrow Wilson* (London: Collier-Macmillan, 1965).

20. Quoted in Olivier Zunz, *Philanthropy in America: A History* (Princeton: Princeton University Press, 2012), 118.

21. Daniel Aaronson and Bhashkar Mazumder, "The Impact of Rosenwald Schools on Black Achievement," *Journal of Political Economy* 119, no. 5 (October 2011): 824–25.

22. Abraham Flexner to V. C. Vaughan, July 7, 1919, Rosenwald Fund Papers, B-2, Fisk University.

23. Quoted in Kenneth R. Manning, *Black Apollo of Science: The Life of Ernest Everett Just* (New York: Oxford University Press, 1983), 156. Just had wanted the Rosenwald Fund to contribute to the creation of a Rosenwald Institute of Zoology at Howard. The Fund did not approve the request but did give $80,000 for five years to support Just's work and to train advanced graduate students.

24. Rosenwald Fund, Executive Committee minutes, June 25, 1929, Rosenwald Papers, 77, 6, UCL.

25. For a full list of African American recipients of Rosenwald Fund fellowships, see Daniel Schulman, ed., *A Force For Change: African American Art and the Julius Rosenwald Fund* (Chicago: Spertus Institute for Jewish Studies, 2009), 157–72.

26. Speech, American Hospital Association, October 20, 1930, Rosenwald Papers, 34, 8, UCL.

27. Quoted in Ascoli, *Julius Rosenwald*, 207.

28. Julius Rosenwald, "Reconstruction and the Negro," n.d., Rosenwald Papers, 34, 7, UCL.

29. National Urban League, *Bulletin*, November 3, 1913, 7.

30. Quoted in Ascoli, *Julius Rosenwald*, 244.

31. Quoted in Diner, *In the Almost Promised Land*, 126.

32. Edwin Embree to Julius Rosenwald, March 12, 1928, Rosenwald Fund Papers, Fisk University.

33. Quoted in Christopher Robert Reed, *The Chicago NAACP and the Rise of Black Professional Leadership, 1910–1966* (Bloomington: Indiana University Press, 1997), 24.

34. Julius Rosenwald to Celia Parker Wooley, 1912, Rosenwald Papers, 14, 3, UCL.

35. Rosenwald Fund, Executive Committee minutes, May 18, 1929, Rosenwald 77, 6, UCL.

36. Quoted in Eric Anderson and Alfred A. Moss, Jr., *Dangerous Donations: Northern Philanthropy and Southern Black Education, 1902–1930* (Columbia: University of Missouri Press, 1999), 62.

37. JR to Mayor William Thompson, May 15, 1915, Rosenwald Papers, 4, 1, UCL.

38. Rosenwald Fund, Executive Committee meeting, July 12, 1929, Rosenwald Papers, 77, 6, UCL.

39. Quoted in Diner, *In the Almost Promised Land*, 8.

40. "A Word from Mr. Julius Rosenwald," *The Crisis* 4, 2 (June 1912): 89.

41. Julius Rosenwald to Edwin Baker, September 14, 1917, Rosenwald Papers, 4, 1, UCL.

42. Quoted in Diner, *In the Almost Promised Land*, 151–52.

43. Ibid, 77.

44. Alexander Dushkin, *Living Bridges: Memories of an Educator* (Jerusalem: Keter, 1975), 97–98.

45. Quoted in Diner, *In the Almost Promised Land*, 178–79.

46. Quoted in Thomas J. Ward, *Black Physicians in the Jim Crow South* (Fayetteville: University of Arkansas Press, 2003), 174.

47. Quoted in Ascoli, *Julius Rosenwald*, 164.

48. William Graves to Julius Rosenwald, February 9, 1923, Rosenwald Papers, 15, 6, UCL.

49. Louis Ginzberg, letter to Emanuel Neumann, in Nathan Isaacs Papers, 3, 4, American Jewish Archives. Thanks to Judah Bernstein for bringing this to my attention.

50. Ludwig Lewisohn, *Israel* (New York: Boni and Liveright, 1925), 25. Thank you to Judah Bernstein for drawing my attention to this reference.

51. Quoted in Diner, *In the Almost Promised Land*, 190–91.

52. Quoted in Jeffrey K. Sosland, *A School in Every County: The Partnership of Jewish Philanthropist Julius Rosenwald and American Black Communities* (Washington, D.C.: Economic and Science Planning, 1995), n.p.

53. Horace Mann Bond, *The Education of the Negro in the American Social Order* (New York: Prentice-Hall, 1934), 140.

54. Quoted in Ascoli, *Julius Rosenwald*, 89.

55. Ibid., 164.

56. Quoted in Diner, *In the Almost Promised Land*, 188.

57. Quoted in Reed, *The Chicago NAACP and the Rise of Black Professional Leadership*, 24.

58. Nannie H. Burroughs, "Julius Rosenwald," Rosenwald Papers, 34, 3, UCL.

59. James Weldon Johnson, "The Shining Life: An Appreciation of Julius Rosenwald," Rosenwald Papers, 33, 10, UCL.

60. W. E. B. Du Bois, "The Passing of Julius Rosenwald," *The Crisis*, February 1932, 58.

Conclusion

1. *Julius Rosenwald: in Memoriam: The Record of a Memorial Meeting Held on Sunday, March 27, 1932, at Twelve o'Clock Noon. Broadcast Through the Courtesy of the National Broadcasting Company Under the Auspices of the American Jewish Joint Distribution Committee* (New York: American Jewish Joint Distribution Committee, 1932), n.p.

2. Irving R. Melbo, *Our America: A Textbook for Elementary School History and Social Studies* (Indianapolis: Bobbs-Merrill, 1937), 212, 204, 211.

3. Julius Rosenwald, Address, May 20, 1912, Rosenwald Papers, 34, 6, University of Chicago Library, Special Collections.

PUBLISHED TITLES INCLUDE:

Rabbi Akiva: Sage of the Talmud, by Barry W. Holtz
Ben-Gurion: Father of Modern Israel, by Anita Shapira
Bernard Berenson: A Life in the Picture Trade, by Rachel Cohen
Sarah: The Life of Sarah Bernhardt, by Robert Gottlieb
Leonard Bernstein: An American Musician, by Allen Shawn
Hayim Nahman Bialik: Poet of Hebrew, by Avner Holtzman
Léon Blum: Prime Minister, Socialist, Zionist, by Pierre Birnbaum
Louis D. Brandeis: American Prophet, by Jeffrey Rosen
David: The Divided Heart, by David Wolpe
Moshe Dayan: Israel's Controversial Hero, by Mordechai Bar-On
Disraeli: The Novel Politician, by David Cesarani
Einstein: His Space and Times, by Steven Gimbel
Becoming Freud: The Making of a Psychoanalyst, by Adam Phillips
Emma Goldman: Revolution as a Way of Life, by Vivian Gornick
Hank Greenberg: The Hero Who Didn't Want to Be One, by Mark Kurlansky
Peggy Guggenheim: The Shock of the Modern, by Francine Prose
Lillian Hellman: An Imperious Life, by Dorothy Gallagher
Jabotinsky: A Life, by Hillel Halkin
Jacob: Unexpected Patriarch, by Yair Zakovitch
Franz Kafka: The Poet of Shame and Guilt, by Saul Friedländer
Rav Kook: Mystic in a Time of Revolution, by Yehudah Mirsky
Primo Levi: The Matter of a Life, by Berel Lang
Groucho Marx: The Comedy of Existence, by Lee Siegel